# LAW AND THE UTOPIAN IMAGINATION

The Amherst Series in Law, Jurisprudence, and Social Thought

EDITED BY

*Austin Sarat, Lawrence Douglas, and Martha Merrill Umphrey*

# Law and the Utopian Imagination

*Edited by*

AUSTIN SARAT

LAWRENCE DOUGLAS

MARTHA MERRILL UMPHREY

STANFORD LAW BOOKS

*An imprint of Stanford University Press • Stanford, California*

Stanford University Press
Stanford, California


Library of Congress Cataloging-in-Publication Data

Law and the utopian imagination / edited by Austin Sarat, Lawrence Douglas, and Martha Merrill Umphrey.
pages cm. — (The Amherst series in law, jurisprudence, and social thought)
Includes bibliographical references and index.
ISBN 978-0-8047-9081-9 (cloth : alk. paper)
1. Law—Philosophy. 2. Utopias. I. Sarat, Austin, editor of compilation. II. Douglas, Lawrence, editor of compilation. III. Umphrey, Martha Merrill, editor of compilation. IV. Series: Amherst series in law, jurisprudence, and social thought.
K486.L39 2014
340.1—dc23

2013043600

ISBN 978-0-8047-9186-1 (electronic)

Printed in the United States of America on acid-free, archival-quality paper

Typeset at Stanford University Press in 10/14.5 Minion

*For my son Ben,*
*with love and thanks for the joy he shares (AS)*

*For Jacob and Milo,*
*with hopes for a better world (LD)*

# Acknowledgments

We are grateful to our Amherst College colleagues David Delaney, Nasser Hussain, and Adam Sitze for their intellectual companionship. We thank our students in Amherst College's Department of Law, Jurisprudence and Social Thought for their interest in the issues addressed in this book. Finally, we would like to express our appreciation for generous financial support provided by Amherst College's Corliss Lamont Fund.

# Contents

# Contributors

SHULAMIT ALMOG is Professor of Law and Director of Doctoral Program of the Faculty of Law at the University of Haifa

LAWRENCE DOUGLAS is James J. Grosfeld Professor of Law, Jurisprudence and Social Thought at Amherst College

NAN GOODMAN is Professor of English at the University of Colorado at Boulder

JAMES MARTEL is Associate Professor of Political Science at San Francisco State University

DIANE MORGAN is a Lecturer in the School of Fine Art, History of Art, and Cultural Studies at the University of Leeds

AUSTIN SARAT is Associate Dean of the Faculty, the William Nelson Cromwell Professor of Jurisprudence and Political Science, and Professor of Law, Jurisprudence and Social Thought at Amherst College

JOHAN VAN DER WALT is Professor of Legal Philosophy, University of Luxembourg

MARTHA MERRILL UMPHREY is Professor of Law, Jurisprudence and Social Thought at Amherst College

# Law and the Utopian Imagination: An Introduction

LAWRENCE DOUGLAS

AUSTIN SARAT

MARTHA MERRILL UMPHREY

In 1922, toward the conclusion of his first book, *Story of Utopias,* the American sociologist Lewis Mumford wrote, "Our most important task at the present moment is to build castles in the sky."[1] In 1929, in his classic work *Ideology and Utopia,* the German sociologist Karl Mannheim offered a similarly emphatic defense of the importance of utopian thinking: "The complete elimination of reality-transcending elements from our world," Mannheim wrote, "ultimately would mean the decay of the human will . . . . The disappearance of utopia brings about a static state of affairs in which man himself becomes no more than a thing."[2] A scant two decades later, a very different tone sounded in the pages of three of the most influential social thinkers of the midcentury. Writing independently, Karl Popper, Lionel Trilling, and Isaiah Berlin essayed critiques of utopianism that, taken together, delivered a broad indictment of utopian thinking. Far from locating in the utopian imagination a vital force for human betterment and social progress, these midcentury thinkers powerfully argued that utopianism paves the way to totalitarianism and that its logical endpoint is not the peaceful community of equals but the death camp. In particular, these thinkers laid bare the particular antagonisms between utopianism and liberal legality—finding in the former a dire threat to the salutary commitments of the latter.

Who, then, writes seriously on the idea of utopia today? The answer would seem to be: almost no one, and least of all scholars of the law. The midcentury critique appears to have carried the day, and a belief in the very possibility of utopian achievements—bracketing for a moment the question of their desirability—appears to have flagged in the face of a world marked by political instability, social upheaval, and dreary market realities. True, one can find in the manifestos of exuberant dot-commers elements or vestiges of utopian thinking—fervent expressions of belief in the Internet's promise of radical equality and unfettered self-expression.[3] One can likewise locate aspects of utopianism in statements of the loose affiliation of groups associated with the "occupy Wall Street" movement.[4] Still, it seems fair to say that utopianism finds itself in a generally moribund state—discredited by a series of critiques penned in the middle of the last century, and marginalized by the dislocations of current political and market processes.

This volume can be seen, then, as a project of exploration and resuscitation. Instead of mapping out the contours of a familiar terrain, our contributors seek to explore the possibilities of a productive engagement between the utopian and the legal imagination. Is it possible to reimagine or revitalize the concept of utopia such that it can survive the terms of the midcentury liberal critique? Alternatively, is it possible to reframe the concept of utopia and the theory of liberal legality so as to dissolve the apparent antagonism between the two? In charting possible answers to these questions, the present volume hopes to revive interest in a vital topic of inquiry too long neglected by both social thinkers and legal scholars.

The term "utopia" first appeared in Sir Thomas More's eponymous novel of 1516, but the concept predated More by two millennia, finding its first and most influential elaboration in the pages of Plato's *Republic.* Over the centuries the utopian imagination has produced a rich and varied literature, including such classics as Samuel Butler's *Erewhon,* Edward Bellamy's *Looking Backward,* and B. F. Skinner's *Walden Two*. Some of these works were no doubt meant to serve as criticism of existing social and political structures; to this day, scholars cannot agree on whether More intended utopia—Latin for "no where," a place the reader is guided through by a character named Raphael Hythloday, or "dispenser of nonsense"—as a bona fide vision or an ironic critique of Elizabethan institutions. Yet whatever the answer to this question, there is no denying that countless real-world social experiments have been launched under the capacious rubric of utopianism.

Our purpose here is not to inventory such experiments; our concern is with the nature of the utopian imagination that has endorsed and stimulated such ventures. In imagining an ideal or perfect community, the utopian imagination has typically eschewed nostalgia. It finds its ideal not in a prelapsarian, Edenic state of innocence; instead, the utopian imagination has tended to fix its gaze on the future, finding its realization not in the dissolution of social arrangements and institutions but in their dialectical transcendence or radical improvement. Certainly one can find aspects of prelapsarian thinking in the utopian imagination—More's vision of the abolition of private property harks back to Plato, just as Plato locates one model of utopia in the lost island of Atlantis—but still the larger fact remains that utopias are not points of return: they are destinations that must be fashioned and engineered. In More's novel, for example, Utopia is an island, but an artificial, not a natural one. Originally a peninsula, the island was created through an ambitious and arduous project of land removal, meant to insulate the community from threats—military and otherwise—from the mainland.

Such engineered communities assume a wide variety of forms in the utopian imagination; still, it is possible to speak of certain commonalities and shared features. Utopias are, first and foremost, communities of harmony and order. In *Utopia and Its Enemies*, political theorist George Kateb described utopias as sharing conditions of "perpetual peace, guaranteed abundance, and conditioned virtue."[5] Work is rewarding and leisure is stimulating. There is no want, strife, or dissension. Virtuous behavior guarantees conditions of peace and plenty for all, while conditions of peace and plenty make possible the cultivation of virtue.

Perhaps the most remarkable example of utopian harmony is found in the pages of *The Republic*, where Plato famously defines justice as "minding . . . one's own business" and performing "the one function in the community for which his nature has best suited him."[6] Justice, in this account, is no more than the harmonious performance of tasks, as Plato posits an affinity between the structural harmony of the parts of the state and the internal equipoise of the well-balanced individual soul. Just as justice "in the state meant that each of the three orders . . . was doing its proper work . . . we may henceforth bear in mind that each one of us likewise will be a just person, fulfilling his proper function, only if the several parts of our nature fulfill theirs."[7] As this passage suggests, it is not the tripartite soul that delivers a template for the state in *The Republic*; rather, it is the harmonious statis of the well-balanced tripartite state that provides a model of the soul—a fact that emphasizes the *conditioned* nature of virtue in a utopian state. For although Plato speaks of persons fulfilling their nature, he recognizes that the inhabitants of his utopia will need to be "induced to make themselves perfect masters each of his [sic] own craft."[8]

We likewise find a link between peace, plenty, and conditioned virtue in More's *Utopia.*[9] More's community provides little in the way of privacy; members of the community work under the watchful eye of omnipresent magistrates; absent are places for social gathering. Taverns, brothels—any place that might make for "secret meeting" are banned.[10] Here, then, Utopia appears as a "no where" in a second sense—as a place where there is nowhere to hide, nowhere for a member of the community to escape the benevolent yet sweeping gaze of the magistrates.

Perhaps the most extreme example of a utopia in which harmonious living amid circumstances of material plenty is achieved through conditioned virtue is to be found in B. F. Skinner's *Walden Two.* As the spokesman for the community simply puts it, "We want a government based upon a science of human behavior":

> We have no truck with philosophies of innate goodness—or evil, for that matter. But we do have faith in our power to change human behavior. We can *make* men adequate for group living—to the satisfaction of everybody."[11]

In *Walden Two,* harmonious and commodious living can be achieved and maintained through a science of behavioral conditioning and engineering.

Given the exceptional lever of order needed to achieve and maintain communities of perpetual peace, guaranteed abundance, and conditioned virtue, we might be tempted to assume that law would play a particularly robust role in the utopian state. As perhaps the most potent tool by which social order is imposed and vouchsafed, law would seem to play an important if not necessary role in the completion of any utopian project. And yet if anything, the utopian imagination has typically displayed hostility toward legal forms and processes.

Some utopias, certainly, contemplate an active role for law in the promotion of a life of peace and plenty. More's *Utopia* envisions a community without private property that, in order to sustain itself, must eliminate "everything that causes, promotes, and fosters intrigue, luxury, [and] jealousy."[12] Here law plays a crucial role: the banning of taverns is but one example of social regulation achieved through and enforced by law. More important, the system of assemblies, councils, and magistrates that promulgate and enforce the law are themselves crucially subject to it. In the words of one commentator, More's island utopia is very much a "law state."[13]

Not so Plato's *Republic.* The guardians of Plato's utopia are philosopher kings, true "lovers of knowledge" who refuse to "linger among the multiplicity of things which men believe to be real" and instead strive "with a passion" to lay hold "upon the nature of each thing."[14] Indifferent to self-aggrandizement or the acquisition of material goods, the philosopher king selflessly dedicates himself to promoting the commonweal. It would be absurd to tie the hands of a ruler whose only ambition is to shape a better and more perfect order. The rule of law has no place in a world ruled by philosopher kings. At best law would be irrelevant, a redundant summary of the guardians' own designs of governance. At worst it would be an encumbrance, a regrettable fetter on the guardians' ability to creatively steer the ship of state on its ideal course. Law is a system born of imperfection, a device needed to restrain rulers who cannot be trusted to restrain themselves. "Genuine guardians" pose no such threat of abuse of power; they "will be the last to bring harm upon the commonwealth."[15]

Of course, in *The Laws*, Plato tells a very different story. Here Plato defends a community ruled by magistrates who, like the ordinary citizens of the community, are ruled by and subject to an elaborate system of laws. As the "Athenian Stranger" who stands in for Socrates in the dialogue asserts, "Mankind must either give themselves [sic] a law and regulate their lives by it, or live no better than wild beasts."[16] However, as this statement suggests, here we have ceased talking about the creation of an ideal community. Plato quite clearly sees the state described in *The Laws* as second best. We accept the law faute de mieux—a necessary tool in a world in which the philosophical truth that anchors *The Republic* is "nowhere to be met with, except in faint vestiges."[17] The true utopia dispenses with regulation by law.

Skinner's *Walden Two* likewise essays a vision of utopia free from legal control. For Skinner, law is nothing more than a primitive form of behavioral engineering. Based as it is on the "use of force or the threat of force," law is a system of coercion "incompatible with permanent happiness."[18] Walden Two, by contrast, is based on an "effective science of behavior" that largely replaces law's reliance on negative reinforcement (namely, "handcuffs, iron bars, and forcible coercion") with techniques of "positive reinforcement."[19] As the spokesman for the community explains, when a person "behaves as we want him to behave, we simply create a situation he likes or remove one that he doesn't like. As a result, the likelihood that he will behave that way again goes up, which is what we want."[20] In *Walden Two*, people behave in a sociable manner not because they are threatened with force if they fail to do so, but because they have been conditioned so as to make such behavior feel voluntary. The science of human behavior has rendered law—an outmoded and inefficient form of behavioral conditioning—obsolete.

If the utopian imagination has displayed hostility to legal forms and processes, the liberal imagination has answered in kind, fervently rejecting utopian thinking. Liberals are not alone in taking issue with utopian thought; Schopenhauer's philosophy of suffering and Nietzsche's philosophy of power sternly call into question the attractions of a world of mindlessly happy people enjoying conditions of peace and plenty. Nor have liberal critics of utopia necessarily concerned themselves with law or with norms and procedures of liberal legality. Precious few legal philosophers or theorists have explicitly written on the subject of utopianism. And yet some of the most influential liberal thinkers of the last century—Karl Popper, Lionel Trilling, and Isaiah Berlin—essayed sweeping critiques of utopianism, critiques that implicitly offer a robust defense of liberal legal forms. Put another way, if utopian thinkers find law an obstacle to the creation of the perfect community, liberal thinkers locate in law a necessary bulwark against the inevitable excesses of utopia.

At first blush, it might seem odd that anyone should see utopian thinking as sinister. One might, pace Nietzsche, view a community of harmony, peace, plenty, and virtue, as dull—but dangerous? Yet Popper, Trilling, and Berlin found dangers aplenty. In both his famous work of 1945, *The Open Society and Its Enemies,* and in a shorter lecture of 1947, "Utopia and Violence," Popper laid bare the perceived connections between utopianism and totalitarianism. While acknowledging the lure of utopianism ("indeed, an all too attractive theory"[21]), Popper insisted that a belief in the perfectibility of society endorses all possible methods toward its achievement, for no means—even the most violent—can be abjured when perfection is the goal. Given the purity of the imagined endpoint, the utopian must be "very thorough in eliminating and stamping out all heretical competing views"[22]—a thoroughness that endorses all manner of force toward the end of the radical transformation of society. Democracy can be smashed, rights suppressed, and enemies ruthlessly eliminated in order to "execute the Utopian blueprint."[23]

Democratic societies, while also committed to social engineering, aim at incremental, piecemeal change. Channeled through legal norms of due process and regulated by the rule of law, democratic social engineering is devoted to the more modest project of improving institutions rather than fundamentally reshaping the very fabric of society. The proper goals of politics and law, for Popper, find elaboration in simple maxims: "Work for the elimination of concrete evils rather than for the realization of abstract goals. Do not aim at establishing happiness by political means. Rather aim at the elimination of concrete miseries."[24] In the final analysis, the difference between the liberal and the utopian ethos finds elaboration in "the difference between a reasonable method of improving the lot of man, and a method which . . . may easily lead to an intolerable increase in human suffering."[25]

Lionel Trilling's 1950 work *The Liberal Imagination* extended Popper's critique.[26] In this book of essays, Trilling did not in the first instance concern himself with the differences between liberal and utopian thought. Rather, Trilling addressed a strand of utopianism that he located within liberalism itself. For Trilling, liberalism represented a singular achievement in the history of political thought, with its greatest contribution the creation of the idea of universal human rights. For Trilling, the liberal notion of human rights constituted, to borrow language more recently used by Samuel Moyn, a "minimalist" ideal—it was dedicated to securing basic principles of justice and protecting the life and dignity of persons.[27]

Within liberalism, however, Trilling detected maximalist strains, impulses that sought to move beyond securing basic rights and that strove instead to transform and perfect institutions in the name of more robust substantive entitlements. This liberal perfectionism or utopianism was, Trilling argued, dangerous, as it sacrificed liberalism's original "lively sense of contingency and responsibility" to the aggressive impulse to organize. "The job of criticism," he argued, was "to recall liberalism to its first essential imagination of variousness and possibility, which implies the awareness of complexity and difficulty."[28] Trilling found this imaginative awareness in nineteenth-century novelists such as Nathaniel Hawthorne and Henry James, literary masters attentive to the moral complexity of human action, the multifariousness of human emotion, and the irreducible range of human character.

That Trilling should locate a challenge to the over-reaching ambitions of liberal perfectionism and utopianism in the novels of literary masters is telling. The utopian imagination has, after all, found expression as often in novelistic form as it has in the political manifesto. All the same, it is hard to ignore that qua novel, the utopian novel invariably fails. The characters perforce lack depth, complexity, and interest. If happy, they display the suspiciously flat happiness of an automaton. Here we need but recall the famous passage in *Walden Two* in which the observers of the community encounter a group of children on their way to a picnic. One observer asks the nursery school teacher whether the children who weren't included on the picnic feel jealousy or envy. The teacher doesn't merely deny this; she responds as if the question were unintelligible, spoken in a foreign tongue, leading the observer to exclaim, "Don't the children . . . ever feel unhappy . . .?" The teacher's "puzzlement" only grows, prompting the guide to observe, "As to emotions—we aren't free of all of them, nor should we like to be. But the meaner and more annoying—the emotions which breed unhappiness—are almost unknown here, like unhappiness itself."[29] It's hard to imagine a more lifeless or terrifying encounter in all of literature.

For Trilling, however, more is at stake than proving afresh the literary proposition made famous by the opening sentence of *Anna Karenina*—that happy communities make for lousy novels. Rather, the fact that one cannot write a substantial novel about a utopian community suggests a defect with the community itself—that conditioned virtue suppresses the energies, ambitions, desires, interests and longings that make humans worthy of artistic and moral attention. It is perhaps no surprise that the strongest utopian novels take the form of dystopias. Dystopias should not be confused with anti-utopias; they follow a logic and impulse altogether different from, say, Cormac McCarthy's *The Road*, a postapocalyptic vision of lone survivors charting their desperate way through the charred and chaotic ruins of civilization. Dystopic novels depict not the collapse of the utopian project but its ultimate nightmarish completion. In the pages of Aldous Huxley's *Brave New World* or Yevgeny Zamyatin's *We*, we encounter the bleak and terrifying sterility that issues from complete stasis, the spiritual morbidity that comes from suffocating harmony maintained through the tireless suppression of individuality. And precisely because they depict the struggle of the lone individual, the isolated resister, against nightmarish mass blandness, dystopian novels, at their best, possess an aesthetic and moral vitality lacking in their earnest, didactic utopian counterparts.

Isaiah Berlin's essay "The Decline of Utopian Ideals in the West" delivers a final influential critique of the utopian imagination.[30] In contrast to Popper and Trilling, Berlin appears, at first blush, to be less interested in presenting a normative argument against utopianism than in charting its intellectual history. In his examination of utopian thought as a "central strand in the whole of western thought,"[31] Berlin claims to detect three basic axioms or propositions to which all such thinking is committed: first, that all "genuine" questions have "only one correct answer, all other answers being incorrect"; second, that a "method exists for the discovery of these correct answers"; and third, that the correct answers "must, at the very least, be compatible with one another." Berlin argues that all utopian thought has been committed to these beliefs—from Plato, through More's "wonderful fantasy," down to and including Marxian perfectionism.

These assumptions, however, have been challenged in the works of other political theorists—most originally, argues Berlin, in the writings of Machiavelli, who first explored the irreducible incompatibility of basic political values and ideals. The German romantic-nationalist Johann Gottfried Herder went one step further, insisting that to judge "one culture by the standards of another" signals a "failure of imagination and understanding."[32] And in the work of liberals such as John Stuart Mill, the challenge to utopianism finds articulate expression in the argument that "men can live full lives only in societies with an open texture, in which variety is not merely tolerated but is approved and encouraged."[33]

Having charted this collision of values—between those who hold on to the promise of the "ultimate salvation of all men," and those who believe "this doctrine to be an illusion," and a dangerous one at that—Berlin stakes out his defense of liberalism in the closing paragraphs of his essay. Invoking Kant's famous observation, "Out of the crooked timber of humanity no straight thing was ever made," Berlin acknowledges that the liberal project, devoted as it is to the promotion of "some kind of equilibrium, necessarily unstable, between the different aspirations of different groups of human beings," is not a "wildly exciting programme"—not the kind of thing to inspire people toward sacrifice and martyrdom. And yet Berlin concludes that this liberal vision, for all its lack of flash and color, just "might yet prevent mutual destruction, and, in the end, preserve the world."[34] If forced to choose between a vision that holds the promise of world preservation and one that risks world annihilation, we need not tarry in our deliberation. At stake in the clash between the liberal and the utopian world view is not simply a competition between irreconcilable political visions—it is ultimately a choice between a politics of tolerance and incrementalism, and one of terror, violence, and possible mass destruction.

Indeed, if we read Berlin through the filter of Popper's earlier work, we can go one step further and say that utopianism is less an alternative political vision to liberalism than a program that contemplates the very elimination of politics. By adopting an agnostic position relative to visions of the good, liberalism defends basic rights, deliberative processes, and legal procedures that enable a vigorous politics of contestation, coalition, and compromise. Utopianism, with its blueprint of social perfection, eschews politics and legislation as proper means of radical societal transformation. And once its blueprint has been engineered into place, utopianism dispenses with politics altogether as vestigial and superfluous.

Can we, however, imagine a vision of utopianism that can survive the liberal critique and entertain a more constructive relationship between law and utopia? This is a challenge recently taken up by Michael Walzer in "Reclaiming Political Enthusiasm." Here Walzer argues that liberalism stripped of utopian longings courts more than mere dullness.[35] "Without the steady pressure," Walzer insists, to create a "new and nobler society," liberalism will "give us only oligarchs and plutocrats."[36] Walzer does not deny the dangers of unfettered utopianism described by Berlin, but he believes that liberalism's commitment to legal procedures—in particular, those subsumed under the concept of due process—establish a necessary bulwark against utopian excess. Thus, while acknowledging the tension between liberalism and utopianism, Walzer appeals to the legal and procedural commitments of the former as a check against the dangers of the latter. If channeled through the deliberative processes of liberal legality, utopian thinking—though anathema to these very processes—can be rendered a useful, and perhaps even necessary, means of invigorating liberal discourse, of guarding against liberalism's tendency to slide into plutocracy.

Russell Jacoby's *Picture Imperfect: Utopian Thought for an Anti-Utopian Age* offers a second valuable attempt to reconcile liberalism and utopianism.[37] Jacoby, a prominent historian and cultural critic, resists the impulse to blame all genocides on utopian perfectionism.[38] As Jacoby notes, "It is, for the most part, nationalist, ethnic, and sectarian passions—not utopian ideals—that drive global violence."[39] At the same time, he recognizes the authoritarian, and even totalitarian, streak in what he calls "blueprint utopianism." Blueprint utopians, Jacoby writes, "map out the future in inches and minutes";[40] they "give the size of rooms, the number of seats at tables, the exact hours at which to arise and retire."[41] And yet the blueprint tradition, Jacoby argues, does not exhaust the field of utopian thinking. Jacoby locates a rival tradition of utopian thinking, "less noticed and well defined," that eschews the drawing of blueprints. He calls these thinkers "iconoclastic utopians":

> Rather than elaborate the future in precise detail, they longed, waited, or worked for utopia but did not visualize it. The iconoclastic utopians tapped ideas traditionally associated with utopia—harmony, leisure, peace, and pleasure—but rather than spelling out what could be, they kept, as it were, their ears open toward it . . . . They did not privilege the eye, but the ear . . . . Against the dominant tradition of blueprints, they offered an imageless utopianism laced with passion and spirit.[42]

Jacoby identifies the origins of iconoclastic utopianism in the Second Commandment's prohibition on graven images and its more mature elaboration in the works of Walter Benjamin, Gershom Scholem, Theodor Adorno and Ernst Bloch, thinkers who imaginatively reinterpreted the "refusal to name the absolute" as a way of preserving "the possibility of redemption."[43] In contrast to blueprint utopians, the iconoclasts did not demand a "renunciation of life" as presently lived; rather, "their pictorial reserve about the future coexisted with attentiveness to the present."[44] If not liberals themselves, the iconoclasts staked a position that could accommodate liberal values and institutional practices. In resisting the impulse to provide "precise dimensions for the future," the iconoclasts offered a vision of utopianism for today's world, a vision that quiets the concerns of Popper, Trilling, and Berlin, but which answers Walzer's disillusionment with liberalism's tendency to slide into soulless proceduralism.[45]

The contributors to the present volume can all be read as vigorously participating in the debate between utopianism and liberalism. Their arguments have different points of departure and trace different trajectories but share two important commonalities. First, they all attempt to move utopian thinking beyond the blueprint model described and critiqued by Jacoby. Second, they strive to reimagine the relationship between utopia and law in a manner that overcomes the somewhat familiar and ossified terms of the liberal critique. In pursuing these dual ambitions, our contributors are dedicated to rescuing utopianism from its association with the great state-sponsored atrocities of the twentieth century, and in so doing, to articulating a fresh vision of the relationship between utopia and law.

Our first chapter, James Martel's "The One and Only Law: Walter Benjamin, Utopianism, and the Second Commandment," squarely addresses Jacoby's challenge. Writing in the wake of World War I and against the looming threat of World War II, Benjamin avoided any vision of utopia based on blueprint. Indeed, Jacoby, in developing the topos of "iconoclastic utopianism," invoked Benjamin as a prime expositor. In uncovering the connections between Benjamin's utopianism and his thinking on law, Martel powerfully extends and enriches Jacoby's discussion.

As we've seen, Jacoby located the spirit of iconoclastic utopianism in Judaism's prohibition of graven images of the Godhead. This prohibition, as inscribed in the Second Mosaic Commandment, provides a powerful trope for a form of speculative utopianism that dares to imagine a more perfect future without arrogantly insisting on the details of its picture. The Second Commandment also holds the key, Martel insists, to Benjamin's understanding of law.

Benjamin was not in the first instance a jurisprudential thinker, but Martel argues that he nonetheless adumbrated a complex and subtle legal theory. As Martel notes, Benjamin insisted that "there *is* a law," one that is "perfect and true"—only "we will never know it."[46] The accents of Kafka are all too clear in this formulation, and it comes as no surprise that Benjamin was deeply moved and influenced by Kafka's writing. For Benjamin, our duty is to "both accept the reality of the law and to come to terms with the fact that we don't have access to it."[47] This creates an acute challenge, as we must avoid surrendering all moral or ethical claims at the same time that we must resist merely "reduplicating the fetishism of law"—that is, the practices of conventional human law-making.[48]

The Second Commandment's prohibition against graven images and forms of idolatry supplies, for Benjamin, an answer to this challenge. The Second Commandment delivers a law against laws; it dictates the removal of "false truths from the scene," without claiming to produce or create "new truths" in their stead, and so safeguards the essential unknowability of the law.[49] Benjamin's entire legal theory, Martel argues, finds expression in the Second Commandment, which defines and exhausts the universe of legal obligation. The Second Commandment is, for Benjamin, the only law, and by implication the only one to which obedience is due.

This radical claim is closely tied with Benjamin's utopianism and, in fact, is an expression and distillation of it. To understand Benjamin's utopian commitments, it is necessary, Martel notes, to first understand his very understanding of reality. For Benjamin, reality must be seen as something of a dream—a product of fetishistic projections and reifications. To contrast the "utopian" with the "real," is, from this perspective, something of a false contrast that belies the irreality of reality itself. Utopianism represents a form of resistance to commodity fetishism, a subversion of existing phantasms of the real. And yet Benjamin likewise rejects the blueprint utopianism of a Fourier as the replacement of one set of fetishistic images and practices with another. Such blueprints of perfection represent for Benjamin nothing more than another practice of idolatry, a simple exchange of fetishisms.

Benjamin's "recuperative approach to utopia" seeks to counter fetishism. The antifetishist, as Martel makes clear, "acknowledges the failures of representation . . . . Rather than seeking for representation to succeed in giving us the object . . . , the anti-fetishist looks for a marker of representation's failures, an aporia that does not overwrite the real of the world with false symbols."[50] The affinity between Benjamin's antifetishistic utopianism and his theory of law now emerges clearly. Indeed, the key to recuperating utopia lies in the attempt to obey the Second Commandment. By submitting to this commandment, we become subjects of a law whose "only goal is the unmasking of the false laws that prevent us from being a subject at all."[51]

Benjamin seeks, then, to radically recast and dissolve the opposition between law and utopianism posited by the liberal critics. At the same time, Benjamin sweeps past the positions of Mather and Kant, the subjects of two later chapters, who understood law—of an international and cosmopolitan character—as a necessary tool toward the realization of their utopian visions. Ultimately Benjamin insists that law and utopianism are inextricably bound—that an anti-idolatrous law does more than merely serve as a means toward realizing an antifetishistic utopia; it authorizes and constitutes such a utopian imagining.

The close but subtle connections between law and utopianism also centrally concern our second chapter, Johan van der Walt's "Law, Utopia, Event: A Constellation of Two Trajectories." Van der Walt begins his discussion with a consideration of Heidegger's deeply opaque but profoundly suggestive notion of *das Ereignis*. Typically though not felicitously translated as the "event," *das Ereignis* stands for the idea that "human worlds emerge *from* and *as*" occurrences; they do not simply exist as modes of "a-temporal presence."[52] The event, as the instantiation of human worlds, traverses "a boundary that human comprehension and perception cannot cross"; it produces an "interface between knowledge and utter ignorance."[53] The notion of the event supplies the linchpin of van der Walt's claim that utopian thinking and law constitute distinct responses to the instantiation of human worlds.

Van der Walt develops this ambitiously synoptic argument in a sweeping genealogy of utopianism. Van der Walt identifies one strain of utopianism with thinkers such as Plato, Saint Francis, Sir Thomas More, and Marx. Key to this strain of utopianism is an element noted at the outset of our introduction—the denunciation and repudiation of private property.[54] In classical Marxism, both property and law were seen as "functions of an interim fallen state of mankind that would come to an end with the proletarian revolution."[55] Van der Walt calls this strain of utopianism "literal," a term that largely tracks the notion we have thus far referred to as "blueprint" utopianism.

He contrasts literal utopianism with what he calls "radical" or "literary" utopianism. By this he most emphatically does not mean to denote the literature of utopias associated with Edward Bellamy's *Looking Backward* or More's *Utopia*. Such works, though presented in novelistic form, remain for van der Walt clear examples of *literal* utopianism. *Literary* utopianism, by contrast, is "an evocative form of non-contestation and non-predication"; it can only "allude to an elusive otherness that withdraws incessantly from all positive specified language."[56] This, of course, sounds a great deal like the strain of iconoclastic utopianism described by Jacoby and associated with the writings of Benjamin in the first chapter.

Van der Walt's notion differs, however, in two important respects. He traces radical or literary utopianism not back to thinkers such as Benjamin, Scholem, and Bloch, but to the postmodern turn and specifically the works of Foucault. And rather than turn to the Second Commandment and its prohibition against *envisioning*, van der Walt turns to the fictional practices of the literary imagination, which alone, he insists, "can *give a sense without naming*."[57]

Literal utopianism, van der Walt insists, seeks to overcome and vanquish law; how, then, can we make sense of the relationship between literary utopianism and law? Benjamin, as Martel reconstructs him, described a special affinity between utopia and law, but did so by virtually defining law out of existence—by reducing the totality of law to a single binding command. Van der Walt's understanding of law, by contrast, is far more capacious and familiar. According to van der Walt, law "responds to the event by acting *as if* it is law."[58] If this formulation sounds obscure, van der Walt insightfully shows that it amounts to no more than a restatement of Hans Kelsen's canonical positivism. In *Pure Theory of Law*, Kelsen famously argued that legal norms inevitably derive their validity from deeper legal norms, the most foundational of which resists validation. For Kelsen, the legal system acts *as if* matters of ultimate validity had been settled; or, to put it somewhat differently, the pure theory of law "turns on the presupposition of valid law and legal validity that never exists in or as fact."[59]

This is not an indictment of legality; rather, it underscores the "*performative act of construction*" upon which the legal system is based.[60] The law labors ceaselessly to distance itself from the specter of its lack of grounded foundation.

The invocation of Kelsen allows van der Walt to argue that law and radical utopianism constitute "two opposite responses to the event"—not contradictory in nature but traveling in opposed directions.[61] Radical utopianism turns to fiction to "undo the world"; it seeks to live "through and in the upheaval."[62] Law, lest it confront its status as fiction, "prudently departs from it."[63] Literary utopianism means to steer us "as close to [the abyss] . . . without precipitating a disastrous fall"; the law, by contrast, strives to "steer us away" from the very "abyssal nothingness" to which "utopian quests incline."[64]

The next two chapters in this book likewise reimagine the relationship between law and utopia, focusing specifically on utopian visions of perpetual peace. As we've noted, the classic blueprint tradition saw perpetual peace as unobtainable in the absence of conditioned virtue. These two chapters, by contrast, describe schemes of perpetual peace attainable in the absence of grand social conditioning maintained through codes of coercion and control. In Nan Goodman's "'What about Peace?': Cotton Mather's Millennium and the Rise of International Law," we travel back to late-seventeenth-century New England, where in 1691 Cotton Mather delivered a lengthy sermon, "Expectanda, or Things to be Look'd for," to the Artillery Corps of the Massachusetts Bay Colony in 1691. In this sermon, Goodman argues that the Puritan theologian adumbrated a radically new vision of millennial peace.

As foretold in the Book of Revelation, traditional Christian scripture saw millennial peace as a consequence of the resurrection of the just. This vision, Goodman claims, underwent a dramatic transformation during the seventeenth century, largely as a result of the sectarian horrors of the Thirty Years' War, which both inaugurated the theory of balanced power in the Peace of Westphalia and also influenced a new generation of jurists, most notably Hugo Grotius, who revolutionized understandings of international law. Assimilating Grotian insights into Puritan teachings, Mather came to understand international law not as a means of enforcing peace but as a tool for constituting it. Less a consequence of the hallucinatory processes of Revelation, millennial peace could be, Mather argued, ushered in and maintained through legal practices of treaty negotiation and diplomacy.

As Goodman makes clear, the figure of the "Turk"—the Ottoman—was central to Mather's thinking. Often cast in Christian writings as the anti-Christ, the Turk, in Mather's register, represented the enemy whom it was possible to engage as a party in peace. The forging of a general peace with the Turk would become a "prophetic sign on a par with the vials and trumpets of *Revelation.*"[65] Employing a rhetoric that slips "repeatedly between the peace of the world and the peace of the millennium," Mather suggests that such a peace would "lie on a spectrum with the peace of the Final Days."[66]

Remarkable in this treatment is the forward-looking vision of Mather's Puritan millennialism. Far from a vision of peace made possible through the dissolution of all difference and the annhilation of all enemies, Mather envisions peace as a cessation of war negotiated through the legal instrument of treaty and managed through diplomacy. Indeed, Mather's millennialism anticipates both the vision of perpetual peace that Kant would articulate a century later and the tenets of contemporary liberal cosmopolitanism, which likewise champion a form of international law that accommodates cultural difference.

Diane Morgan's "*Globus terraqueus:* Cosmopolitan Law and 'Fluid Geography' in the Utopian Thinking of Immanuel Kant and Joseph-Pierre Proudhon" complements and extends Goodman's analysis. As Morgan observes at the outset of her chapter, Kant is not typically thought of as a utopian thinker; it was, after all, Kant to whom Berlin repaired in penning his critique of utopianism. As we recall, Kant's uncharacteristically quotable observation, "Out of the crooked timber of humanity no straight thing was ever made," supplied a precis of Berlin's liberal critique of utopianism. Yet the utopianism that Morgan detects in Kant's thinking eschews detailed blueprints and so avoids conflict with his "crooked timber" remark. Though it may be a stretch to claim that Kant's thinking anticipates the "iconoclastic" utopianism described by Jacoby, it would also be wrong to treat Kant as a drafter or planner of utopian schemes. Rather, his utopianism, in its commitment to perpetual peace secured through a federation of states and cosmopolitan law, can be read as an extension of the position Goodman ascribes to Cotton Mather.

Morgan begins by laying out Kant's defense of utopian thinking as a wholly speculative enterprise. The "perfect state may never indeed come into being," Kant writes; "nonetheless this does not affect the rightfulness of the idea."[67] For such "mere ideas" or "concepts of reason" can produce real effects both in "the realm of morality" and in "relation to nature."[68] Put another way, if we "wish to expand understanding beyond given experience," it helps to have a "*focus imaginarius*" that can function as a "productive heuristic device."[69] For Kant, the *focus imaginarius* supplies a sense of the "whole"—in this case, a vision of the global, which makes possible and facilitates thinking about cosmopolitan law. This is crucial, Morgan argues, as cosmopolitan legality emerges as the central achievement of Kant's utopianism.

In contrast to conventional legality, which runs the risk of suppressing cultural variety if wedded to coercive practices and a particular blueprint of international perfection, cosmopolitan law, Morgan notes, relies on a concept of the "world as a whole," something that exists less as a physical or historical fact, and more as a heuristic construct.[70] In this regard, cosmopolitan law resists the empirical at the same time that it avoids a totalizing hegemonic logic of abstraction. As Morgan argues, Kant's vision of perpetual peace, by wedding ideas of international and cosmopolitan law, pushes us toward pluralism, "a way of thinking which considers itself and behaves not as a world unto itself but as a simple citizen of the world."[71] This, again, is altogether different from the pluralism we encounter in our final chapter's discussion of *Blade Runner*, where plural practices are subtended by dystopic instrumentalities of control. Instead, Kant's pluralism, based on both a federation of states and cosmopolitan legality, makes possible an enduring peace that allows both freedom and respect for what is "mine and thine."[72]

A rather less sanguine picture of the relationship between utopia and law is taken up by our final contributor, Shulamit Almog. In "Dystopian Narratives and Legal Imagination: Tales of Noir Cities and Dark Laws," Almog offers a close examination of two dystopian films, Jean-Luc Godard's *Alphaville* and Ridley Scott's *Blade Runner. Alphaville,* more explicitly than *Blade Runner*, fits the classic model of the dystopia that we earlier associated with Zamyatin's *We* and Huxley's *Brave New World*. Like the worlds portrayed in these novels, *Alphaville* depicts a society nightmarish in its regulation, order, and stasis; here we encounter the familiar picture of dystopia as not the rejection of blueprint utopianism but its perfection. More radical than the community in *Walden Two*, which sought to control and eliminate antisocial emotions, and so mold humans adequate to the task of communal living, Alphaville aims to extirpate *all* emotion. A tyranny of logic, run by computers and enforced through an elaborate institutional legal system of coercion and punishment, works to turn the inhabitants of Alphaville into soulless, obedient subjects.

*Blade Runner*, by contrast, would appear to fit imperfectly into this dystopic tradition. Far from sterile and relentlessly well ordered, the futuristic Los Angeles pictured in the film seems to brim with vitality, variety, and urban excitement—as one commentator put it, "the nightlife looks terrific."[73] And yet for all the apparent vibrancy of its urban landscape, the world of *Blade Runner* does represent a classic dystopia for one segment of its population—the Replicants whom the film's antihero is charged with eliminating. In *Blade Runner*, the Replicants are subjected to forms of control even more extreme than anything used on humans in *Brave New World* or *Alphaville.* Replicants appear human in all respects and yet are literally manufactured: their behavior is programmed, their function clearly delineated, and even their termination is subject to central planning. The pluralism of languages, cultures, and identities that characterizes this futuristic Los Angeles is made possible by a system of forced enslavement kept in place by a technocratic elite and elaborate structures of coercion.

Here, as in *Alphaville,* the dystopic order is maintained by a "threatening, invisible, and arbitrary law,"[74] and yet the vision we encounter in *Blade Run-*

*ner* is arguably all the more disturbing as the city's surface vitality obscures the subterranean structure of regulation and control. In *Alphaville*, mechanisms of control are omnipresent and unavoidable; in *Blade Runner*, as in More's original *Utopia*, which likewise tolerated and benefited from slavery, the communal pleasures are facilitated by legally entrenched practices of coercion and control. In this respect, *Blade Runner* can be read as offering a trenchant response to the critiques of Popper and company, who saw liberal pluralism as standing against utopia's totalizing impulse. *Blade Runner* suggests that liberal pluralism and dystopic micromanagement can exist side by side—and that the latter can subtend the former. Far from liberal legality as supplying the necessary and sufficient corrective to utopian excess, *Blade Runner* suggests a more dynamic and indeed troubling relationship between law and utopia, in which the practices of a ruthlessly totalizing law, as applied to certain communities, smooth the way to the flourishing of others.

By way of conclusion, we return to the closing paragraphs of van der Walt's chapter, which nicely pull together the differing trajectories of law and utopianism traced in this volume. As we have noted, Popper, Trilling, and Berlin repudiated utopianism in the name of liberalism and liberal legality. By contrast, Mather, Kant, and Benjamin sought to overcome the tension between utopianism and law by both recasting the terms of utopian striving and redefining what counted as law. Van der Walt, however, defends *both* law and utopian thinking as necessary *and* as necessarily separate. Dangers arise, van der Walt suggests, only when law seeks to service the utopian and when the utopian attempts to dispense with law. Such a conclusion, we submit, must be read in the spirit in which it is offered—not as a definitive blueprint meant to chart the only possible relationship between law and utopia, but as a gesture to stimulate future imaginings.

## Notes

1. Lewis Mumford, *The Story of Utopias* (New York: Boni and Liveright, 1922), 307.

2. Karl Mannheim, *Ideology and Utopia: An Introduction to the Sociology of Knowledge*, trans. Louis Wirth and Edward Shils (New York: Harcourt, 1985), 262–63.

3. Even this spirit has flagged in recent years. For an early and influential expression, see John Perry Barlow, "A Cyberspace Independence Declaration," http://w2.eff.org/Censorship/Internet_censorship_bills/barlow_0296.declaration.

4. See, for example, Todd Gitlin, "Occupy Wall Street Is Chaotic, Romantic and Utopian—and That's a Good Thing," http://www.newrepublic.com/article/politics/96254/occupy-wall-street-protest-social-movement#.

5. George Kateb, *Utopia and Its Enemies* (New York: Free Press, 1963), 20.

6. Plato, *The Republic*, trans. Francis MacDonald Cornford (Oxford: Oxford University Press, 1972), 127.

7. Ibid., 139–40.

8. Ibid., 111.

9. Sir Thomas More, *Utopia*, trans. Ralph Roybynson (Boston: Bedford, 1999).

10. Martin E. Marty, "'But Even So: Look at That': An Ironic Perspective on Utopias," in *Visions of Utopia*, ed. Edward Rothstein, Herbert Muschamp, and Martin E. Marty (New York: Oxford University Press, 2003), 63.

11. B. F. Skinner, *Walden Two* (New York: Macmillan, 1976), 182.

12. More, *Utopia*, 9.

13. Ibid., 11.

14. Plato, *The Republic*, 197.

15. Ibid., 111.

16. *Dialogues*, 1443–44.

17. Ibid.

18. Skinner, *Walden Two*, 180.

19. Ibid., 243–44.

20. Ibid., 244.

21. Karl Popper, "Utopia and Violence," reprinted in *World Affairs* 149, no. 1 (Summer 1986): 3–9, 5.

22. Ibid., 6.

23. Ibid.

24. Ibid., 7.

25. Popper, quoted in Russell Jacoby, *Picture Imperfect: Utopian Thought for an Anti-Utopian Age* (New York: Columbia University Press, 2005), 55–56.

26. Lionel Trilling, *The Liberal Imagination: Essays on Literature and Society* (New York: New York Review Books, 2008).

27. Samuel Moyn, *The Last Utopia: Human Rights in History* (Cambridge: Harvard University Press, 2010), 223.

28. Trilling, *The Liberal Imagination*, 44.

29. Skinner, *Walden Two*, 91–92.

30. Isaiah Berlin, "The Decline of Utopian Ideas in the West," in Berlin, *The Crooked Timber of Humanity* (London: John Murray, 1990).

31. Ibid., 24.

32. Ibid., 38.

33. Ibid., 46.
34. Ibid., 48.
35. Michael Walzer, "Reclaiming Political Utopianism," *Utopian*, December 14, 2009, http://www.the-utopian.org/post/2410107552/reclaiming-political-utopianism.
36. Ibid., 7.
37. Jacoby, *Picture Imperfect*.
38. He resists, for example, the Eric Weitz's argument that explains Nazi, Soviet, Cambodian, and Serbian genocide in terms of a regime's utopian and murderous commitment to a vision of ethnic purity. See Eric Weitz, *A Century of Genocide: Utopias of Race and Nation* (Princeton: Princeton University Press, 2003).
39. Jacoby, *Picture Imperfect*, xxii.
40. Ibid., xiv.
41. Ibid., 32.
42. Ibid., 33.
43. Ibid., 127.
44. Ibid., 141.
45. Ibid., 144.
46. Martel, 12.
47. Ibid., 13.
48. Ibid., 14.
49. Ibid., 17.
50. Ibid.
51. Ibid., 40.
52. Van der Walt, 5.
53. Ibid., 6.
54. Ibid., 15.
55. Ibid., 16.
56. Ibid., 24.
57. Ibid., 25.
58. Ibid., 31.
59. Ibid., 34.
60. Ibid., 48.
61. Ibid., 35.
62. Ibid., 42.
63. Ibid.
64. Ibid., 50–51.
65. Goodman, 28.
66. Ibid.
67. Kant, quoted in Morgan, 6.

68. Ibid.

69. Ibid., 8.

70. Ibid., 21.

71. Kant, quoted in ibid., 23.

72. Kant, quoted in ibid., 17.

73. Stephen Rowley, *False LA: Blade Runner and the Nightmare City,* quoted in Almog, 18.

74. Almog, 19.

# The One and Only Law: Walter Benjamin, Utopianism, and the Second Commandments

JAMES R. MARTEL

## I. Introduction

The question of the relationship between law and utopia seems a contradiction in terms when you think that law is about judgment, order, and rules, while utopia seems to be about nothing at all. How then can utopian thought have anything at all to say about legal theory when it seems to have no basis or purchase in the real world that law operates within? What would be the value of thinking about law from the perspective of imagining societies and forms of practice that do not (by definition) even exist? Yet to think this way—and to ask these kinds of questions—is to make certain assumptions about both law and utopianism. When we assume that law is purely a matter of facts on the ground, of how law is practiced, and what goes by the name of justice, we risk naturalizing a status quo that is in fact constantly in a state of flux (hence, depoliticizing the ways in which that change occurs). Similarly, when we dismiss utopianism as being completely cut off from reality, we risk, once again, ascribing to our current conceptions of reality a certain sense of inevitability or fate which we feel powerless to change.

The value, then, of connecting legal to utopian thought comes from the way that both can serve as ways to rethink our contemporary practices by mutually calling the assumptions that we make about these practices into question. When we understand law not as a fixed set of practices per se but as a series of principles and guidelines that help determine those practices, we see the benefit of submitting those principles to utopian thought. Utopian thought is useful precisely because it begins with a basic rejection of how things operate in the contemporary context (and hence helps to make us open to new ideas, new possibilities). Similarly, when we think about utopian thought in terms of legal theory, it helps to anchor and specify the nature of that thought, so that what we think and the ways we think about utopia remain in the service of human actors and actual human situations.

In this essay I will examine the question of the relationship between law and utopianism by looking at one particular thinker, Walter Benjamin, who, in my view, is uniquely well suited for considerations of this intersection.[1] Benjamin's life work is devoted to exactly the central issue that connects utopianism and the law—namely, how to question what we take as basic and unchangeable reality and, further, how to act in ways that are lawful and just even as we don't have access to what reality really "is." In this essay I will argue that Benjamin has something critical to offer us about the notion of law, the nature of utopian thought, and, most critically, the intersection between law and utopia. He shows us how to turn our backs on virtually the entirety of what we think of as law, without fundamentally abandoning law itself. He also shows us how to engage in utopian thinking without succumbing to the unreality that utopianism inherently operates within. In Benjamin's hands, both law and utopia are radically reconceptualized and, in that reconceptualization, we have a chance to revisit law afresh, to think about its fundamentals without being guided by long-established patterns of thinking and doing that tend to replicate existing practices and ideologies.

In thinking about the theme of "Law and the Utopian Imagination" in terms of Benjamin then, we must proceed, first, to uncover what his own legal theory actually is and, secondarily, to examine what his notion of utopia is and how it works. Both of these steps are critical: if Benjamin has no effective legal theory, then we needn't worry about whether he is utopian or not (or rather, his utopianism, taken in the ordinary sense of that word, is confirmed for us). If he has a legal theory but it is "utopian" (again, taken in the ordinary sense of the word), then it doesn't much matter what his legal theory is since it would seem to be of no actual use to us.

Therefore, I will attempt first to delineate what a properly Benjaminian sense of law would be, what we are and are not obliged to do in terms of such a law, and, secondarily, to think about what Benjamin actually means by the term "utopian" and how this influences or illuminates our understanding both of his theory of law and its practicability. I will argue that in fact Benjamin does have a theory of law, but it boils down to obeying only one law: the Second Commandment's prohibition against idolatry. From this one law, I will show, we can surmise an entire style of legal ethics and obligation (in other words, we can derive from this one law all the validity and authority that are normally ascribed to law more generally, albeit in an entirely different manner). Moving on to his notion of utopianism, I will argue that his utopianism is oriented only toward a world that is ensconced in idolatry (that is to say, our world, a world that does not obey the only law that Benjamin requires of us). Taken from the perspective of a world that is not idolatrous (a world that is "nowhere" to be found in our own world), it is we idolaters who live in a phantasmic utopia; reality itself can only be dimly imagined via acts of "utopian" imagination.

By looking at Benjamin's work on the subject, we can think more deeply about the connection between law and utopia more generally; Benjamin's work offers us a particularly well thought out example of what the utopian imagination can do for the study of law. In his work we can see how a way of thinking that is inherently esoteric and unmoored from reality can, in fact, have very tangible and practical implications, can in fact completely undo and remake the notions of law that we tend to take for granted (or accept as inevitable).

## II. Benjamin's Law

Let me begin this inquiry then by turning to the question of the law and what legal theory, if any, we can find in Benjamin's work. In terms of such a contribution, Benjamin leaves us in a strange position. On the one hand, in his "Critique of Violence," Benjamin sets out a very comprehensive overview of the law, ranging from natural to positive law. Here, he sets out the parameters of law as we understand it, its basis for authority. On the other hand, via his notion of divine violence, also promoted in that essay, he offers a vision of a law-destroying deity that upends and subverts all human contrivances. If law is both the foundation of political authority and also, in its divine manifestation, the undoing of the same, what does this say about our actual practices? What kind of law are we permitted in the face of divine interference?

In this section, I will argue that for Benjamin divine interference does not completely undermine law as a human practice; instead—as already suggested—it leaves us with only one law, the Second Commandment against idolatry. Insofar as the act of divine violence is itself an act explicitly directed against idolatry, it offers a celestial model for law that serves us on earth as well. To obey one single law may seem like a recipe for anarchy (and indeed, I will argue that it is, but not in the usual negative sense that many bring to that term). It seems to diminish law to a mere pith, a singularity that cannot address the complexity of human life and experience. In fact, however, I will argue that this one law is the only law that we need. This law protects us from the ossification of law as a whole. It prevents law from being "bastardized" by myth (to use Benjamin's own term).[2] With it we are given just what is required for law to function as a way to safeguard the human polity and no more. Indeed, as I will go on to argue, for Benjamin, all other law is not only superfluous but actually distorts and interferes with this one true law. Collectively, these essays lay out the basis for Benjamin's understanding of law.

### *Divine vs. Mythological Violence*

To make this argument more clear, let me lay out some of Benjamin's basic claims in the "Critique of Violence" along with a corresponding essay, "The Right to Use Force," which offers useful commentary and elaboration on the better-known essay. These essays were written very closely in time (1921 and 1920, respectively, although only the "Critique" was published in Benjamin's lifetime).

In the "Critique," Benjamin runs through many distinctions in law, including between the aforementioned natural and positive law and between law-making and law-preserving violence. The key distinction in this essay, however, as I read it (and many others as well), is that between divine and mythic violence. As is often the case with one of Benjamin's essays, as you move along through the work, the ground that the reader has assumed at the beginning becomes upended and subverted by later iterations in the text. Not unlike the usurpation of law that Benjamin attributes to divine violence in the essay, we as readers are left similarly upended, without recourse to those easier answers and assurances that the essay seemed to supply us with at the beginning.

The introduction of the distinction between mythic and divine violence, which comes about two thirds of the way into the essay, calls into question much of the careful work that Benjamin had painstakingly laid out (and without any foreshadowing) in the earlier portions of the essay. The iterations of law that he has catalogued are revealed to be instances of mythic law—that is, law that is idolatrous, a false, human-derived stand-in for divine law.

Benjamin introduces this final distinction by asking, "[W]hat kind of violence exist[s] other than all those envisaged by legal theory"?[3] In other words, what force or power of authority exists beyond the confines of the human imagination? He asks this because as he sees it, there is a chronic "insolubility of legal problems."[4] For Benjamin, despite the various distinctions that we make within the law, no form of it can serve as its own ground or foundation; no form of law that human beings derive on their own can ever actually produce true justice.[5] Benjamin tells us: "[It] is never reason that decides on the justification of means and the justness of ends: fate-imposed violence decides on the former, and God on the latter."[6] Here we see that the law—such as we know it—is produced randomly, without recourse to any actually true principles. In this way, the law takes on the character of fate: a random destiny that we cannot resist.

For Benjamin there *is* a true and perfect law—God's divine law—but as human beings we are fated never to know it. In introducing the distinction between mythic violence and divine violence, Benjamin is distinguishing between the truth of law as we imagine it (that is, as a myth, a human projection onto God), and what it actually is (as divine, something that lies only in the mind of God).

Benjamin furnishes an archetypical example of mythic violence by considering the punishment of Niobe. In the Greek myth that bears her name, Niobe bragged that while she had fourteen children, Leto, the mother of Apollo and Artemis, only had two. In revenge, Apollo and Artemis slew her children one by one (in some renditions, they leave one child of each gender alive to achieve parity). Niobe was then turned into a weeping rock, forever mourning the loss of her children. After connecting this kind of mythic violence directly to lawmaking violence, Benjamin notes:

> The function of violence in lawmaking is twofold, in the sense that lawmaking pursues as its end, with violence as the means, *what* is to be established as law, but at the moment of instatement does not dismiss violence; rather, at the very moment of lawmaking, it specifically establishes as law not an end unalloyed by violence but one necessarily and intimately bound to it, under the title of power.[7]

In other words, such an action does not eliminate violence in its manifestation but rather preserves it in the heart of the legal process. Niobe, Benjamin notes, is not killed but lives on, "more guilty than before through the death of the children."[8] As opposed to divine violence, which is based on the principle of justice and which (therefore) definitively settles matters—and hence the need for more violence or law—for Benjamin, mythic violence is endless, unresolvable. He tells us that "power [is] the principle of all lawmaking."[9] Law is in the end only force or violence (as is often noted, the German term that Benjamin employs, *Gewalt*, applies to both); it has no other basis for existing than the simple exertion of power, even as it attributes that power to divine or other external sources.

Mythic violence is thus very much a product of the human world; it seems to come out of nowhere and has no source besides humanity's own conception. The law that it produces therefore remains in an ambivalent limbo, always vulnerable to change and exposure (Benjamin speaks of the "mythic ambiguity" of law).[10] Such ambivalence, as we have already seen, becomes disguised as fate, as undeniable destiny, in order to avoid exposing the vulnerability of law. Thus, for Benjamin, "violence . . . bursts upon Niobe from the uncertain, ambiguous sphere of fate."[11] Without the authority and finality of an act truly marked by justice (that is, an act of divine violence), law—the product of mythic violence—is always grasping for as well as presuming a truth that it does not possess (hence it is idolatrous).

Benjamin writes further of this:

> Far from inaugurating a purer sphere, the mythic manifestation of immediate violence shows itself fundamentally identical with all legal violence, and turns suspicion concerning the latter into certainty of the perniciousness of its historical function, the destruction of which thus becomes obligatory.[12]

Benjamin responds to this fundamental ambiguity in law with a call to destroy the law—or rather, it is not that he calls for its destruction but notes that it is always in the process of being destroyed. For Benjamin divine violence, a force that comes from without the human realm (and, as we will see further, is in fact not really a form of violence at all), is the answer to the problem of mythic law. Benjamin famously tells us that "just as in all spheres God opposes myth, mythic violence is confronted by the divine."[13]

Benjamin contrasts the story of Niobe with the story of Korah as an example of divine violence, a violence, that is to say, which definitively answers the question of justice and that leaves no ambiguity in its wake. In this story, Korah led a group of Levites in a rebellion against God's authority as instantiated by Moses and Aaron. While Niobe was left alive as a testament to a power that has to reveal itself over and over in order to exist (insofar as its basis for authority is tenuous and unresolved), Korah's punishment is decisive and leaves no sign: Korah and his followers are simply swallowed up by the earth, decisively settling the question of their idolatrous (that is, mythic) challenge to God's authority.

Benjamin says of this (in another passage of the "Critique" that is very well known):

> God's judgment strikes privileged Levites, strikes them without warning, without threat, and does not stop short of annihilation. But in annihilating it also expiates, and a profound connection between the lack of bloodshed and the expiatory character of this violence is unmistakable.[14]

Here there is no sign (no blood) but there *is* an end to punishment. Niobe's punishment cannot end because the law that it produces would end along with it. Korah's punishment brings with it its own expiation; not only is the sin forgiven, it is erased, removed from the world entirely as if it did not exist. Benjamin writes:

> The dissolution of legal violence stems . . . from the guilt of more natural life, which consigns the living, innocent and unhappy, to a retribution that "expiates" the guilt of mere life—and doubtless also purifies the guilty, not of guilt, however, but of law.[15]

What is left in the wake of Korah's idolatry is a space that has been freed from (mythic) law (but not from guilt, not from our original obligation to divine law, which remains in effect).

Here then is the crucial difference between mythic and divine violence. Mythic violence requires the sign or idol to perpetuate itself, whereas divine violence brings nothing new into the world. Instead it merely removes its own idolatry, leaving a blank aporia in its place. Korah's idolatry was undone in a single moment, and in the space that he once occupied, we find a chance for a new beginning.

Such acts of divine violence, Benjamin goes on to tell us, are "defined, therefore, not by miracles directly performed by God but by the expiating moment in them that strikes without bloodshed and, finally, by the absence of all lawmaking."[16] The annihilation that divine violence instigates, Benjamin is careful to point out, is not purely and totally destructive. It is annihilating, "but it is so only relatively, with regards to goods, right, life and suchlike, never absolutely, with regard to the soul of the living."[17] The destructive power of divine violence is not meted against human beings per se (although of course Korah was a human victim of it) but rather toward the idolatry that we foment. As Benjamin tells us:

> Mythic violence is bloody power over mere life for its own sake; divine violence is a pure power over all life for the sake of the living. The first demands sacrifice, the second accepts it.[18]

## *"The Right to Use Force"*

The arguments that we find in the "Critique" are both reinforced and expanded upon by Benjamin's earlier essay, "The Right to Use Force."[19] Part of this essay echoes the same language we find in the "Critique." In "The Right to Use Force," Benjamin contrasts "the violent rhythm of impatience in which the law exists and has its temporal order" with "the good (?) rhythm of expectation in which messianic events unfold."[20] He goes on to write that although we think that "in a constitutional state, the struggle for existence becomes a struggle for law," in fact the reverse is the case, insofar as "law's concern with justice is only apparent, whereas in truth the law is concerned with self-preservation."[21] Once again we see that (mythic) law is not concerned with preserving human life but rather with preserving its own existence over and above the human life it is charged with protecting.

The one way in which "The Right to Use Force" differs from or expands upon the "Critique" comes when Benjamin considers our options as legal subjects. One option, that he entitles "ethical anarchism," denies that either the state or the individual has any right to violence at all. In this vision it appears that we must turn our back on the law entirely, eschewing all forms of mythic violence, all lawmaking as a solution to the perils that face human beings.[22]

Benjamin tells us that such a response is "fraught with contradiction as a political plan," and further that it is "invalid."[23] Yet he does not condemn this position entirely. He tells us that such a stance can "elevate the morality of the individual or the community to the greatest heights in situations where they are suffering because God does not appear to have commanded them to offer violent resistance."[24] Benjamin offers a concrete example of this approach to law:

> When communities of Galician Jews let themselves be cut down in their synagogues without any attempt to defend themselves, this has nothing to do with "ethical anarchism" as a political program; instead the mere resolve "not to resist evil" emerges into the sacred light of day as a form of moral action.[25]

Here we see an example of the possibility of how to live (or die, as it were) without following mythic law. Without presuming that they could know anything about God's will, these communities of Galician Jews simply suffered the law of others without responding with any kind of responding violence of their own.

Yet if this is touted as an option for legal subjects—however ambivalently Benjamin's support seems to be—this example seems like a formula for perfect passivity. Rather than being a meaningful, political response to the arbitrariness and ultimate instability of law, the notion of refusing to respond to force in any way suggests a recipe for total defeat and the death of political community (in this case, quite literally).

Benjamin himself, as we have seen, offers that this example does not suggest a "political program." He is not offering this example therefore, as a model for resistance to a system of law that is not just. Yet there is a way in which this example allows for the possibility of resistance in ways that might not normally be recognized as such. The story of the Galician Jews at the very least suggests the possibility of refusing the law even in the direst of circumstances.

And this refusal can actually take a more positive form for Benjamin as well, one that affirms our ability to make many choices in the face of law. Benjamin concludes "The Right to Use Force" by arguing that "a truly *subjective* decision [in terms of the response to force] is probably conceivable only in the light of specific goals and wishes."[26] In other words, in the face of mythic law (and without access to true law), Benjamin won't call for a systematic formula for how to measure our actions; he does not seek to replace one conception of law with another. What he leaves us with instead is a very different way to think about the law, a subjective, local, and temporary response.

### *Wrestling with the Law*

Here I return to my argument that for Benjamin, we do not need to give up on law entirely despite the fact that we receive it in only in a "bastardized" form.[27] Similarly, in the face of a deity that tells us nothing and serves only to destroy those myths we develop in the absence of clear divine guidance, we do not need to give up on the possibility of either justice or law. Recall that for Benjamin there *is* a law, a perfect and true one, and there *is* justice but we will never know it. Thus our duty is both to accept the reality of the law and to come to terms with the fact that we don't have access to it.

Such a state of affairs leads to a peculiar attitude vis-à-vis actual laws, including laws that have been handed down to us from the divine. In the "Critique," Benjamin speaks, for example, of how we must approach the divine commandment "Thou shalt not Kill." He writes of this that

> neither divine judgment nor the grounds for this judgment can be known in advance. Those who base a condemnation of all violent killing of one person by another on the commandment are therefore mistaken. It exists not as a criterion of judgment, but as a guideline for the actions of persons or communities who have to wrestle with it in solitude and, in exceptional cases, to take on themselves the responsibility of ignoring it.[28]

Actually the original German here is even stronger in terms of what it advocates than the English translation I have used; in German Benjamin uses the phrase "und in ungeheuren Fällen die Verantwortung von ihm abzusehen auf sich zu nehmen haben," in which *abzusehen* does not mean "ignore" so much as "look away from" (literally), or, more forcefully, "abandon."[29] Here, we see quite clearly that we cannot receive this commandment as a knowable, actionable policy (that is, as an objective truth), one that dictates our behavior in all cases. Divine law is, by definition, unknowable to us. Whereas mythic violence "will be recognizable as such," in part because it is of human derivation, divine violence and its expiatory power "is invisible to men."[30] We must therefore be prepared to "abandon" law in its particular manifestations (just as moments of divine violence "cleanse" us of law).

Yet to abandon laws does not mean to abandon law itself, taken in its most absolute sense as divine command. Despite the invisibility of law, we remain ethically "on the hook" (as Alenka Zupancic tells us too) for what law demands of us.[31] We are still subject to God's commandments (although, as we will see shortly, there is only one that we absolutely must obey). For Benjamin, were we not responsible at all, we could conclude that "What pleases is permitted."[32] However this is not the case (he says that such a conception "excludes reflection on the moral and historical spheres, and thereby on any meaning in action, and beyond this on any meaning in reality itself, which cannot be constituted if 'action' is removed from its sphere").[33] To avoid either giving up on moral and ethical claims altogether on the one hand, or merely reduplicating the fetishism of law—the basis of mythic violence—on the other, we must struggle against the ossification of all law by treating it "not as a criterion of judgment [since that province belongs to God alone] but as a guideline for action."

For Benjamin, in making such decisions, we must "wrestle in solitude," either as a community or as an individual. The Galician Jews made one such decision. In the "Critique," Benjamin notes that Jews more generally "expressly reject . . . the condemnation of killing in self-defense," thereby modifying the Sixth Commandment (or at least not taking it literally).[34]

As we have already seen, for Benjamin we can only make truly "*subjective* decision[s] . . . in the light of specific goals and wishes." If divine violence clears the earth (at least temporarily, at least in one place or another) of the fetishism of law that we have received and created, Benjamin is telling us that the rest is entirely and absolutely up to us.

### *The Only Law: The Second Commandment*

Such a proposition may appear at first glance to be truly amoral and quite awful, insofar as it suggests that different people and communities can and will make different decisions about law and force for different reasons. Why is this not just a recipe for relativism, and a horrible, endless relativism at that?

My first response to such a concern is that we already do live in a world marked by endless relativism; by turning arbitrary decisions into "laws" (for Benjamin, "all mythic, lawmaking violence . . . is pernicious"), we ensure that randomness is enshrined in the heart of our political community (albeit a randomness that is enforced universally within the bounds of a sovereign entity).[35] At the same time, I don't think that the decisions we make about the use of force that Benjamin describes in the two essays under consideration are actually either random or relative. Instead, I would argue that there is a method at play in Benjamin's treatment that serves as a critical guide for us. Even if this method does not always produce the same results (that is, even if it doesn't mean, as is the case with proscriptive laws, that we would make the same decision in the same context over and over again), it yet offers a coherence and ethical substance to our approach to law that does not constitute merely a surrender to purely negative or nihilistic forces.

It is this "positive" aspect of Benjamin's approach to law (at the risk of using such a loaded term in an entirely different context) that, in my view, suggests we can speak of a law in Benjaminian theory despite the appearance that he is adamantly opposed to law in all of its guises. In this instance, I would argue, as already suggested, that the law Benjamin would have us follow (and the only law he would have us follow) is not the Sixth Commandment but the Second.

Although Benjamin does not refer to it all the time or in all of his work, the commandment against idolatry, I would suggest, is one of the key elements that unites his work. We see his concern for this commandment in virtually every aspect of his political and legal theory. We see it in his rejection of commodity fetishism, in his theological rendering of the fall of Adam and humanity's removal from paradise (in many ways for Benjamin these two events are deeply connected). We see it in his admiring claim about Franz Kafka that "No other writer has obeyed the commandment 'Thou shalt not make unto thee a graven image' so faithfully.[36]" For Benjamin, the phantasmagoria is itself the product of fetishism and idolatry, and our contestation of it must be absolute.

Benjamin's concern with the Second Commandment reflects his background in Judaism, but in his hands, I would argue, it takes on a very different valence. In this case, the Second Commandment requires not only that we do not engage in idolatry but also that we actively battle against all manifestations of the truth (for they must be idols), even if that truth takes on the form of God or the divine itself (because any idea that we have of God or God's truth must, by definition, be an idol).

In this sense, we emulate God's own acts of divine violence to overturn and subvert those myths that present themselves to us in God's name. We do this without the sure knowledge that what we are doing is just, but Benjamin's method of combating idolatry offers us a way, as already mentioned, to link our individual and collective acts of resistance to create some kind of cohesive and enduring form of politics—that is to say, it does amount to a binding law, only one that takes on a radically different form than we generally associate with law.[37]

### *The Second Commandment and the General Strike*

To get a clearer sense of what that form would actually be, we need to look at a further example that Benjamin provides in the "Critique"—namely, that of the revolutionary general strike. By examining a concrete instance of what obeying one single law at the expense of all others might look like, we get a better idea of the political and legal upshot of such a radically divergent practice. In looking at this example we can ask ourselves if a "law" of this type actually serves us in ways that we would desire. Would it continue to provide some of the functions of law that we have come to expect from it, such as protection and order? And, if not, should we not just then accept the "bastardized" version of law that mythic violence represents as the best we can do under the circumstances (that is, better bad laws than no laws at all)?

Although he does not make the connection completely explicit, I argue that in many crucial ways, Benjamin's treatment of the general strike in the "Critique" is aligned with (although crucially not an example of) divine violence. In both instances, as we will see further, an action serves not to produce new truths but simply to remove false truths from the scene. In this way, both the general strike and acts of divine violence are instances of anti-idolatry (although only the general strike is an instance of engaging in the Second Commandment).[38]

Benjamin begins his discussion of the general strike by noting that (not unlike the example of Galician Jews) it appears to be a "non-action" and hence not a real threat to the state—that is, it is seen as something that leaves the state it's monopoly on "action," and hence violence, as the terms are generally understood.[39] In fact, for Benjamin the general strike *is* nonviolent, insofar as it does not partake of the usual phantasms for which violence—that is to say, all forms of lawmaking and mythology—is engaged in (for this same reason, I'd argue that divine violence is not, properly speaking, an instance of actual violence either, but something of a completely different order and category).

Distinguishing between the political strike and the general strike (or rather engaging with Sorel's distinction between them), Benjamin argues that while the former is merely a change of commanders over the state (and hence, remaining within law), the latter is outside of law and violence altogether. He writes:

> Whereas the first [political] form of interruption of work is violent, since it causes only an external modification in labor conditions, the second, as a pure means, is nonviolent. For it takes place not in readiness to resume work following external concessions and this or that modification to working conditions, but in the determination to resume only a wholly transformed work, no longer enforced by the state, an upheaval that this kind of strike not so much causes as consummates.[40]

The notion of the general strike as "pure means" suggests once again the kind of "truly *subjective* decision[s]" that we must engage with in the face of divine laws that we cannot know. For Benjamin to speak of the general strike as "pure means" suggests turning away from ends (which are the province of God alone). It means, once again, to embrace the subjective as our only possible response to the unknowability of law. This accords with something that Benjamin argues in the *Origin of German Tragic Drama* when he writes: "Subjectivity, like an angel falling into the depths is brought back by allegories, and is held fast in heaven."[41] We see here, as in the case of the general strike (and the example of the Galician Jews as well) that subjectivity, although itself a product of the fall, is our path back toward truth, not insofar as it shows us truth, but insofar as it suggests and dramatizes our failure to know truth. To embrace our subjectivity as such is to acknowledge our failure to know the law (or, our failure to know anything at all, as is expressed by allegory in Benjamin's schema). In that knowledge, we are freed, however temporarily or partially, from the idolatry we constantly foment and subscribe to; the aporia of law is kept open, unknown, and unknowable. In this way, too, what appears to be totally passive, inert, and a "non-action" can have a radical and subversive effect in the world. Here, failure itself becomes the chief weapon, the strongest asset that we can possess as befits our obedience to the Second Commandment.

This failure is at the heart of what distinguishes the revolutionary general strike, in Benjamin's view, from other (compromised) forms of political action. In once again considering the difference between a political and a general strike, Benjamin writes that "the first of these undertakings [that is, the political strike] is lawmaking, but the second [the general strike] anarchistic."[42] In this way we see that anarchism (which links us back to the previous discussion of "ethical anarchism" as well) can offer a way for human beings to act that is not itself lawmaking, not mythic, not even violent at all. To engage in anarchism means in effect to turn our failure to obey the law into a weapon that annihilates mythic law itself (without producing some new law, new truth, or new idol in its wake). Anarchism, in this way, emerges as that political creed which follows only one law: the Second Commandment.

As already mentioned, in this way too, we see a way for human beings to act in the world in ways that are not inherently and automatically idolatrous. As I have already argued, the general strike is coordinated with or corresponds to an act of divine violence (once again without becoming one and the same, which would mean to reduce the general strike, and our anarchist tendencies more broadly, to another form of idolatry). The discussion of divine violence follows almost immediately after Benjamin's discussion of the general strike in the "Critique." While partial or political strikes are essentially acts of extortion for Benjamin, seeking to intimidate the state into sharing its goods with one class or another, the general strike is, like God's elimination of Korah, both the annihilation and expiation of the crime of state capitalism. There is no deal to be cut or compromise to be reached, but simply a great sweeping undermining of the lawmaking violence that the workers oppose. This also accords with Benjamin's view that the coming of the messiah and the act of human revolution are simultaneous, even overlapping (but not identical) moments.

The fact that it is possible for human beings to engage in nonviolent and law-subverting behavior means that we are not condemned either to idolatry or to passivity in the face of false laws. As already suggested, when we think of the model of the Galician Jews and the general strike as being in the same mode, we can see that our own definitions of what constitutes a passive or active response is itself largely determined by our context. Both of these examples show that it is possible not to participate in law, as we understand it. Even more boldly, they offer that it is possible for human beings, and not just God, to erase law entirely and leave nothing at all in its wake.[43]

Perhaps most vitally, the example of the general strike gives us a clear formula for the kinds of coordinated actions that we can see as promoting an effective resistance to the phantasmagoria. When we see the general strike as disobeying all the mythic laws we normally follow and simultaneously as obeying the one law that we all must follow instead, we get a concrete, tangible example of how following the Second Commandment would actually serve us. It shows how the Second Commandment is not a merely negative feature (such as the example of the Galician Jews might imply) but can be a program for large-scale action. Rather than serving as a font for relativism and the complete absence of law (a sense of anarchism that is truly bereft of order—the nightmare of anarchism that is produced out of the capitalist and liberal imagination), the Second Commandment in this case serves as a font of authority, as a way to create community and action. Here, law serves as a guide for politics—it prevents our actions from being merely reactive, random, and uncoordinated. With his analysis of the general strike, we get the clearest idea of how Benjamin's legal theory is a basis for a political ordering as well.

### *Anarchism and Community*

Here we see that something *is* left in the wake of both acts of divine violence and the human response (let's call it acts of anarchism). What is left are simply the human communities that already existed, those that may have been formed through mythic violence (and hence what we know of as law) but which have an existence that is distinct from—which is to say, not entirely or only produced by—that mythology. Such communities exist in the midst of law and mythology. This view harkens to what I was earlier calling (however problematically) Benjamin's "positive" theory, those aspects that are not entirely bound up with the pure, destructive force that comes from acts of divine violence as well as corresponding human acts of "nonviolence" (that is, the revolutionary general strike). It also recalls Benjamin's claim, already noted, that "[m]ythic violence is bloody power over mere life for its own sake; divine violence is a pure power over all life for the sake of the living."[44] It is the living, the human beings that are not totalized by their own idolatry, that remain left over in the space where idolatry itself has been cleared.

It is this community that is exposed and rendered legible when we obey one law only. Benjamin offers a bit more insight on this community and the nature of its political practices when, in "The Right to Use Force," he discusses how:

> the term "anarchism" may very well be used to describe a theory that denies a moral right not to force as such but to every human institution, community, or individuality that either claims a monopoly over it or in any way claims that right for itself from any point of view, even if only a general principle, instead of respecting it in specific cases as a gift bestowed by a divine power, an *absolute power*.[45]

Here we see more clearly how force (or *Gewalt*) is not legitimate as a thing that is owned (or thought to be owned) by an individual or a community. To engage in this kind of violence is to remain bound by law and myth; it is to seek to extort or carve out a place at the table for a particular constituency (as the example of the political strike suggests). But a violence or force that recognizes "a gift bestowed by a divine power, an *absolute power*" becomes something altogether different (and hence, not a force or violence at all). This divine and absolute power is not ours, but when we act in accordance with it—that is to say, when we clear ourselves of the idolatry we project onto the divine—then a different political relationship, one that Benjamin here gives the label of anarchism, becomes possible. As opposed to "general principles" of Kantian-style categorical imperatives and other systems of legal and more philosophy that seek to avoid or turn away from the subjective, as we have already seen, Benjamin turns *toward* the subjective as a way to avoid the idols that pose as objective truth. He does this by aligning the subject with the objective truth that really is objective, the "*absolute power*" that has nothing to do with terrestrial affairs or human intentionality (but of which we, therefore, know nothing at all).

It is thus in our existence as entirely subjective beings, in our material practices, and those side relationships that occur in the shadow of the laws that we make and hold to, that we find anarchist practices that can be recuperated or recognized.[46] Such relationships are not innocent of law, insofar as they have been formed in the expectation of law and justice. But the removal of law by acts of divine violence and revolutionary action allows these communities to emerge in the space emptied of law's domination, in a terrain I'm tempted to call "postlegal," although a fidelity to Benjaminian conceptions of time discourages such easy and progress-oriented terms. Also, it is not the case that this community has no law at all, for as we have seen, it does have and obey law, but only one.

## III. Benjamin and Utopia

Having laid out an argument about Benjamin's understanding of law, I now turn my focus to the other issue at hand—namely, the question of utopianism. As previously noted, Benjamin's notion of law and his notion of utopianism are linked by a common thread insofar as the conception of a society that obeys only one law seems "utopian," impossible, anachronistic, useless. Furthermore, insofar as Benjamin considers utopianism quite extensively—especially in terms of his work on Charles Fourier (and in a light that could be considered positive)—it is important to understand Benjamin's own notion of utopianism to see whether it may pose the kind of political dead-end that is often ascribed to utopian theory more generally. Our attempts to understand Benjamin's legal theory are useless if they come from a thinker who does not offer an effective, actionable understanding of the political. Thus the connection between utopianism and law in Benjamin's work is critical; if we are to obey only one law, we must come to understand how it is possible to move from current conditions—in which the law itself serves as a phantasm—to a situation in which our obedience to the Second Commandment becomes possible. How do we get from here to there? In this section of the paper, I will argue that Benjamin's utopianism can be considered realistic after all when we realize that the "reality" that we subscribe to is, for Benjamin, only a fetishistic dream and the true reality—the one that his utopianism seeks to access—seems literally "nowhere" even as it in fact forms the material context in which we live and operate (but are unaware of because of our devotion to commodity fetishism and the phantasmagoria).

Before making such an argument, we can see that there are in fact many reasons to be concerned that Benjamin's theory is not realistic or practicable. Besides the example of the general strike and a few favorable (but highly cryptic) comments about anarchism, we have seen that Benjamin doesn't offer us much in the way of concrete suggestions about a path toward revolution or political change. Even if we leave his legal theories out of our considerations, Benjamin is often admired but he is rarely taken seriously as a political thinker and often considered "utopian."[47] This may be, in part, a reflection of the relative lack of guidance that he gives us in political matters.

Among many of those who were heavily influenced by Benjamin, a large degree of borrowing and admiration is mixed with a sense that Benjamin is similarly too far removed from ordinary politics to be of much use for practical matters. Derrida, for one, whose influence by Benjamin is (self-admittedly) immense, nonetheless writes that Benjamin is "too Heideggerian, too messianico-marxist or archeo-eschatological for [him]."[48] More generally, Benjamin tends to be seen as falling between the two stools of his Marxism and his messianism insofar as his reputation as a political thinker is concerned.

### *Benjamin's Utopia*

For all of these reasons, it seems as though Benjamin might not be able to help us after all. Even if his legal thought is attractive, if it is only a beautiful idea that can never be implemented, what is the point of thinking about it further? To better understand this (and to see why we should in fact continue with our consideration of his understanding of law), we must engage more closely with the question of Benjamin's utopianism and where it leaves us, politically and legally speaking.

In more recent scholarship, there have in fact been important attempts to come to terms with Benjamin's utopianism in ways that do not preempt a revolutionary, actionable outcome. By looking at what Benjamin himself had to say about utopianism, these scholars give a better sense of the ways that his political and legal theory are perhaps not so impossible or anachronistic after all (and hence vital for our consideration of Benjamin's law as well).

Margaret Cohen investigates Benjamin's understanding of utopian thought by recognizing that he sees it as pointing to actual, albeit unrealized, revolutionary potential in the collective psyche. For Cohen, Benjamin sought to investigate collective hopes, dreams, and images "even if in a degraded and ambivalent form."[49] It is these degraded dreams (that is, dreams that seem, on the face of them, to be useless for a leftist political agenda) that interest Cohen in Benjamin's work. Contrasting Benjamin to Freud, she tells us:

> Freud emphasized the destructive power of the libido, viewing culture as based on repression. For Benjamin, in contrast, the wish images of the dreaming collective are the utopian longing for a better future whose advent could be promoted, once its content had been articulated.[50]

Here, utopianism is not merely useless dreaming but rather holds within it a trace of resistance in a population that has otherwise completely succumbed to the phantasmagoria. In a way that is very typical of Benjamin, we find that the phantasms of commodity fetishism can be subverted only by other fantasies, fantasies that often take on the generally absurd form of futuristic visions of collective harmony, as we find with the most prominent utopianists of the late eighteenth and early nineteenth centuries, such as Saint-Simon and Fourier himself.

For Cohen, such a strategy is very serious when seen in light of Benjamin's larger methods. In looking at Benjamin's treatment of the commercial arcades that were built in Paris in the mid to late nineteenth century (and the subject of his monumental and never finished *Arcades Project*), Cohen describes how this project could be at once a culmination of mindless consumerist utopianism and a revelation and disruption of commodity fetishism (and hence, idolatry) all in one:

> Displaying commodity as pure fetish, completely severed from its links to production and use, the arcades offered a privileged perch to contemplate the commodity's

> powerful fascination, the pleasure and desire it inspired. In doing so, they not only revealed the workings of reification, but are linked, in however corrupted a manner, to the utopian aspirations of a dreaming collective. These aspirations . . . can be read as a degraded yearning for a society abolishing private property, even though this yearning took the form of an activity that was decidedly for profit.[51]

Cohen also notes how for Benjamin, the very iron construction materials of the arcades "took the capitalist reduction of all relations to questions of use and profit and turned it against bourgeois ideas of beauty."[52] Thus in both its abject fetishism—one so extreme that it becomes legible as such—and in the way it is materially shaped and formed, we see an opportunity (but just an opportunity) for the arcades—to take just one example—to be subverted by their own expression (this too is very much in keeping with Benjamin's methods whereby "art's last line of resistance coincide[s] with the commodity's most advanced line of attack").[53]

In her own study of *The Arcades Project*, Susan Buck-Morss similarly describes Benjamin's understanding of utopia as being an expression of the "wish image," a dream of progress that animates each era in its turn. In *The Dialectics of Seeing*, she cites a long passage from him in the *Arcades Project* that begins with a citation by Jules Michelet: "Every epoch dreams of the one that follows it."[54] Benjamin's own quotation follows in her analysis:

> To the form of the new means of production which in the beginning is still dominated by the old one (Marx), there corresponds in the collective consciousness images in which the new is intermingled with the old. These images are wish images, and in them the collective attempts to transcend as well as to illuminate the incompletedness of the social order of production. There also emerges in these wish images a positive striving to set themselves off from the outdated—that means, however, the most recent past. These tendencies turn the image fantasy, that maintains its impulse from the new, back to the ur-past. In the dream in which every epoch sees in images the epoch that follows, the latter appears wedded to elements of ur-history, that is, of a classless society. Its experiences, which have their storage place in the unconscious of the collective, produce, in their interpenetration with the new, the utopia that has left its trace behind in a thousand configurations of life from permanent buildings to ephemeral foundations.[55]

We see here as well that the utopian dream of a classless society is held by multiple generations. Each moment of dreaming is connected to other moments in ways that are possibly (and mutually) subversive. Yet crucially, in her own comments on this citation, Buck-Morss points out that Benjamin does not see these wish images—and, by extension, the utopianism of a figure like Fourier—to be revolutionary as such. She tells us that

> Benjamin was reluctant to rest revolutionary hope directly on imagination's capacity to anticipate the not-yet-existing. Even as a wish image, utopian imagination needed to be interpreted through the material objects in which it found expression, for (as Bloch knew) it was upon the transforming mediation of matter that the hope of utopia ultimately depended: technology's capacity to create the not-yet-known.[56]

In other words, neither the arcades of nineteenth-century Paris nor the writings and actions of Charles Fourier do anything, in and of themselves, to advance the revolutionary spirit that they indirectly manifest. It is true that Benjamin sees in Fourier, and in utopianism more broadly, a striving for the very kind of classless—and I would critically add (nearly) lawless—society that he looks for himself. But, at the same time, in many ways, Benjamin directly condemns the ideas of Fourier insofar as they remain in their purely fetishistic, uncritical mode.

In the citation from Benjamin that Buck-Morss considers above, we see for example the way in which utopian thinkers look for "the new" and also toward a bright and progressive future. Yet, in his later 1939 updating of the *Exposé* that begins (or at least anticipates) the *Arcades Project* (and which therefore comes from a later version of the *Exposé* that Buck-Morss quotes from above), Benjamin offers the following: "Newness is a quality independent of the use value of the commodity. It is the source of that illusion of which fashion is the tireless purveyor."[57] Newness, for Benjamin, is part of an apparatus that makes the never endingness of commodity fetishism appear to be heading somewhere, offering false hope in a static modern environment that he elsewhere considers to be a kind of hell.

In other works, Benjamin also condemns the idea of thinking about the future in the kind of utopian style that we see Fourier himself engaged with. Very famously in his "On the Concept of History," Benjamin writes:

> We know that the Jews were prohibited from inquiring into the future: the Torah and the prayers instructed them in remembrance. This disenchanted the future, which holds sway over all those who turn to soothsayers for enlightenment. This does not

> imply, however, that for the Jews the future became homogeneous, empty time. For every second was the small gateway in time through which the Messiah might enter.[58]

Here, the attempt to "fill" the future with imagination and with projections is seen to be a kind of idolatry that actively interferes with the potential arrival of the messiah (and hence a violation of the Second Commandment).

Thus we see several ways that Benjamin is set against some of the main tenets of utopianism as it is practiced. We see his criticisms of the utopianists' obsession with the future, with the new, as well as their strong belief in technology as salvation. Perhaps more to the point, Benjamin explicitly breaks with utopian thought in the "Critique of Violence," for example, when he writes: "Taking up occasional statements by Marx, Sorel rejects every kind of program, of utopia—in a word—of lawmaking—for the revolutionary movement."[59] Here Benjamin points directly to the lawmaking and hence fetishistic nature of utopianism itself. He reminds us that utopianism itself is not free from fetishism but operates from deep within it.

Yet, as is once again very typical of him, none of this absolutely condemns utopianism, and particularly Fourier's version of it, in Benjamin's eyes (and technology does have a role to play in Benjamin's notion of revolution as well). We should bear in mind that being a fetishist is, for Benjamin, not the end, but the beginning of resistance insofar as we are all fetishists (Benjamin included). That the utopianists partake in the kinds of delusions that mark other fetishists should not therefore surprise us (and we should not take Benjamin's condemnation of such tendencies as being absolute).

Indeed, for all of his skepticism, Benjamin concedes that utopianism in general, and Fourierism in particular, corresponds in some ways to his own thought. In Konvolute W—the part of the *Arcades Project* dedicated to Fourier—Benjamin writes:

> Fourier's conception of the propagation of the phalansteries [his communal housing] through "explosions" may be compared to two articles of my "politics": the idea of revolution as an innervation of the technical organs of the collective (analogy with the child who learns to grasp by trying to get hold of the moon), and the idea of the "cracking open of natural teleology."[60]

This passage alludes in part to a fragment that Benjamin wrote entitled "A Different Utopian Will." This was written in 1936 in conjunction with the second version of the "Work of Art in the Age of Its Technological Reproducibility."[61] In this fragment, Benjamin explicitly describes the role that he sees for utopianism to play in revolutions. To understand the passage I am about to cite, it is helpful to understand that in the fragment, as well as in the larger "Work of Art" essay it is related to, Benjamin distinguishes between a "first" nature—a question of bodies and organisms—and a "second" nature—a matter of technology and the social. Expanding upon the citation that we saw in Konvolute W, Benjamin writes:

> Revolutions are innervations of the collective—attempts to dominate the second nature, in which mastery of elemental social forces has become a *prerequisite* for the higher technical mastery of elemental natural forces. Just as a child who has learned to grasp stretches out its hand for the moon as it would for a ball, so every revolution sets its sights as much on currently utopian goals as on goals within reach. But a twofold utopianism will asserts itself in revolutions. For not only does the collective appropriate the second nature as its first in technology, which makes revolutionary demands, but those of the first, organic nature (primarily the bodily organism of the individual human being) are still far from fulfilled. These demands, however, will first have to displace the problems of the second nature in the process of humanity's development.[62]

Here we get a better sense of how, for Benjamin, utopianism is a mistaken goal that allows for an actual one. Like a child grasping for the moon, utopianism is a dreamlike expression of a longing; but, just as a sleepwalker will sometimes inadvertently do something in the world that has real effects, the action of the utopian thinker can similarly have dramatic—and revolutionary—consequences, or at least lay the groundwork for revolution despite his or her own full buy-in to the phantasmagoria. For Benjamin, the presence of new technologies (such as filmmaking, as described in the "Work of Art" essay, and ironwork, which he discusses in *The Arcades Project*) enables a "twofold utopianism" in which both technological and bodily questions can be addressed. Here again, we see how for Benjamin the extremes of fetishism are revealed to be a potential basis for the subversion of fetishism more generally. Out of the dream of utopia, a revolution might just be born.

### Recuperation and the Fall

In order to better appreciate Benjamin's understanding of utopianism, of what can be retrieved from utopian acts (or how those acts can be potentially subversive), we must look more deeply at his basic cosmology. In his *Origin of German Tragic Drama* especially, Benjamin lays out a political theological understanding of the world that shows how and why what could be called a recuperative approach to utopia is viable.[63] As already suggested in the earlier discussion of law, for Benjamin, fetishism is a product of the fall. Critically, for Benjamin the fall does not introduce an autonomous form of evil into the world:

> [It] is said of God after the creation: "And God saw everything that he had made, and, behold it was very good." Knowledge of evil therefore has no object. There is no evil in the world.[64]

When Benjamin writes "there is no evil in the world," he does not mean that human beings are not in fact fallen, or that they are not distant from God. Rather, he means that evil, such as it is, exists entirely within human subjectivity. It is our hubris, our misreading of the world around us, that puts us at a distance from God (and hence from ourselves, from our own material existence). This can be said to be Benjamin's understanding of the origins of human alienation. It is once again fetishism, the hubristic belief that we have the ability to know the things of the world unproblematically that leads to our undoing.

And Benjamin means one other thing when he writes that "there is no evil in the world." It means that no one is so fallen, so corrupted by fetishism, as to be beyond recovery (by the same token, no one is so innocent of fetishism as not to be in need of recovery). Benjamin sees in the fetishist an attempt, however misguided, to read the world the way it was originally perceived by Adam. In the *Origin* Benjamin tells us that Adam did not represent but *named* the objects of the world:

> Adam's action of naming things . . . confirms the state of paradise as a state in which there is as yet no need to struggle with the communicative significance of words. Ideas are displayed, without intention, in the act of naming.[65]

Naming does not involve human intention—the hubristic desire to control or dominate; it is a simple act of recognition or acknowledgment. Since the fall, instead of naming we only have representation, an attempt to reproduce the lost facticity of paradise. Since both the fetishist and the antifetishist engage in representation (albeit in a very different way), we see that fetishists are not purely evil but rather pursuing the good according to their own warped perceptions of the world. Their attempts at representation offer a dim reflection or imitation of Adam's original act. The difference between the fetishist and the antifetishist for Benjamin is not that the antifetishist could have direct access to the thing itself. Rather, the antifetishist (that is, the one who obeys only one law) acknowledges the failure of representation, our distance from the thing itself. Rather than seeking for representation to succeed in giving us the object (as the fetishist does), the antifetishist looks for a marker of representation's failure, an aporia that does not overwrite the real things of the world with false symbols.

Far more than Marx or Adorno (depending on how you read them), Benjamin is willing to work with what we have—that is, he refuses to completely condemn the manifestations of the phantasmagoria—because he sees such phenomena as the only mechanisms at our disposal. For Benjamin we have no objective purchase, no space free from phantasm from which to plot our assault on fetishism. Any attempt to think "clear" of the phantasmagoria, to observe false consciousness and objective reality, is, for Benjamin, instantly suspect as just more of the phantasmagoria posing as its own overcoming.

With the above insights, we can see that the recuperation of utopianism is possible in Benjamin's schema because the wishes that it conveys are not inherently evil wishes. They are, as we have already seen (and as Cohen and Buck-Morss explain) the wish for a classless society, a kind of ur-history that harkens back to Adam's life in paradise (even if his theological view isn't always present in Benjamin's work, it is always important to keep it in mind, because it underlies and makes a coherent whole out of his disparate ideas and writings). The fetishist doesn't know she is fallen and so seeks to find her fulfillment in a sense of future, novelty, and progress that guarantees a return to a state that she in fact has never left (for Benjamin God never abandoned us; it is we who have, in effect, abandoned God). Thus rather than condemn a belief in novelty and the future (in other words, a belief in a form of utopianism that is present in every one of us), Benjamin seeks to recover from that viewpoint the valuable and actionable possibilities that it carries within it.

Another way to think about this is to argue that for Benjamin, the very aspects of phantasmagorical utopianism that serve capitalism and reaction can be made into weapons that undermine those very things, returning the subject who engages in them (and, by extension, the larger community as well) to the things that they unconsciously wish for when they are trapped in a dream of a perfect—and idolatrous—future.

Buck-Morss suggests this strategy when she argues that "[s]lumbering within the objects, the utopian wish is awakened by a new generation that 'rescues' it by bringing the old 'world of symbols' back to life."[66] She goes on to write:

> In his 1936 essay, "The Storyteller," Benjamin described the fairy tale as a mode of cultural inheritance that, far from participating in the ideology of class domination, keeps alive the promise of liberation by showing that nature—animals and animated forces—prefers not to be "subservient to myth," but rather, "to be aligned with human beings" against myth. In this sense, merely by rescuing for historical memory Fourier's vision of society, the historian becomes a teller of fairy tales. Fourier's utopian plans, in which nature and humanity are in fact allied, challenge the myth that industrialization had to develop as it has, that is, as a mode of dominating both human beings and the natural world of which they are a part.[67]

We see here an indication both of how the materials that compose the myths of the phantasmagoria can be turned against it, as well as the price we pay when we remain subservient to that mythology. The phantasmagoria, by giving us a sense of our inevitable mastery over the objects of the material world (including one another), in fact makes us subservient to it. (Benjamin ends the Introduction to the *Exposé* of 1939 by writing that "humanity will be prey to a mythic anguish so long as phantasmagoria occupies a place in it.")[68]

We also get a sense in the above passage from Buck-Morss that specific utopian ideas and figures, like Fourier, have a big role to play in this regard. By thinking of another future (even while being enslaved, at least to some extent, to commodity fetishism), Fourier's utopianism serves as a kind of counternarrative to disrupt the sense of inevitability that comes with the development of capitalism and commodity fetishism. His future is as false as the future that capitalism promises, but as another, different future it nonetheless interferes with the sense of inevitable destiny (or "fate") that capitalism puts forth. It is a blow to the totalizing power of lawmaking even as it is itself just another instance of the same phenomenon (or at least strives to be).

Fourier's sense of the harmony of nature and humanity (Benjamin cites Fourier as saying that "the phalanstery is a machine made of human beings") also harkens, however accidentally (or rather not accidentally but as a result of an unconscious connection to the dreams of ur-history), to a kind of reunification with the material world, the very world that our fetishism otherwise distances us from.[69]

Once again in Konvolute W, Benjamin collects citations and quotations about Fourier that illuminate some of this radical possibility in Fourier. For example, he cites from Joseph Ferrari's "Des Idées de l'école de Fourier" ["The Ideas of the Fourier School"], where Ferrari writes that "[with Fourier] the world turns to its antitype, as dangerous and savage animals enter the service of mankind: lions are used for delivering the mail. The aurora borealis reheats the poles; the atmosphere, at the earth's surface, becomes clear as a mirror; the seas grow calm; and four moons light up the night. In short, the earth renews itself."[70] Images such as these suggest, in a dreaming, nonrevolutionary form, the revolutionary potential to alter the world.

When we enlist a thinker like Fourier into the service of a revolution he neither knows about nor desires (so intent is he on his own sort of "revolution"), we see that the basis of his work can serve as a platform for totally unimagined outcomes. We see that the future we (and he) yearn(s) for may not be what we/he expect(s). Benjamin concludes his earlier (1935) *Exposé* by writing: "With the destabilization of the market economy, we begin to recognize the monuments of the bourgeoisie as ruins even before they have crumbled."[71] When monuments to an idolatrous future become, instead, harbingers of their own failure, the failure of fetishism itself, we are finally on a revolutionary path, the path of antifetishism.

## *A Different Kind of Future*

We can already begin to see to some extent how a concern with recuperating utopia is therefore also, in effect, an attempt to obey the Second Commandment. Although in the previous section on law, we briefly considered what living under only one law might look like, we see here that to get to that point, we first must contend with all the ways that we do not (yet) obey that law. From the perspective of someone (that is, all of us) who lives under conditions of capitalism and fetishism, it is highly unclear how we can obey only one law; it is much easier, it seems, to obey all the other laws that capitalist notions of sovereignty and legality impose on us. But our examination of Benjamin's utopianism permits us to see that to some extent, our devotion to one law is already possible—in some ways already happening—even under conditions of capitalism and the phantasmagoria.

If we just look at the example of Benjamin's consideration of Fourierism and the future, for example, we see that although Benjamin exhorts us not to think about the future—lest we contaminate it with the "homogeneous empty time" that already (falsely) constitutes the present—by linking Fourier's future-oriented visions to a distant "ur-history," Benjamin is not so much acting as a "soothsayer" but is rather engaging with an entirely different temporality. Such a temporality can only be expressed from within our own ordinary (and fetishistic) understandings of time.[72] By shifting the focus from fetishism to antifetishism—that is, by reading Fourier according to a different register—Benjamin can redeem Fourier and, by extension, the rest of us as well, bringing us, not to a shining new future, but to a present that we occupy but do not recognize. While such a place seems "nowhere" to us (that is, a utopia in a different sense) because we have withdrawn ourselves from its reality, we see that even in the height of our delusion, we have given ourselves signs of its ongoing presence, a necessary prerequisite to the ability to engage in politics and revolution in ways that challenge the "reality" of the world we (think we) occupy.

### *III. Law and Utopianism*

It is this other sense of utopianism as the harbinger of antifetishism that is most important to stress in thinking about the requirement to follow the Second Commandment and only the Second Commandment. Utopianism speaks of a fantasy realm, a false future that is "nowhere"" on earth. The very use of the term indicates our disconnection from reality, our sense that it might be possible to climb up out of reality itself and go somewhere better and different. Yet, when we subject our worldview to Benjamin's cosmology, our understanding of utopia shifts dramatically. When we realize that what we call reality is anything but, we can see, as previously noted, that it is we who have in fact come to occupy a "utopia" of sorts; it is we who live nowhere real, nowhere at all. Our dreams from within this context (what goes by the label of "utopian") are in fact dreams from nowhere that are about somewhere—that is, about the actual, material world that is not distorted by fetishism (a world, it should be stressed, that we will never know perfectly but that we can at least experience without the alienating certainties that are the hallmark of the phantasmagoria).

It is for this reason that a Benjaminian project to obey the Second Commandment cannot avoid an engagement with utopianism. In Benjamin's hands, utopianism is like a door in a dark room. We dreamers who inhabit this room may see it as a door to another (better) part of the house, but when we open it, it lets in a flood of light, illuminating our situation in ways that would never have (otherwise) occurred to us (and in ways we probably wouldn't have wanted). More accurately, what comes in is not a flood of light but an even greater darkness. In "Fate and Character," Benjamin speaks of a "sun . . . which casts [a] shadow."[73] Rather than illuminating things more clearly (our hope for truth as fed by Plato's myth of the cave), this incoming shadow would render things so black that we would have to give up on the possibility of seeing at all. Bereft of such false hopes, we may finally begin to think about and engage with the world that we actually live in.

Such an understanding helps us to think more clearly about the nature of law itself. We tend to think of law as a set of absolute commands that cannot be avoided without punishment. Benjamin's notion of law is no less authoritative, no less absolute when taken as a divine edict, but it functions in the human realm as a kind of antiauthority and antiabsoluteness. Within the context of the phantasmagoria, command is itself a fetish; the requirement to follow mythic law is meant to come to us in the form of unavoidable demands, commandments that are not to be questioned. We require the anticommandment (that is, the Second Commandment when it is itself taken out of its fetishistic context) in order to resist the siren call of phantasmic law.

Yet this is not to say that Benjamin's law is purely negative; its effect in the world—its authoritative basis—is tangible and immediate: when we obey this commandment, our reward is a break from the idolatry that otherwise determines us. When we disobey, our punishment is similarly instant—the perpetuation of idolatry. We see in this consideration of the Second Commandment that there remains a deep and necessary connection between law and commandment but that connection can only be understood through its negative impression, the effect it has on the myriad false commandments that normally compose our world.

Although such a commandment seems infinitely removed from our sense of reality, as we have seen, the effects of engaging with it are immediate and tangible. This is true even in terms of our most basic individuality; by following this one law (and only by following it) we can finally be said to come into our own as subjects. While under conditions of fetishism, we remain merely objects of the law, when we obey the Second Commandment, we become law's subjects. To say this does not imply that we are controlled at that point by God. To subscribe to such a view would be to reintroduce a kind of total command for human beings which is the hallmark of the phantasmagoria. Instead, we become subjects who are capable (but not assured) of self-determination through the instrument of a law whose only goal is the unmaking of false laws that prevent us from being a subject at all. This is the kind of radical—and profoundly secular—freedom that Benjamin's political theology makes available to us.

In thinking more about the practical and tangible effects of Benjamin's theory of law and its connection to utopianism, we should be careful not to conclude that until we actually get away from, or completely break with, capitalism, we can't follow the Second Commandment. It should be clear by this point that we can (and must) obey the commandment regardless of our situation. Although Fourier qua Fourier is not quite obeying the Second Commandment, we can find a kind of lawfulness in his relative disobedience, something that enables us to look for other, perhaps more effective, forms of disobedience, and lawfulness, as well.

To be an antifetishist and hence, to follow the Second Commandment, we must not only disrupt the festishes that pass for reality but we must also engage in the steady and constant recuperation of antifetishistic possibilities from our various idolatrous acts and gestures (like Fourier's). We must see, once again, that in many ways we are already obeying the Second Commandment, that even the fetishist "obeys" this commandment in her or his own distorted way. Armed with this knowledge, we can see that it is not impossible to obey this commandment; we can and do obey it all the time. The question then changes from "Can we obey the Second Commandment?" to "How can we best obey the Second Commandment?" At this point, it becomes a matter of strategy and politics rather than faith or hope.

### *A Community Without (Much) Law*

By way of reaching toward a conclusion, we may be permitted to speculate further about following the Second Commandment in expressly political terms. Here we can return to a question that we already began to raise at the end of the earlier section about law: What would a community do or look like if it obeyed only this one law? What would it be like in practice? Perhaps more accurately, we can ask at this point what would a community look like where obedience to the Second Commandment was not just accidental or episodic but sustained and widespread, the basis for the community itself?

Would such a community appear "law-like" to us at all? Given that Benjamin tells us that we can (and, indeed, must) "abandon" at times the commandment against killing, what, if anything, would stop one person from murdering others in such a community? How would we still punish people (if at all)? With what authority and on what basis? In thinking about such things, we must be careful not to fall back into the unredeemed aspects of the utopianism of Fourier and others. Such an idealist reading of Benjamin's law is perilously easy to make. One could argue, for example, that if a community obeyed only the Second Commandment, but really obeyed it, then, without idolatry, there would be no "crime." Insofar as God's punishment expiates sin, it seems that a community without (much) law would also be a community without (any) sin (a reflection, it would seem of Augustine's vision of the City of God, in which even the desire to sin is finally removed from us).[74]

Such a vision is tempting insofar as it seems to finally resolve the "problem" of law, but it is important to note that such an outcome is actually highly unlikely—even impossible—in Benjamin's schema. For Benjamin, the lure of fetishism is strong and unlikely to depart from the world anytime soon (if ever). Furthermore, we must suspect any permanent leftist paradise as just another reiteration of the promises of future salvation that are the hallmark of the phantasmagoria itself. For Benjamin, we will never again live in a paradise where we have no sin to worry about (recall that divine violence removes mythic law but not our guilt). The very notion of obeying one law that fights against idolatry suggests that idolatry itself will be a factor of our existence for as long as human beings exist.

It might help to think further about Benjamin's "utopianism" (if that is really what we should call it) in terms of a story that Agamben cites referencing Benjamin (among others). Agamben writes:

> There is a well-known parable about the Kingdom of the Messiah that Walter Benjamin (who heard it from Gershom Scholem) recounted one evening to Ernst Bloch . . . . "A rabbi, a real cabalist, once said that in order to establish the reign of peace it

> is not necessary to destroy everything nor to begin a completely new world. It is sufficient to displace this cup or this bush or this stone just a little, and thus everything" . . . Benjamin's version of the story goes like this: "The *Hassidim* tell a story about the world to come that says everything there will be just as it is here. Just as our room is now, so it will be in the world to come; where our baby sleeps now, there too it will sleep in the other world. And the clothes we wear in this world, those too we will wear there. Everything will be as it is now, just a little different."[75]

In this way we can see once again that the world that Benjamin seeks is in most ways identical to the world that we already live in. As previously noted, Benjamin's own version of "utopia" *is* in fact the world that we live in, but we ourselves do not realize this, so intent are we on our fetishism and misreading. Instead of offering us a full guide to moral, ethical, and legal behavior (such as we already have now in myriad forms), Benjamin's version of law forces us to face a world without such firm (and fetishistic) guidance. As we have already seen, we would be (and already are) forced to "wrestle in solitude" (both individually and collectively) with our judgments. The distance between law and politics, firmly separated under conditions of phantasmagoria, would effectively vanish if we followed only one law; our political actions would all be grounded in the one law (as we already saw in the discussion of the revolutionary general strike).

Thus Benjamin's understanding of law does not deliver us to a happy paradise where we know what to do and ethics are easy to apply. We would still have all the problems and impulses (and clothes and babies) that we do now, but what we would also have, what would be different, is the ability to avoid being determined by phantasms. Even without those phantasms, there are no assurances that what we did was just; true justice, for Benjamin, is the province of God alone. But it would mean that we could have the chance to gesture at justice, to decide, collectively, what justice would mean for us. We would do it without the certainty of delusion, without the phantasms of law and sovereignty that override and render into the background the kinds of daily acts of antifetishism, subversion, and resistance that already mark our life in the world.

Finally, to return to the larger questions of law and the utopian imagination that Benjamin helps us think further about, we can see that although in our present ways of thinking, these two concepts are seen as completely separated, even unrelated, for Benjamin they form what he would call a constellation, a juxtaposition of ideas (and/or also times, persons, objects) that serve to mutually subvert one another. This mutual subversion is not undertaken for the sake of subversion itself; it is not a purely negative or nihilistic impulse. Instead, we can see that the acts of utopian imagination that Benjamin both investigates and engages with himself allow us to revisit the law, to think about what law might be (or is) when it is disengaged from the onslaught of rules, traditions, ways of thinking, and other factors that tend to reproduce our conceptions of law even when we seek to oppose or overturn them.

Utopianism in this argument serves as a powerful tool by which to do something that is otherwise difficult or even impossible: to rethink the nature of law. Whether we consider this as working in a moderate sense, as a tool that can help reform law, or in a radical sense, as is the case with Benjamin, whereby we think about the law down to (and arguably even beneath) its foundations, we see that the utopian imagination is a powerful way to engage with law and legal theory. What Benjamin's offers in particular is a way to avoid utopianism falling into the very trap of unreality that motivates it in the first place. If the utopian imagination serves to challenge the status quo in terms of law, it can also very easily smuggle in more of the same. In his own rendition of this question, Benjamin guards us against the occult reintroduction of the legal status quo. What I have been calling Benjamin's one law, the Second Commandment against idolatry, perpetually serves as a way to avoid replacing one set of idols with another. Here, we see that law is reduced almost to nothingness, but in its very "not quite nothingness," we see the strength and resilience of law, its endurance even in the light of its myriad false forms.

## Notes

1. Benjamin is well known as a theorist of aesthetics and literary criticism. He is also known for his philosophy of history and his theory of language. Yet while his "Critique of Violence" is a widely read essay (one of Benjamin's best known, in fact), Benjamin's reputation as a political and legal theorist is significantly less developed. The "Critique of Violence" has been foundational for contemporary theory, especially in terms of the way that Derrida interprets it in his own essay entitled "Force of Law." Yet it remains the case that Benjamin's contribution to legal philosophy is largely screened through Derrida's intervention rather than being taken on its own terms. See Jacques Derrida, "Force of Law: 'The Mystical Foundation of Authority,'" in *Deconstruction and the*

*Possibility of Justice*, ed. Drucilla Cornell and Michael Rosenfeld (New York: Routledge, 1992).

2. Walter Benjamin, "Critique of Violence," in *Walter Benjamin: Selected Writings, Vol. 1, 1913–1926*, ed. Marcus Bullock and Michael W. Jennings (Cambridge, MA: Harvard University Press/Belknap, 1996), 252.

3. Ibid., 247.

4. Ibid.

5. For more on this, see Peter Fitzpatrick, *Modernity and the Grounds of Law* (New York: Cambridge University Press, 2001).

6. Benjamin, "Critique of Violence," 247.

7. Ibid., 248.

8. Ibid.

9. Ibid.

10. Ibid., 249.

11. Ibid., 248.

12. Ibid., 249.

13. Ibid.

14. Ibid., 250.

15. Ibid.

16. Ibid.

17. Ibid.

18. Ibid.

19. This essay, which exists only as a fragment, was a commentary on an essay by Herbert Vorkwerk by the same name.

20. Walter Benjamin, "The Right to Use Force," in *Walter Benjamin: Selected Writings, Vol. 1, 1913–1926*, ed. Marcus Bullock and Michael W. Jennings (Cambridge, MA: Harvard University Press/Belknap, 1996), 231 [question mark in original].

21. Ibid., 232.

22. Unfortunately, Benjamin tells us that his clear rejection of this vision comes in an essay he wrote called "Life and Force" that was published in the early 1920s and is now lost. Ibid., 234.

23. Ibid., 233.

24. Ibid.

25. Ibid.

26. Ibid., 234.

27. Benjamin, "Critique of Violence," 252.

28. Ibid., 250.

29. Walter Benjamin, "Zur Kritik der Gewalt," in *Gesammelte Schriften*, Band II.1 (Frankfort: Surkamp Verlag, 1980), 201. I am grateful to Marc de Wilde for pointing this out to me.

30. Benjamin, "Critique of Violence," 252.

31. See Alenka Zupancic, *Ethics of the Real: Kant, Lacan* (New York: Verso, 2000), 27.

32. Benjamin, "Critique of Violence," 241.

33. Ibid.

34. Ibid., 250.

35. Ibid., 252.

36. Walter Benjamin, "Franz Kafka: On the Tenth Anniversary of His Death," in *Walter Benjamin: Selected Writings, Vol. 2, 1927–1934*, ed. Michael W. Jennings, Howard Eiland, and Gary Smith (Cambridge, MA: Harvard University Press/Belknap, 1999), 808.

37. I make this argument at much greater length in a forthcoming book that has part of the same title as this essay: *The One and Only Law: Walter Benjamin and the Second Commandment* (Michigan University Press, forthcoming, 2014).

38. Here we see why these actions can never be identical, since it is ludicrous to think of God as actually following a divine commandment that is meant for human beings.

39. Benjamin, "Critique of Violence," 239.

40. Ibid., 246.

41. Walter Benjamin, *Origin of German Tragic Drama* (New York: Verso, 1998), 235.

42. Benjamin, "Critique of Violence," 246.

43. Although I would add here that human beings are able to do this only because of God's acts of divine violence.

44. Ibid.

45. Benjamin, "The Right to Use Force," 233.

46. Although I won't develop the argument here, in a related book I argue that by aligning ourselves with the material objects that serve as the fetishes that organize the phantasmagoria, we can take part in their own inherent resistance to the fetishism we project onto them. See James Martel, *Textual Conspiracies: Walter Benjamin, Idolatry and Political Theory* (Ann Arbor: Michigan University Press, 2011).

47. For more on Benjamin and utopianism, see, for example, Michael David Szekely, "Rethinking Benjamin: The Function of the Utopian Ideal," *Cultural Logic* 9 (2006); Detlef Mertins, "The Enticing and Threatening Face of Prehistory: Walter Benjamin and the Utopia of Glass," in *Walter Benjamin and the Arcades Project*, ed. Beatrice Hanssen (New York: Continuum, 2006): 225–39; Michael Löwy, *Redemption and Utopia: Jewish Libertarian Thought in Central Europe: A Study in Elective Affinity* (Stanford: Stanford University Press, 1988): 95–126; and Richard Wolin, *Walter Benjamin: An Aesthetic of Redemption* (Berkeley: University of California Press, 1994).

48. Derrida, "Force of Law," 62.

49. Margaret Cohen, "Benjamin's Phantasmagoria: The Arcades Project," in *The Cambridge Companion to Walter Benjamin*, ed. David S. Ferris (New York: Cambridge University Press, 2004), 202.

50. Ibid., 205.

51. Ibid., 212.

52. Ibid.

53. Walter Benjamin, *The Arcades Project* (Cambridge, MA: Harvard University Press/Belknap, 1999), 22 ].

54. Susan Buck-Morss, *The Dialectics of Seeing: Walter Benjamin and the Arcades Project* (Cambridge, MA: MIT Press: 1999), 114.

55. Ibid. See also Benjamin, *Arcades Project,* 4 (albeit with a somewhat different translation; I use Buck-Morss's since it is part of her analysis).

56. Buck-Morss, *The Dialectics of Seeing,* 114–15.

57. Benjamin, *Arcades Project,* 22.

58. Walter Benjamin, Thesis XVIII, B, in "On the Concept of History," in *Walter Benjamin: Selected Works, Volume 4, 1938–1940,* ed. Marcus Bullock and Michael W. Jennings (Cambridge, MA: Harvard University Press/Belknap, 2003), 397.

59. Benjamin, "Critique of Violence," 246.

60. Benjamin, *Arcades Project,* 631 [W7,4].

61. The same idea also appears as a footnote in the "Work of Art in the Age of Its Technological Reproducibility," in *Walter Benjamin: Selected Writings, Vol. 3, 1935–1938,* ed. Howard Eiland and Michael W. Jennings (Cambridge, MA: Harvard University Press, 2002), 124.

62. Walter Benjamin, "A Different Utopian Will," in *Walter Benjamin: Selected Writings, Vol. 3, 1935–1938,* ed. Howard Eiland and Michael W. Jennings (Cambridge, MA: Harvard University Press, 2002), 135.

63. Much of this same argument is made in Benjamin's famous essay "On Language as Such and the Language of Man," in *Walter Benjamin: Selected Writings, Vol. 1, 1913–1926,* ed. Marcus Bullock and Michael W. Jennings (Cambridge, MA: Harvard University Press/Belknap, 1996).

64. Benjamin, *Origin of German Tragic Drama,* 233.

65. Ibid., 37.

66. Buck-Morss, *The Dialectics of Seeing,* 274.

67. Ibid., 275–76.

68. Benjamin, *Arcades Project,* 15.

69. Ibid., 626 [W4,4].

70. Ibid., 630 [W6,4].

71. Ibid., 13.

72. Another way to think about this is that, even as Fourier does exactly what Benjamin says not to do, he is *also and simultaneously* engaged in undermining and calling into question the basis for the fetishistic future he subscribes to. *This* is the aspect of Fourier that Benjamin would seek to recover.

73. Walter Benjamin, "Fate and Character," in *Walter Benjamin: Selected Writings, Vol. 1: 1913–1926*, ed. Marcus Bullock and Michael W. Jennings (Cambridge, MA: Harvard University Press, 1996), 206. Benjamin is speaking here specifically of the "shadow of the comic action" as a kind of antidote to the doom of fate. For an analysis of this essay, see Samuel Weber, "Towards a Politics of Singularity," in *Crediting God: Sovereignty & Religion in the Age of Global Capitalism*, ed. Miguel Vatter (New York: Fordham, 2011), 241.

74. See Saint Augustine, *City of God* (New York: Modern Library, 1994).

75. Giorgio Agamben, *The Coming Community* (Minneapolis: University of Minnesota Press, 1993), 53.

# Law, Utopia, Event: A Constellation of Two Trajectories

JOHAN VAN DER WALT

*Prelude*

Ladies and gentlemen, about what am I actually speaking, when I talk from *this* direction and in *this* direction about the poem?

. . . the poem would thus be the place, where all tropes and metaphors want to be taken into the absurd.

Topos research? Surely. But in the light of that which must be researched. In view of the u-topos.

Meine Damen und Herren, wovon spreche ich denn eigentlich, wenn ich aus *dieser* Richtung, in *dieser* Richtung . . . von dem Gedicht spreche?

. . . das Gedicht wäre somit der Ort, wo alle Tropen und Metaphern ad absurdum geführt werden wollen.

Toposforschung? Gewiß! Aber im Lichte des zu Erforschenden: im Lichte der U-topie.[1]

## I. Introduction

We begin with the prelude above because of Celan's invocation of the word "U-topie" in the last line. We do so because Celan's invocation of "U-topie" in this line reflects the fundamental transformation of the utopian imagination in the course of the twentieth century. This transformation became abundantly evident in certain prominent trends in twentieth-century philosophical thinking. Philosophy's role in this transformation was probably as performative as it was constative. Philosophy, or at least some philosophy, reflected or registered this transformation clearly but in doing so also contributed to it. The transformation of the utopian imagination was, however, not just the work of philosophers. It was also reflected in and effected by artistic and literary intuitions. Celan's lines cited above—the reflection of a poet on poetry—was surely an eminent case in point.

The trend of philosophical, artistic, and literary thinking at issue here can be described, very broadly, in terms of a resistance to the way language and the exigencies of clear communication reduce the utterly incomparable uniqueness of *singular entities* or *persons* or *events* to repeatable and generic instances of fixed identity and stable meaning. At issue in this trend is what one might call, following Theodor Adorno, a negative-linguistic quest for the nonidentity of singular existence that transcends or exceeds the identity-forging thrust of conceptual language. This negative-linguistic quest is utopian because of the way it contemplates the possibility of the impossible, as Jacques Derrida put it when he received the Adorno prize in 2001.[2] It contemplates completely noninstrumental relations between individuals that would not subject anyone to the systematic instrumentalization at work in all generalizing conceptual schemes.

The law, insisted Adorno, lies at the far end of this identity-forging thrust of conceptual language. According to him the law is evidently a kind of hyperconceptual language, the extreme generic thrust of which ignores and suppresses the nonidentity and irreducible otherness of singular existence. The quest for nonidentity that is at issue in the thinking that Adorno called "negative dialectics" thus constitutes an endeavor to move as far away from the identity-forging quest of law and of all language that rests content with generic or generalizing predication. Negative dialectics and the law thus move in opposite directions, and it is exactly these opposite directions or trajectories of language that Celan appears to contemplate with the invocation of two directions—from *this* direction and in *this* direction (aus *dieser* Richtung, in *dieser* Richtung). Section IV (The Utopian Response to the Event) will return to Celan to elaborate this point further.

Why does one refer to the *transformation* of the utopian imagination in the philosophical, artistic, and literary movements that have been announced here? In what way did philosophers like Adorno and poets like Celan change the utopian imagination? What was the utopian imagination like before twentieth-century philosophy and poetry and art changed it? The utopian imagination began with Plato and endured for many centuries—in the thoughts of thinkers such as St. Francis, More, Rousseau, and Marx—as a very topical and typical denunciation of private property. It typically viewed private property as the source of all social injustice and all forms of societal alienation. The utopian imagination thus became a very predictable and generic socialist resistance against the institution of private property before it turned—already to some extent in the work of Marx and then very evidently in the work of Adorno and other neo-Marxists—into a much more radical questioning of linguistic or conceptual propriety as such. This radical questioning of linguistic propriety—what Celan describes in the lines quoted above as the wish of language itself to turn around and away from its regular quest for meaning so as to reach back into the absurd—was, however, surely not just a Marxist or neo-Marxist development. It reflected a broader movement in twentieth-century thinking that was also clearly evident in the strands of twentieth-century philosophical thinking that became known as phenomenology, poststructuralism, and deconstruction. And, as already mentioned, it was also clearly discernible in prominent literary and artistic sensibilities of the twentieth century. Section II of this essay (The Transformation of the Utopian Imagination) will trace this development from Plato to Foucault (and Artaud) and ultimately to the Italian novelist Italo Calvino.

Italo Calvino's novel *If on a Winter's Night a Traveller* is brought into the discussion of the transformation of utopian thought that follows because of the way it clarifies, along with Celan's invocation of the "absurd," what was ultimately at stake in this transformation. A utopian imagination that resists linguistic and conceptual propriety as such disqualifies itself logically from just pursuing an alternative conception of normative propriety. It can no longer entertain an alternative social vision that is more proper than ones that are currently deemed proper or improper. It cannot even contemplate the notion of nonalienated social relationships that are more *proper* to human existence than the societal alienation that results from private property relationships. At issue in this utopian imagination has to be something that can in no way be called "proper" or "more proper." This is why the notion of the *event* entered and changed the utopian imagination and why it still signals a core element of utopian thinking today. This is how the utopian imagination became radically non-normative. It turned into a quest for any occurrence that disrupts propriety in every possible sense of the word. And it neither sought nor offered any justification for this quest. Silently but evidently, its concern with the event was simply assumed to resist the identities that social construction imposed on existence. "Madness beyond insanity," Foucault calls it. Celan, we saw, makes mention of the "absurd." Calvino, we shall see, calls it "an upheaval that still has no name [and] has not yet taken shape." Following what one might loosely call the tradition of phenomenological thinking, I will rely on the notion of the "event" to denote this "upheaval with no name," this "absurdity" and this "madness."

However, the understanding of the event that will be elaborated in this essay will not be confined to the currency it received in the utopian imagination. In fact, it may well be the unwonted epistemological merit of the utopian imagination to have drawn social scientific attention to a concept that can be used as an analytical point of departure from where not only the utopian but also the nonutopian imagination can be described instructively. This is what will be done in this essay. Informed by a phenomenological concern with the event, the absurd appearance or emergence of singular existence, and informed by Celan's prompt in the lines above, this essay will describe the relation between law and the utopian imagination in terms of an inception of two trajectories of responsibility. These two trajectories of responsibility, the legal and the utopian, take leave of one another from the moment they emerge from the event that catapults *both* of them into existence. The utopian imagination does therefore not have an exclusive claim or relation to the event. The law too is fundamentally related to the event. The law is also a response to the event, albeit a very different response.

In other words, legal and utopian thinking have a *common point of departure*, departing from which they move in *opposite directions*. The relation between law and the utopian imagination can thus be described in terms of a *nonoverlapping contiguity*. They touch one another—or may have touched one another—once, for reasons of emerging from or having emerged from a common point of departure. But they then take leave and let go of one another, or have done so, for the sake of pursuing two different responsibilities or two different responses. Responses to what? one may well ask. Law and utopian thinking, phenomenology suggests, are two responses to the event from which they emerge. They are two modes of responsibility that emerge from and respond to a primordial event or happening. But they respond to the event from which they emerge in two very different ways.

It might help to contemplate here the picture of two wrist-locked trapeze artists flung into space from an origin of which they will henceforth only have a vague and ever vaguer memory. The relationship between them commences the moment their wrists unlock (all pluralities and all relationships can be said to commence with the "unlocking of wrists"). The relationship between law and the utopian imagination commences the moment they take leave of one another so as to summersault into two different trajectories. And the breathtaking questions will of course always be whether, when, and how they might ever touch or be in touch again. Can they remain in some kind of orbit, perhaps orbiting around one another, sometimes coming closer, sometimes moving far apart, or must they simply move on and move off in completely different directions, ultimately becoming indifferent to and oblivious of one another?

It is along the lines drawn above that this paper will scrutinize the relationship between law and utopian thinking and the different trajectories that they must maintain should they seek to sustain some significant relationship between them. It will proceed to do so as follows. After the discussion of the transformation of European thinking in Section II, Section III will explain what is meant by the notion of the primordial event from which law and utopian thinking emerge and commence with their divergent trajectories. Sections IV and V will look at the respective trajectories of utopian thinking, on the one hand, and legal thinking, on the other. Section VI thereafter explores the way in which the two trajectories of law and the utopian imagination can be considered to relate to one another. It does so by invoking the notion of a *Stoic difference* regarding the different trajectories of law and utopian thinking. *Stoic difference* concerns the way the different and divergent trajectories of law and the utopian imagination can be understood as a differential relationship that results from two different responses to significant events. The different trajectories of law and utopian thinking need not render them *indifferent* to one another. But the return of renewed wrist-locked continuity between legal and utopian discourses is no longer to be hoped for. The time for that kind of utopian thinking is over, at least in modern and postmodern societies that may wish to lay claim to the acrobatic act called liberal democracy. This act turns on the sustenance of an essential distance and difference between law and the utopian imagination.

## II. The Transformation of the Utopian Imagination

The utopian imagination evident in More's *Utopia* is typical of Renaissance humanism. More was a close friend of Erasmus, one of the most prominent humanists of the time, and *Utopia* is significantly influenced by core ideas of Erasmus. Crucial among these ideas were the identification and denunciation of private property as the source of most social ills. Erasmus's *Adagiorum chiliades* commences with two adages that he attributes to Pythagoras: "Friends have everything in common," and "Friendship is equality." At issue in the text is a discussion of Plato's communist portrayal of the ideal society. The best kind of city and the finest laws, suggests Plato, are to be found where the Pythagorean adages are maintained throughout the city.[3]

The identification and denunciation of private property were, however, not the only and most likely not the most pervasive features of Renaissance humanism. Renaissance humanism, at least as far as the history of legal theory is concerned, was pervasively informed by readings of the Stoic philosophers. And the teachings of the Stoic philosophers, and the broad legacy of these teachings in Renaissance and later Western legal thought, hardly require a denunciation of private property. They may well be understood to have sustained, quite to the contrary, the institution of private property.[4] The difference between the utopian and the legal response to the event announced above can therefore be said to have found an early or prototype expression in the difference between a Platonic/humanist denunciation of private property and the Stoic acceptance of the way private property appears to have become an inevitable social arrangement. One already notices here, in these two responses to property in Renaissance humanism, the emergence of the two opposite trajectories of law and utopian thinking.

A central feature of the Stoicism that Renaissance legal thinking rediscovered was the belief in a conception of universal human reasonableness that can be articulated positively and, at least ideally, positively embodied in personal ethics and social institutions. The rational school of natural law thinking of the seventeenth century (*Vernunftrecht*) can be traced directly to these Stoic roots.[5] This humanist conception of reason as an intrinsic characteristic of human existence was pervasive during the sixteenth century. Influenced as it was by Stoicism, it was quite expectedly also markedly apolitical and ahistorical. Stoicism was from its very beginnings onward an ethical or moral response to the pervasive political disempowerment of Greek citizens under the centralized imperial reign of Alexander. No longer able to take part freely in a political community that was sufficiently local to allow and require active participation in the life of the city, the Stoics sought and found existential meaning in a personal ethics and inner morality that turned on the idea of the natural rationality shared by all of humanity.[6] The idea of moral universalism, the origin of which Alain Badiou would attribute to St. Paul,[7] was already significantly present among the Stoics, and it is plausible to accept that the Pauline universalism of early Christianity was a derivative of Stoic universalism.[8] Moral universalism, however, is not a key element of the utopian response to the event that we are tracing. In fact, the moral universalism of the Stoics is in a fundamental way nonutopian. As will become clear in the next section, and partly already in the next paragraph, the Stoic concern with moral universalism is much more characteristic of law's response to the event. It is characteristic of the decidedly nonutopian trajectory of the legal response to the event.

Pauline Christianity inherited a second characteristic from Stoic thinking. Alongside the moral universalism that it preached, Stoic thinking famously also contemplated and practiced a dispassionate regard for the obvious imperfections of the human being. It understood that the very universalism that it contemplated was subject or exposed to these imperfections. The Stoics observed that universal rationality and reasonableness were constantly threatened and tarnished by human irrationality and unreasonableness. Their response to this constant standoff between the reasonable and the unreasonable was not to pursue the final triumph of the former over the latter. Their response to this standoff consisted in cultivating a dispassionate way of life that would ultimately contain instead of aggravate the threat that human imperfection posed to the moral universe to which all humans belonged. This dispassionate response had two sides, a personal or private and a public side. The personal side consisted in cultivating an inner calm that would not be upset by the unreasonable behavior of others.[9] The public side consisted, ultimately, in the articulation of a rational system of law that would prevent human imperfection and irrationality from ruining the minimum standards of rationality without which no human coexistence and commerce would remain possible.

Roman law was in fundamental respects a legacy of the Stoic concern with the minimum standards of reasonable sociability that sustain communal life. There was clearly a good measure of Aristotle in the mix of ideas that went into Roman law, but to the extent that the Aristotelian elements in Roman law comprised concerns that were not already assimilated by Stoicism (thus passing through Stoicism to Roman law), they were surely not more utopian than the Stoic influences on Roman law. We shall return to the Stoicism embodied in Roman law and in law as such in Section VI. Suffice it now to make one last observation regarding the universalistic ethics and morality of the Stoics on which Roman law turned before we return to the trajectory of utopian thinking. This universalistic morality should not be confused with that which contemporary positivist theories of law may want to describe as a conflation of law and morality. Roman law maintained a tangible distinction and difference between law and morality.[10] But it did turn on basic principles of universal reasonableness. As such it did turn on something akin to that which Hart described as the "minimum content of natural law" without which law can hardly survive as law.[11] That this conception of a *minimum* content of morality or natural law hardly confronts one with a utopian response to the event surely requires no further contestation.

The Stoicism that informed early Christian thinking received eminent expression in St. Paul's instruction—in Romans 13—to the Christian community in Rome to respect and abide by the laws of the emperor. Earthly rulers were ultimately appointed by God. This was the beginning of a line of Christian political and legal thought that would become central in the work of St. Augustine and would ultimately inform Luther's denunciation of the peasant revolts of 1525.[12] Giorgio Agamben recently rearticulated this line of thinking in a brilliant reading of St. Paul to which we shall return presently. It brought to the fore the Christian idea of two relatively separate spheres of existence, the earthly and the heavenly. St. Augustine articulated this idea in books 18 to 20 of his major work, *De Civitate Dei,* in terms of the reign of two cities, the City of God and the earthly city. In doing so, he bequeathed a form or mode of political thinking to European political thought that is crucial for any attempt to come to terms with the European tradition of utopian thinking and, more specifically, with the trajectory of the utopian response to the event that has been introduced above as the core theme of this essay. The crucial conception at issue here concerns the idea of *history* or *History.* Books 18 to 20 of *De Civitate Dei* relate the relation between the heavenly and earthly city in terms of a grand historical narrative. They relate St. Augustine's vision of history as the unfolding of God's eternal plan. The history of the world concerns the part of the plan in which the heavenly and earthly cities exist alongside one another in a constant state of conflict and tension. This phase of the plan, however, only prepares the way for the full revelation of God's glory and the final triumph of the heavenly over the worldly city at the end of time and history.[13]

Karl Löwith and Jacob Taubes observed more than half a century ago that the great modern philosophies of history of Hegel and Marx were secularized rearticulations of Augustine's grand Christian narrative.[14] Their observations in this regard surely qualify Koselleck's understanding of history as a discovery of the modern age.[15] The idea of linear *history*, as something qualitatively different from ancient *chronicles* that turned on cyclical or seasonal conceptions of time, surely already raises its head with Judeo-Christian Messianic expectations regarding a future king that would come to liberate and/or redeem the faithful from the woes of earthly existence. And St. Augustine's *De Civitate Dei* can surely be understood as the first grand philosophical and/or ontological articulation of this idea in European and Western political thought. Our present concern with the trajectory of the utopian response to the event requires that one take a closer look at especially the Christian idea of history, for there is an ambivalence in this idea of history that is crucial for the understanding of the difference between utopian and legal thought. This ambivalence would surface in the significant difference between the Hegelian and Marxist philosophies of history that would emerge from this Christian conception. The Hegelian narrative would sustain a Stoic element of Christian thinking that the orthodox Marxist narrative would abandon in no uncertain terms.

As already mentioned, St. Augustine justified the authority of earthly law and earthly rulers with reference to St. Paul's instruction to the Christian community to abide by the laws of the secular sovereign. St. Augustine integrated the authority of secular law in God's overall scheme of the world on the basis of this instruction. God's greater wisdom ordained that the complete revelation of his glory first pass through a phase of partial and imperfect revelation, and this phase of imperfect revelation necessitated the institutions of earthly authority and earthly law.[16] A thorough engagement with St. Augustine's oeuvre is not possible here. Suffice it therefore, for purposes of highlighting what one might venture to call an essential Stoic element in Christian thought, to rely briefly in what follows only on the instructive reading of St. Paul that Agamben articulates in *The Time that Remains*.[17] St. Paul's letter to the Romans, argues Agamben, concerns an instruction on how to live in *the time that remains* until the return of the Messiah and the final revelation of God's will and justice. St. Paul instructs the Christian community to respect the law, but also to live under the law *as if not* (ὡς μή) under the law. The messianic time in which the Christian community lives, pivots on this *as if not* experience. At issue in this *as if not* experience of messianic time is not only a faithful refusal to identify earthly life with the fullness of God's glory but also a resigned equanimity regarding the imperfections and evident injustices that prevail in this interim phase of God's ultimate plan.[18] This resigned equanimity of the faithful vis-à-vis earthly imperfection can be highlighted as the crucial Stoic element in Christian thinking. The Stoics also had to come to terms with the evident contradiction that permeated their thinking. They had to reconcile their faith in the existence of natural reason in which all humans shared with the undeniable irrationality and failures of natural reason that often prevail in human affairs and consequently require regulation by coercive law.

The ambiguity regarding the possibility of earthly perfection evident in Stoic and Christian political thinking surely renders both these traditions of political thought significantly *nonutopian,* or at least *incompletely utopian.* Both these traditions of political thought contained some "utopian" elements. Both entertained counterfactual notions (the redeemed Christian community, on the one hand, and the rational brotherhood of mankind, on the other). But they reconciled these "utopian" elements with the plain evidence of their imperfect realization on earth. It is important to note, however, that certain trends in Christian thinking did at times edge closer to a full or fuller utopian imagination, especially when one takes the denunciation of the institution of private property as a key element of this imagination. Especially of note in this regard is the insistence of the followers of St. Francis that they never owned property. According to the Franciscans, they only used and consumed the clothes they wore and the food they ate: they never owned any of them. For a while the argument received papal protection under the *Exiit qui seminat* bull published by Pope Nicholas III in 1279, but it became increasingly exposed to critical refutation as the Franciscans became a powerful force in Catholicism that eventually controlled vast material resources. Especially Dominicans began to point out the hypocrisy evident in the Franciscan denial of ownership against a background of considerable affluence. Pope John XXII eventually withdrew the papal sanction of the Franciscan claim not to own property in his *Quia vir reprobus* bull of 1329. It is nevertheless important to note, in this regard, how William of Ockham sought to justify the Franciscans' claim that they did not own property. The Dominicans accused the Franciscans of heresy, because the claim that Jesus and the disciples did not own property suggested that everything they used and consumed was used and consumed unlawfully. Ockham argued in response that Jesus and the disciples never claimed property rights of the goods they used and consumed under positive or earthly law (*ius fori*). They were never required to do so, for no one ever contested their right to use and consume these essential goods. As such, they simply received the right to consume what they consumed from the law of the heavens (*ius poli*).[19]

The implication of the Franciscan claim and Ockham's defense of this claim was evidently that the Christian community could already begin to live a heavenly life on earth. The Franciscans clearly claimed that Christians could actually live *outside* the law or *without* law, not only under the law *as if not* under the law. Especially evident in this more radical Christian ethic is a watershed separation of the utopian and the legal, a watershed separation that would henceforth inform the markedly less ambiguous conceptions of morality and ethics evident in especially Marxist philosophies of history. The central line in these Marxist philosophies would denounce property and the laws of the state that sustain property as functions of the phase of history characterized by class struggle. The classic line of Marxist thinking would regard property and law as functions of an interim fallen state of mankind that would come to an end with the proletarian revolution, the dismantling of the state, the dissolution of law, and the inauguration of an administration of goods for which no law is required.[20] It is doubtful whether this Marxist vision still envisages any significant role for ambiguity and for Stoic resignation in the face of human imperfection in the postrevolutionary, posthistorical, and therefore *futureless* "future" of redeemed humanity. Emphasizing such a continued need for Stoic resignation in the face of imperfection has nevertheless not been its conspicuous trademark. And it is a good question whether recognition of the need for Stoic resignation in the face of imperfection would not have blown the whole project with little delay, for it would surely have reintroduced recognition of the need for some form of coercive regulation of social coexistence that former times (times before the grand proletarian revolution) candidly called "law."

The Hegelian philosophy of history is significantly different from the grand

Marxist narrative in this regard. For Hegel the ultimate end of history would not deliver us from the need for law. For him, the ultimate goal of history was, in fact, the materialization of a legal system based on the *idea* of individual freedom, not the materialization of human freedom as such. There is enough textual evidence that suggests a significant measure of Stoic resignation regarding the gap between the historical *materialization of the idea* of freedom and the materialization of freedom itself in Hegel's philosophy of history and law.[21]

The great European and Western philosophies of history would appear to have gone out of fashion for a considerable while now. One of the significant beacons in this change of fashion can surely be found in Jean-Francois Lyotard's annunciation of the postmodern condition of knowledge in terms of the end of the era of grand historical narratives.[22] What happened to utopian thinking in the wake of this postmodern turn? Did it disappear along with the grand modern narratives of history? It is in response to this question that this essay ventures one of its main theses or hypotheses: to the contrary, the European or Western utopian sensibility *radicalized* in the course of the postmodern turn in the sense of *returning to roots* that the great modern philosophies of history only served to obscure. One might say that the great European debate between those in favor and those against the institution of private property finally lost its fascination and gave way to a radically different understanding and exploration of the utopian sensibility in the Western imagination. In the process, an articulation of the utopian intuition came to the fore that was no longer content simply to denounce the institution of private property, but shifted its focus to a more radical resistance—namely, the resistance to the very notions of *propriety* and the *proper* that ultimately informed and conditioned not only the institution of private property but also the rather *typical* and *topical* denunciations of property as *unnatural* and *improper* that have been around since Pythagoras and Plato and include among their legendary subscribers St. Francis, Erasmus, Rousseau, and Marx. It is not entirely clear whether More actually belongs to this list, or whether he articulated, instead, significant incredulity regarding the insight into the impropriety of private property that ensued from utopian conceptions of true human nature.[23]

Suffice it to say that More's *Utopia* provides one with a *typical* and *topical* articulation of the link between *proper human nature* and the *impropriety of private property* in Western utopian thinking, irrespective of whether he himself meant to endorse or satirize this link. And suffice it to observe further that a different line of thinking would emerge prominently in the second half of the twentieth century. This line of thinking would analyze not only private property but also all intimations of linguistic and normative propriety in terms of temporarily dominant and ultimately contingent outcomes of material power relations. Michel Foucault's inquiry into the constructed nature of the distinction between sanity and insanity and his invocation of a madness beyond this distinction as the real abode of liberty remains one of the principal beacons in this development. Friedrich Nietzsche's genealogical unmasking of the power relations that inform dominant conceptions of norms and normativity was of course a nineteenth-century precursor of the postmodern turn against the grand narrative sustenance of propriety.[24] But let us stay with Foucault for a crucial statement regarding the literary and artistic turn to (and into) a madness beyond constructions of sanity and insanity, for one notices in this statement Foucault's lucid regard for this madness as a return to the beginnings of time and the primal emergence of worlds to which we turn in Section III, below:

> It is indeed a question of that *Sleep of Reason* which Goya, in 1797, had already made the first image of the "universal idiom"; it is a question of a night which is doubtless that of classical unreason, that triple night into which Orestes sank. But in that night, man communicates with what is deepest in himself, and with what is most solitary.[25]
>
> The madness of Nietzsche, the madness of Van Gogh or of Artaud, belongs to their work perhaps neither more nor less profoundly, but in quite another way. The frequency in the modern world of works of art that explode out of madness no doubt proves nothing about the reason of that world, about the meaning of such works, or even about the relations formed and broken between the real world and the artists who produced such works. And yet this frequency must be taken seriously, as if it were the insistence of a question: from the time of Hölderlin and Nerval, the number of writers, painters, and musicians who have "succumbed" to madness has increased; but let us make no mistake here; between madness and the work of art, there has been no accommodation, no more constant exchange, no communication of languages . . . . Artaud's madness does not slip through the fissures of the work of art; his madness is precisely the *absence of the work of art,* the reiterated presence of that absence, its central void experienced and measured in all its endless dimensions . . . . By the madness that interrupts it, a work of art opens a void, a moment of silence, a question without answer, provokes a breach without reconciliation . . . .

> There is no madness except as the final instant of the work of art—the work endlessly drives madness to its limits; *where there is a work of art, there is no madness*; and yet madness is contemporary with the work of art, since it inaugurates the time of its truth. The moment when, together, the work of art and madness are born and fulfilled is the beginning of the time when the world finds itself arraigned by that work of art and responsible before it for what it is.[26]

We shall return below (Section IV) to engage more incisively with the key observations in this passage. Suffice it to begin here with only a general question: What was at stake in the pervasive twentieth-century resistance to propriety and the proper and the very notion of sanity that underpins propriety and the proper? At stake was not only the resistance to the proper and propriety but also the most extreme resistance to the *topical* and *typical* that condition notions of propriety and the proper, an extreme resistance that borders on complete madness and opens up a void, a question without answer, a breach without reconciliation. To return to the lines of Celan with which this essay began: At stake was a concern with the *u-topos* and the absolutely nontypical, the *absurd*. Ultimately at stake was a literary and artistic resistance to any language or idiom that has become current; a resistance against the reduction of language to currency, cliche, and coinage. As far as Marxist or neo-Marxist versions of this radical resistance against the proper is concerned, one might want to refer in this regard, following Jean-Luc Nancy, to *literary Marxist* resistances to the commodification of meaning—that is, to the primary *commodification of language* that underlies whatever secondary modes of commodification—economic, moral, and so forth—take place in any society. At issue in this *literary Marxism* was or is a shift from typical and topical utopianism to a radical utopian concern with the *atypical* and *nontopical*—that is, a shift from cliched conceptions of socialist utopias that simply impute the same basic or natural needs to every individual, to an artistic and aesthetic exploration of the absolutely unique and singular manifestation and experience of existence.

Marx himself can surely be said to have made a crucial contribution to the opening of this *literary Marxist* register with his acute analysis of law in terms of the commodification, not only of labor, but also of the laborer him/herself. A crucial passage from the 1875 *Critique of the Gotha Programme* is especially significant in this regard. "Law," wrote Marx in 1875,

> can by its nature only consist in the application of an equal standard, but unequal individuals (and they would not be different individuals if they were not unequal) can only be measured by the same standard if they are looked at from the same aspect, if they are grasped from one particular side, e.g., if they are regarded as workers and nothing else is seen in them, everything else is ignored.[27]

Adorno would rearticulate this thought ninety-three years later in *Negative Dialectics*, one of the pivotal texts in what one might call *the twentieth century turn from literal to literary Marxism.* Adorno wrote in 1968: "Right is the primeval phenomenon of irrational rationality. It makes the principal of formal equivalence the only applicable norm. It cuts all sizes over the same last. Such equality, in which differences perish, surreptitiously privileges inequality."[28]

It is important to note the use of the word "particular" in the English translation of the passage from the *Critique of the Gotha Programme.* "Particular" would have been an apt literal translation for the German words "*partikuläre*" or "*besondere.*" But the word Marx used is "*bestimmte,*" the literal English translation of which would be "determined." The degree of deviation from literal correspondence in this translation is felicitous, however, for it allows one to appreciate the *generically determined* nature of all particulars. It therefore also allows one to discern how ill suited the concern with *the particular* is as far as the radical utopian engagement with the atypical, nontopical, the absolutely unique and absolutely singular is at stake. As Scott Veitch points out poignantly in his contribution to a highly instructive volume of essays on this thematic, the particular is always already a constructed or determined universal.[29] Jean-Luc Nancy's exploration of a *Literary Marxism* similarly points out the array of surreptitious comparisons that always already inform invocations of the particular; hence his recourse to the word "singular" instead of "particular" for purposes of naming the key concern of the literary Marxist project.[30]

It is therefore important to note in this regard that Marx's concern in the passage quoted above is not with *the particular*. At issue for him is *a critique of the particular*; a critique of the particular ways in which the law determines general categories of comparison. The passage reflects an acute awareness of the determined or generated and ultimate generic nature of any positive assessment of value and worth, however specified or specific such evaluation may strive to be. The roots of commodification can be traced to specification.

Marx's and Adorno's concern in both these passages quoted above must therefore be with differences that cannot be specified or assessed positively. They are concerned, in other words, with *difference* that manifests as *difference* and nothing else. To come back to the central theme of this essay, the radical utopian concern with the atypical, nontopical, the unique and the singular is thus a concern with *difference* that manifests itself as *difference* and nothing else. It is a concern with absolute nonidentity, as Adorno put it.[31] This of course implies that the radical utopian concern that has been announced so boldly here cannot be articulated positively. The radical utopian concern cannot be constative. Concerned as it is with difference that manifests itself as difference and nothing but difference, the radical utopian project can only allude to an elusive otherness that withdraws incessantly from all positively specified language. This is why the radical utopian project cannot be anything but a *literary project* that presents whatever it seeks to present (the word "representation" is deliberately avoided here) in an evocative form of noncontestation and nonpredication. The radical utopian project must present itself as evocative and effective fiction that elicits an experience of difference and otherness without inviting comparison and without raising claims to comparable truths.

Difference that manifests as difference and nothing but incomparable difference is evidently what Italo Calvino is getting at in his enigmatic novel *If on a Winter's Night a Traveller.* A crucial passage from the novel reads as follows:

> The book I would like to read now is a novel in which you sense the story arriving like still-vague thunder, the historical story along with the individual's story, a novel that gives the sense of living through an upheaval that still has no name, has not yet taken shape.[32]

This passage calls for extensive commentary, and we will return to pay more attention to it in Section IV, below. Suffice it for now only to note well the notion of "an upheaval that has no name [and] has not yet taken shape" invoked in the last line. The cue that this invocation gives one is this: the literary utopian quest for the unnameable ends in a concern with nothing but a nameless and shapeless disruption of regular and predictable courses and patterns of existence that are well known and well named. If there is anything that is truly nameless and truly absurd, it is surely an upheaval or event that disrupts what we regularly know about and expect from the regular courses of existence. And if there is anything like a real event that is truly an upheaval with the disruptive force that merits being called an upheaval, it surely must remain absolutely nameless. Let us take a closer look at what is at issue when we invoke notions such as upheavals and events.

## III. The Event, the Common Point of Departure of Legal Thought, and Utopian Imaginations

We have it from physicists that the physical universe derives from something like a big bang.[33] Lack of expertise in this field of knowledge prohibits any closer engagement with this idea in what follows. Suffice it for now simply to point out some resonance between this natural scientific explanation of the origin of all things and the understanding of the origin or emergence of worlds in the tradition of philosophical thinking that Edmund Husserl called into social scientific currency with the philosophical method that he called phenomenology. One need not engage here with the structural mutations in the course of which Husserl's philosophical *method* transformed into a specific mode of philosophical thinking in the work of a number of key philosophers of the twentieth century, among the most prominent of whom are Martin Heidegger, Maurice Merleau-Ponty, Hannah Arendt, Jacques Derrida, and Jean-Luc Nancy. The engagement with *the event of the world* is a prominent concern in the thinking of all these philosophers, and the exposition of the event that figures as the common point of departure of the utopian and the legal in this paper draws deeply from the work of all these thinkers. No attempt will be made here to illuminate significant critical differences between them. At issue in what follows will simply be a thought that can be drawn from the work of all of them—namely, the suggestion that the human world does not just exist as a mode of atemporal presence. The human world emerges *from* and *as* an event. Or, to put it more precisely, and to register the irreducible plurality that is at play here: human worlds emerge *from* and *as* events. They happen. They arrive. They do not simply exist in the atemporal or significantly less temporal modes of presence that lay or everyday experience might attribute to sticks and stones and other inorganic entities, as if these objects might also exist "beyond" or "outside" the human world (the grand epistemological puzzle of former times that current epistemology no longer considers meaningful).[34]

What is the event? How does a world happen? How does it emerge from that which one may decide to call *nothingness* for lack of any word that would reach effectively into the abyssal linguistic void at issue here? Considering the way the event traverses a boundary that human comprehension and perception cannot cross, the event must be taken to comprise at least two basic components to which one can refer as the knowable and the unknowable, or the known and the unknown. The event can accordingly be described as the very occurrence of the known and the unknown. The event produces an interface between knowledge and utter ignorance. It also produces a register of this interface. It brings forth renewed constellations of mute incomprehension and articulate understanding. The event is the differential hinge between the *sheer potential* of new registers and new constellations of knowledge/ignorance and comprehension/incomprehension that constitute human worlds. The event is also the very *emergence* of these registers and constellations. Utter ignorance and mute incomprehension are phrases that one may plausibly use to invoke the abyssal boundary of the event, the abyssal limit that emerges from the event or from which the event emerges. It is this abyssal boundary that Lyotard invokes when he suggests that no living person, not even survivors of the camps, really knows or knew fully what the holocaust was.[35] It is this same abyssal limit that Derrida invoked when he said that we shall never comprehend the meaning of 9/11.[36] The event, or the aspect of the event that produces knowledge and language, concerns a finite sip from infinite shorelines.[37] What subsequently comes to be called "knowledge" retains, at best, an accurate aftertaste, or rather, an aftertaste the accuracy of which has not turned stale.

## IV. The Utopian Response to the Event

We can now return to the three articulations of the utopian imagination invoked above—namely, Foucault's madness beyond insanity, Calvino's nameless and shapeless upheaval, and Celan's absurd poetry. For now that we have some idea of what is at issue when phenomenology invokes the notion of *an* or *the* event, we can also begin to fathom the transgression or transcendence of linguistic propriety that is at stake in the madness, absurdity, and upheaval that Foucault, Calvino, and Celan contemplate.

"By the madness that interrupts it, a work of art opens a void, a moment of silence, a question without answer, provokes a breach without reconciliation where the world is forced to question itself," writes Foucault in the passage quoted above.[38] "There is no madness except as the final instant of the work of art—the work endlessly drives madness to its limits," he continues. "[M]adness is contemporary with the work of art, since it inaugurates the time of its truth. The moment when, together, the work of art and madness are born and fulfilled is the beginning of time when the world finds itself arraigned by that work or art."[39]

Times begin and worlds commence to take shape in the intimate and close partnership between madness and art, suggests Foucault. "The world finds itself arraigned by and responsible before" this partnership. And yet, art is not madness and madness not art. Art and madness are only contemporaries, contemporaries that accompany one another in that moment (that triple night into which Orestes sank [and still sinks]) when temporality commences, when time begins. But they are not the same, there is already a parting between them. "Artaud's madness does not slip through the fissures of the work of art; his madness is precisely the *absence of the work of art. . . . [W]here there is a work of art, there is no madness.*"[40] Art is already sane and worldly enough (reasonable enough/presentable enough in public spaces) to be part of the world that is responsible before the partnership between art and madness. Art is already the *world's* response to madness. It is itself part of the world's "responsibility before" its partnership with madness. It straddles madness and the world that emerges from madness. Art is thus both arranged (part of the world that arranges it, notwithstanding the way it arraigns the world) and deranged (irreducibly in partnership with madness).

The poem, suggests Celan, likewise straddles meaningful language and an absurdity that is devoid of meaning. Celan tells us that the poem is the place—*der Ort*—where literary modes of language (tropes and metaphors—*Tropen und Metaphern*) want to be taken into the absurd. Alongside this first invocation of place as *Ort* he almost immediately introduces another word that signifies "place"—namely, *topos*. He introduces *topos* in conjunction with research, or *-forschung*. At issue for him, then, is the research of place—*Toposforschung*. But the sense of the *place* that is at issue in this research of place understood as *topos* is evidently different from the sense of place that is denoted by the word "*Ort*." The latter "place" invokes a locality, a spatial abode. At issue for him in the research of place as *topos* is evidently a place in language, a linguistic place, in other words. European languages have been denoting this linguistic place, at least since Aristotle, with the word "*topic.*" A topic is a focus point of a discussion, conversation, or text. It is also a *typical* focus point of a discussion. A topic is thus through and through a typical place *in* language and more specifically the form or mode in which this typical place takes place *in* language. Celan links *topos* or topic directly to tropes and metaphors. At issue for him are the modes and metaphors—that is, the ways in which language produces topics.

However, Celan is only concerned with tropes and metaphors and the ways of language in the light of that which is to be researched—namely, the nonplace, the *U-topie.* The last line of the prelude starts in the form of an elliptic question: "*Toposforschung?*" The question at issue here is evidently this one: Is the poem the research of topos or topic[s]? Or, in view of the elaboration with which we have begun here: Is the poem or poetry the research of a typical place in language? Indeed/*Gewiß*, answers Celan, but only in the light of the nonplace—*aber im Lichte der U-topie*—where the typical topics and typical tropes of language want to become completely untypical and nontopical. At issue for him in the abode of the poem is the nonplace where language wants to become absurd—*wo alle Tropen und Metaphern ad absurdum geführt werden wollen.* Celan's concern with the poem is clearly the concern with language that turns around and away from its identity-forming typicality and topicality. It is time to turn around—*Es ist Zeit, umzukehren*—stresses a line that follows almost directly after the ones quoted above.

The about-turn that the poem effects is nevertheless never complete. The poetic quest for the absurd that would turn completely away from language, from typical enough tropes and metaphors, would become unreadable. It would cease to be poetry. Celan is duly of aware of this. The poem that would reach the absurd that it sets out to reach—the complete or absolute poem—does not exist.[41] The poem that exists, the readable poem, is ultimately a failed attempt at straddling utopian absurdity and typical and topical language. In the language of Foucault invoked above: the poem is ultimately too much part of the world to sink completely into the madness of Artaud and the triple night of Orestes. The readable poem, however couched in a distant and strange self-designed darkness,[42] is still too intelligible to embody the very idiocy of Goya's

*Idiot.* It cannot become this "shrieking and twisting" convulsion that, according to Foucault, "promises the birth of the first man and his first movement toward liberty."[43]

One will never name it, but one might be edging here—via Foucault and Celan—toward a sense of what might be at stake in Calvino's invocation of "an upheaval that still has no name" in *If on a Winter's Night a Traveller.* Calvino himself stresses that the novel that he contemplates does not name anything. It only "gives the sense of living through an upheaval that still has no name," that is, of living through something that cannot be named. It is important to reflect carefully on this *giving of a sense* that *does not name,* for not only is the straddling of language and absurdity—in Celan—and language and madness—in Foucault—again at stake here. It is also at stake in a way that throws more light on the enigmatic boundary that is crossed and not crossed in this straddling. One must begin by noting the tautological character of the whole phrase "give a sense of living through." "Sensing" is the essence of "living through." "Living through" is first and foremost a matter of *sensing. Giving a sense* or *giving sense* therefore already facilitates or constitutes an instance of "living through." At issue in the novel or in the response to the novel is therefore *not an imagination* of living through something. At issue is not an "as if" we are living through some event. The novel *gives* the sense. It gives, affords and facilitates nothing less than *an actual living through.* The novel allows for living through an event. As such, it does not concern the mere imagination of an event. It does not concern or entail an "as if" experience. As far as any *as if* experience is at all relevant here, it is the negation or the inversion of the *as if* that is really at stake in the novel. The real sense or experience of the novel is, in fact, an *as if not* experience. Reading entails vivid and visceral experience, as vivid and visceral as any other bodily experience; as vivid and visceral, perhaps, as a nosebleed. Sometimes it might take nothing less than a nosebleed to disrupt the experience of reading. Engaged reading produces the momentary sense of no longer being tied *by* the language *to* which reading is irreducibly tied. The actual experience of reading is therefore a matter living under (the law of) language *as if not* living under language.

The objection that the opposite is true, the objection that reading is an imagined experience and therefore an *as if* experience and not an *as if not* experience, contemplates a disembodied imagination from the perspective of which the very real existential threshold- or boundary-crossing experience of reading and the profound utopian role that this experience plays in human existence cannot be appreciated. The utopian and redeeming force of reading literature with which Agamben engages in *The Time that Remains*[44] is incomplete but real.[45] Literature produces par excellence the *as if not* (ὡς μή) experience of messianic time, the experience of living under the law *as if not* living under the law. Reading *is* the redemption that takes place in the midst of and under law, the redemption that renders the experience of law unreal. What law? In the case of literature it is the general laws of language and linguistic reference that are concerned. It is the liberation from these laws that opens up a utopian or u-topical space that delivers the reader from the constraints of typical and topical language.

This redeeming utopian experience nevertheless remains incomplete. The sense of an upheaval that has no name and cannot be named, produced or induced by reading, remains irreducibly clouded in mystery. It is always inaccurate or untrue in a fundamental sense. Literature, suggests another passage from *If on a Winter's Night a Traveller*, is irreducibly *apocryphal* in the double sense of the word. Not only is true literature "false" or falsifying. It is false and falsifying because it derives from a mystery that cannot be revealed. Calvino writes:

> Apocrypha (from the Greek *apokryphos*, hidden, secret): (1) originally referring to the "secret books" of religious sects; later to texts not recognized as canonical in those religions which have established a canon of revealed writings; referring to texts falsely attributed to a period or to an author. . . . Perhaps my true vocation was *that of an author of apocrypha*, in the several meanings of the term: because writing always means hiding something in such a way that it then is discovered; because the truth that can come from my pen is like a shard that has been chipped from a great boulder by a violent impact, then flung far away; because there is no certitude outside falsification.[46]

The work of art does not embody madness, wrote Foucault with reference to Artaud. The truly absurd poem does not exist, insisted Celan. The novel derives from the secret, but falsifies it, suggests Calvino here. But the falsification at issue here is crucial for the utopian experience. The secret does not have an independent existence that then becomes falsified by language so as to leave the reader only with a sense of mystery. No, it is the other way round. The falsification wrought by language produces the mystery. The secret has no place of its own. It is not a place. It is the nonplace, the *u-topos.* The irreducible falsification effected in language and art calls forth the u-topos, the split and threshold between Artaud's madness and the work of art, the poem and the absurd, the novel and its apocryphal origins.

We commenced with the proposition that the event is the common point of departure of both legal and utopian discourses. These discourses take leave of one another, we contended, because of the way they respond to the event in radically different and in fact in directly opposite ways. The utopian and the legal take leave of one another because of the fundamentally opposite or inverse trajectories of their respective responses to the event. It should now have become clear that utopian discourses concern an origin-oriented concern with the very event from which they emerge. As such, they entail much more than mere attempts to step away from privatization and private property, as the classical history of utopian discourses would suggest. The radical utopian discourses of the twentieth century make clear that they seek to step back from the very notions of propriety and the proper that inform and condition discourses of private property in the first place. They do so in the hope of sustaining an experience with the absolute singularity and ineffability of the event. The *absurd*, Celan calls it. *Madness* is Foucault's word for it. Calvino calls it *an upheaval with no name. An upheaval with no name* is an apt denotation for the ineffable event or the ineffability of the event that precipitates the beginnings of time and the origins of worlds.

The trajectory of literature—that is, the radical utopian trajectory of literature—consists in an incessant return to the nameless event from which this trajectory itself emerges like a shard flung forth from a violent impact. Literature is the incessant obsession with returning to the event from which it derives. It is the utopian obsession to return to the event that flung it into language but to which it cannot return fully without losing its status as language completely. As Celan explains with reference to Buchner's *Lenz*, it simply seeks to return to or recall a date—Lenz's journey through the mountains—that it cannot recall from the inside of language from where it is doomed to commence.[47] That is why serious poetry and serious literature always put their linguistic status—their status as language—at risk. Not being able to return fully, however, literature ultimately remains the obsession to maintain sufficient proximity to the event. It is the obsession to maintain at least such proximity to the event as would still allow for the real sense of living through, living, or reliving the event. This is where significantly atypical and nontopical u-topian sensibilities have arrived today. This is the trajectory of its response to the event. The time has come now to look at the very different trajectory of the law's response to the event.

## V. Law's Response to the Event

If it is correct to say that the trajectory of law's response to the event is the exact inverse (180 degrees) of the trajectory of the utopian and literary response to the event, and if it is also correct to say that literature shares with the experience of messianic time the experience of living under the law (living under the law of language, in the case of literature) *as if not* under the law, the following statement should offer an accurate assessment of the law's response to the event: law responds to the event by acting *as if* it is law. Law's response to the event is not really or is surely not fully *an instance* of law. It is much rather a matter of staging itself or styling itself as law. The question whether all of this is correct or not need not be addressed directly in what follows. Suffice it simply to say for now that the assessment of law that has just been offered here is exactly the assessment of law's status that one finds in Hans Kelsen's pure theory of law. According to Kelsen, law never quite exists. The existence of law cannot be posited or asserted (*gesetzt*). The existence of law must be presupposed (*vorausgesetzt*). One must deal and work with the law *as if* (*als* ob) it exists.[48] And this is so, argues Kelsen, exactly because of the way the law is, in the final analysis, always a response to an event.

Why does Kelsen argue in this way? He argues thus because of the problematic and ambivalent status of the foundational norm, or *Grundnorm,* in his pure theory of law. The pure theory of law requires that every legal norm in the hierarchical system or pyramid of the law be fully validated by a higher norm. This would appear to be reasonably feasible in a legal system where one apparently already has legal norms in place that can and must be invoked as validation for all other legal norms lower down in the system of law. The problem is, however, that the foundational norm, or *Grundnorm,* at the apex of the legal system that is required to validate the rest of the legal system, itself lacks a higher norm that could validate it. The foundational norm thus remains fundamentally *unvalid* or *un-validated* (as opposed to invalid and invalidated). And if the foundational norm remains unvalid, the whole system of law supposedly validated by the foundational norm also remains fundamentally unvalid. Not only can a pure theory of law thus not assert the validity of the foundational norm. A pure theory of law cannot assert the validity of any legal norm. A pure theory of law must therefore rely on a whole series of presuppositions through which the law is held to be law. The pure theory of law deals with nonlaw and works with nonlaw *as if* it is law.

In what sense can and must one say that all of this is the inevitable consequence of the law's response to the event? One can and must say this because of the way real or empirical legal norms are always a response to some or other urgent historical exigency. This is true of national constitutions (or transnational conventions or treaties)—the empirical or impure instantiation of what should have been a pure foundational norm—and all other legal rules that are based on such national constitutions or transnational conventions. National constitutions or transnational conventions assess and respond to a historical situation that calls or at least appears to call for the inauguration of a new jurisdiction and the installation of a new legal system. What happens in this historical moment of assessment and response can obviously not qualify, ab initio, as valid. The assessments and responses that take place here eventually receive validation in the course of an extended process of nonlegal intervention and/or lack of intervention: the validity that eventually emerges from a function of a mixture of historical and sociological commitment, contentedness, acquiescence, and adequate familiarity that usually goes by the name of "legitimacy."

Compared with validity, legitimacy is a vague and diffuse notion. It is therefore also a highly contentious notion. Legitimacy can therefore not be invoked under circumstances where some or other crisis or conflict demands recourse to the constitution or convention as an instance of law by which everyone can be expected to abide, for the contentiousness of the situation will most certainly spill into, contaminate, and inundate whatever "legitimacy" may have existed or may have appeared to exist before and up to the moment of crisis. Every instance of significant crisis would therefore reopen the initial assessment of and response to the historical exigency that the constitution or convention *was supposed* to have settled. The enduring existence of constitutions and constitutional law surely depends on sufficient degrees of legitimacy (contentedness, acquiescence, familiarity) as Hart points out well with the assertion that the effective survival of legal systems depends on sufficient levels of *internal aspect*.[49] But it should also be clear that no constitution would constitute law and found law if such constitution and foundation of law were to depend on legitimacy. Legitimacy (sufficient commitment, contentedness, acquiescence, familiarity) is exactly what is in question or in crisis when we seek recourse to law. Legitimacy can therefore not be invoked as an answer to legal questions, for law is exactly that to which we turn, not to answer or resolve questions of legitimacy, but to terminate them. We terminate a question of legitimacy by *supposing* or *presupposing* that we have law that terminates the question.

This is the crucial move of Kelsen's pure theory of law. The pure theory of law turns on the presupposition of valid law and legal validity that never exists in or as fact. Factually or empirically speaking, "law" or what was or is supposed to be "law" will always run the risk of disintegrating and evaporating in the face of legitimacy questions. Law only exists as long as adequate numbers of sufficiently powerful individuals continue to *presuppose* the *prior*, a priori, and therefore *precedent* existence of law (which of course would historically only happen—this is Hart's point—as long as adequate levels of legitimacy or adequate levels of *internal aspect* prevail). The pure theory of law considers law to pivot on the act of purification that takes place when questions of legitimacy are terminated or substituted by presuppositions of validity. This act of purification is the sacrificial heart of law. The ancient rites of sacrifice were essentially rites of purification, and law will never sever its definitional ties with these rites.[50]

What happens at the level of constitutional law also happens at every lower level of law that depends on the constitution. Constitutional questions may sometimes appear to be settled. A legal dispute may appear only to involve the contentiousness of some or other lower level rule of law, say some rule of private law. The identification of a valid and applicable private law rule again turns invariably on a sacrificial act of purification that settles the dust and impurity of some social ambiguity. There would have been no dispute or conflict had there not been ambiguity. Ambiguity is the essential impurity that law has to terminate. The sacrificial termination of ambiguity is the essential purification that produces pure law. The impurity of social ambiguities that informs private law disputes had better be dealt with adequately at the level of private law adjudication, for this impurity surely harbors the potential of contaminating the whole system of law right up or into its constitutional roots. The need to do so has never been addressed adequately in the pervasive literature on the so-called horizontal application of constitutional rights.

The event—a date; an occurrence; a sudden irruption of discontent; the irruption of ambiguity that conditions discontent—is the essential impurity to which the sacrificial purification of the law responds. It should already be clear that the trajectory of this purification is one of *distancing*. Law distances itself from the event. It takes leave of the event. Its trajectory is exactly the opposite of the literary utopian or radical utopian response to the event. Law and radical utopian literature constitute two opposite responses to the event. As such, they relate to one another by taking leave of one another. They only begin to relate to one another when they begin to take leave of one another. Those who would wish to propose a different, closer, overlapping, mutually informative or wrist-locked relation between law and utopian literature should first try to imagine the dark eye of an ancient and eternal hurricane, the *u-topos*, the pure impurity of the event, the nothingness in which all is still one and nothing relates to nothing.

## VI. Stoic Difference and Indifference—Some Concluding Thoughts

Martha Nussbaum's work *Upheavals of Thought* presents her understanding of emotions as upheavals of thought as a neo-Stoic position.[51] She takes from the Stoics the conviction that emotions are evaluative cognitive appraisals. But in doing so she also takes leave of two fundamental tenets of Stoicism. The first concerns the conception that the cognitive content of emotions is invariably misleading. The second concerns the ethics of emotional indifference that the Stoics developed on the basis of their general distrust of emotions. She rejects both these positions and seeks to develop instead a more nuanced view that recognizes the way emotions can lead moral judgment astray, but by realizing that they remain indispensable for sound moral judgment.[52] We are moving to the end of this essay, and the short engagement with her formidable argument that follows does not do justice to it. However, it is instructive to briefly compare the key arguments in *Upheavals of Thought* with the assessment of the relation between law and the utopian imagination that has been articulated in this essay.

In contrast to the Stoic denunciation of the distorting role of emotions in moral deliberation, Nussbaum seeks to rehabilitate emotions as an instructive source of moral deliberation. According to her, emotions provide sound moral deliberation with an essential relation to reality without which moral judgment would not even become the existential issue that it is for humans. Emotional responses provide moral deliberation with an indispensible *aboutness.* They render moral deliberation reality- or object-related.[53] They are the upheavals that call forth moral deliberation. In this regard her thoughts would seem to resonate strongly with the engagement in this essay with Calvino's invocation of an *upheaval with no name or shape.* However, Nussbaum's concern is surely not with the literary utopian return to this nameless and shapeless upheaval. The trajectory of her thinking in *Upheavals of Thought* is evidently the trajectory of law, the trajectory through which the law distances itself from upheavals or events. Her concern is more with legal than with moral judgment, but the crucial thrust of moral and legal judgment is the same as far as their respective relations with the utopian imagination are concerned. At issue in both is the articulation of sound acts of generalizable judgment (at which all reasonable people should eventually arrive) with recourse to which one can extract and distance oneself from the immediate chaos of the event.

Forceful emotions enter the hurricanes with which worlds begin and end and they draw us into their obliterating chaos. Only when they subside do we find ourselves able and necessitated to withdraw from the event and re-establish degrees of equilibrium by means of sound moral and legal judgment. Utopian literature resists this withdrawal and seeks to re-enter the event. It continues to live through and in the upheaval or seriously attempts to do so. It pivots on a relentless and obsessive *aboutness.* One might diagnose it psychoanalytically as a serious case of melancholy, if not hysteria.[54] Law prudently departs from the *aboutness* of the event. Law is not *about* the event. It relates to the event by leaving it behind. Whether it does this with some regret depends on the extent to which it consciously recognizes that it does so, as Kelsen's pure theory of law does.

Nussbaum's assessment of the relation between law and literature is quite in line with the trajectory of her thinking in *Upheavals of Thought.* According to her, good literature can contribute to good legal judgment. It is a source of sound legal insight. It moves in the same direction in which the law moves. Her views in this regard are not implausible. There may well be a genre of "literature" that is simply aimed at moral enlightenment and legal instruction. Such "literature" would indeed move on parallel lines and in the same hermeneutic direction that law moves. But this kind of "literature" would surely not be helpful as far as the attempt to understand the relation between law and the utopian imagination is concerned.[55] It would not be concerned with the shapeless and nameless *aboutness* that Celan discerns in Lenz's journey through the mountain. It would be concerned with re-establishing desired degrees of stability and equilibrium in the wake of the devastation that results from this shapeless and nameless *aboutness*, not with this *aboutness* as such. In this respect, Nussbaum's engagement with the relation between law and literature is surely not utopian.[56]

Be it as it may, a reassessment of the legacy of the Stoics indeed appears uncircumventable for any thorough engagement with the relation between law and utopian thought. The thoughts that have been developed in this essay nevertheless call for a reassessment of Stoic ethics that differs significantly from the one on which Nussbaum embarks in *Upheavals of Thought*. It calls, in fact, for the question whether the concept of Stoic indifference was not in fact informed or at least accompanied by a radically differentiated ethics that one may plausibly call *Stoic difference*.

The massive hermeneutic weight and textual evidence that inform the concept of Stoic indifference is undeniable. At issue in this concept is the common reading and conception of Stoic ethics that has prevailed for millennia—namely, the conception that Stoic ethics turn on the ability to remain calm in the face of the painful imperfections of this world. Stoics reconcile themselves with the world and with fate.[57] In this respect they are fundamentally nonutopian. This assessment of Stoicism is accurate, but it fails to do justice to its complex legacy. We have already noted the ambiguity of the Stoic mind-set above. We noted the conception of and faith in universal reason that informs Stoic visions of natural law. But we also noted that the Stoics entertained no illusions regarding the actual materialization of this universal reason. From this perspective, at least, it seems wrong to impute *indifference* to them. Indifference may well be imputed to the Cynics, a school of philosophy closely related but significantly different from Stoicism, but not to the Stoics themselves. Considered carefully, the Stoic regard for universal reason and natural law, on the one hand, and human imperfection, on the other, may well justify an understanding of Stoic philosophy in terms of an acute regard for the fundamental tensions, differences, and differentiations that condition human existence. It is instructive to highlight two of them:

(1) Human existence is conditioned by faith in universal principles of reason, on the one hand, and a pervasive failure to comply with them or to articulate them consistently, on the other.

(2) Human existence is conditioned by profound yearnings for existential fulfillment, on the one hand, and acute wariness regarding the disastrously destructive potential of these yearnings.

These two tensions may well be counter sides of the same coin. Quests for existential fulfillment may well be the root cause of disastrous and destructive failures of reason. Attempts to maintain or restore compliance with principles of reason may well stem from wariness regarding the catastrophes to which quests for existential fulfillment may lead. Should there be any substance to the way the relation between law and utopian aspirations has been articulated in this essay, it may well be because law and utopian aspirations represent the quintessential trajectories along which compliance with principles of reason and quests for existential fulfillment take leave of each other. John Rawls's distinction between public reason and comprehensive worldviews and his articulation of the tensions between them may well be one of the most incisive articulations of this insight in contemporary political and legal theory. Rawls is acutely aware of the way compliance with principles of public reason frustrate deeper or fuller existential quests. He writes:

> As institutions and laws are always imperfect, we may view that form of discourse as imperfect and in any case as falling short of the whole truth set out by our comprehensive doctrine. Also, that discourse can seem shallow because it does not set out the most basic grounds on which we believe our view rests.[58]

Must one conclude with Rawls that law, in comparison to utopian aspirations or comprehensive worldviews,[59] is existentially shallow? Not necessarily. Rawls, in any case, does not suggest that law *is* shallow. It only *seems* shallow, he writes. Considering the remarkable *existential* achievement that becomes evident when relatively faithful compliance with law and relatively effective sustenance of legal systems manage to steer clear of the disastrous abyssal nothingness or u-topos to which utopian quests incline, law can hardly be deemed shallow. Law is existentially conditioned and marked by the abyssal depths from which it manages to steer clear. A regard for the vertiginous cliffs from which the law has managed to step back is enough to make one realize that the law is far from shallow. Its apparent shallowness is, in fact, an inverse depth. It moves along the same trajectory of profound utopian quests and aspirations, but does so in the opposite direction. The more profound the utopian aspirations become with which law has to contend and compete in the wake of abyssal events, the more profound becomes the law's inverse depth.

The relation of law to the literary radicalization of utopian sensibilities that this essay articulates should be understood in the same way. The more the generalizing language of law and general legal concepts can retain a memory of the way they take leave of the radical literary concern with the abyssal mystery of existence and the nongeneralizable singularity of the event, the more will their unique achievements—their inversely singular achievements—become evident. Law need and must therefore not be informed by utopian literature. It must be informed and remain informed about the way its own trajectory relates to the historical events from which it too is flung into existence. And a regard for this trajectory demands or consists in an acute awareness of how the law differs from and takes leave of utopian literature.

The twentieth-century radicalization of the utopian discourse that required or precipitated its turn into a literary discourse—that is, into a suggestive, experimental, and ultimately sublimely poetic discourse (as opposed to typical predicative or propositional discourses about ideal social arrangements)—can be understood as a response to the disastrous totalitarian political projects of the twentieth century that resulted from propositional, predicative or literal utopian discourses.[60] Whether this response has turned utopian thinking into a private concern with no political and therefore no legal significance, and whether there might not be some indirect feedback loops between the opposite trajectories of utopian literature and law—feedback loops that may indeed lead back to the realm of politics—is a different question that one must reserve for another inquiry.[61] One must also reserve here for another inquiry the question whether the twentieth-century transformation of the utopian imagination described in this essay—its radical turn away from the resistance to private property and toward a more fundamental resistance to linguistic and normative propriety—has not in fact contributed to a global entrenchment of existing property relations in the course of the twentieth century. Suffice it to conclude for now that the literary utopian turn surely effected a certain depoliticization of utopian thinking. But suffice it also to suggest for now that this depoliticization of utopian thinking may well have been a response to a political exigency, a response through which politics, at least in some parts of the world, became liberal politics by ridding itself of destructive obsessions with ultimate origins and ends. Cast in the terminology of physics and the scientific discourse about the primal event that flung the universe into existence, the literary utopian turn may well have been a felicitous development that temporarily and precariously stabilized the irreducible exposure of *matter* to *antimatter* and rendered possible, for a further while at least, the option of muddling through on this careening mud ball called earth.[62]

Does the description of the constellation of *law, utopia, event* and the two trajectories on which this constellation pivots ultimately turn on little more than a Stoic endorsement of liberal politics? The invocation of Rawls's thoughts on the relation between public reason and comprehensive worldviews in the previous section surely seems to suggest so. One cannot address the question here whether this same constellation might not also account for the essential tensions that are bound to inform political and legal dispensations that are definitively nonliberal. My suspicion is that it does indeed. My suspicion is that any nonliberal political dispensation, say any fundamentally Marxist or communitarian political dispensation, would only be able to stabilize itself institutionally to the extent that its literal utopian imaginations can be displaced by literary utopian imaginations.

Be it as it may, if it is a liberal politics that happens to be endorsed and stabilized by the *law, utopia, event* constellation elaborated in this essay, it is surely a ruefully respectful liberalism that is at stake here, a liberalism that recognizes profoundly the extent to which it suppresses and takes leave of the primordial *aboutness* that catapults it into existence. Political liberalism generally aims to be a level-headed and dispassionate affair. Hysteria is not its way. However, as long as it continues to find the question regarding the relation between liberal democratic law and the utopian imagination compelling, liberalism's Stoic prudence will remain tangibly haunted by nagging melancholy. And at times this Stoic prudence and nagging melancholy will hardly be distinguishable.

This should not be surprising. Notwithstanding the two very different and opposite directions of their respective trajectories, law and the utopian imagination continue to traverse the same contaminated and contaminating space that opens up in the wake of the event.

## Notes

I wish to express my thanks to the participants in the Amherst College Jurisprudence Seminar on March 14, 2012, for their encouraging comments on an earlier draft of this essay, but especially for the probing and critical observations that allowed me to sharpen the key thoughts elaborated here significantly. Thanks also to Jeff Ellsworth for a meticulous reading of the final draft.

1. Paul Celan, "Der Meridian," in Celan, *Gesammelte Werke,* 5 vols. (Frankfurt a. M: Suhrkamp, 1983), III, 199.

2. Compare Jacques Derrida, *Fichus* (Paris: Galilée, 2002), 19.

3. Compare David Wootton's introduction to Thomas More, *Utopia* (Cambridge: Hackett Publishing, 1999), 8.

4. Michel Villey, *La Formation de la Pensée Juridique Moderne* (Paris: Quadrige/PUF, 2009), 420.

5. Ibid., 533: "Si Grotius mentionne les thèses d'Aristote, le plus souvant pour les combattre et sans les avoir bien comprises, on constatera que Cicéron prévaut dans son système et qu'il transporte surtout la morale stoïcienne dans le droit."

6. Alisdaire Macintyre, *A Short History of Ethics* (London: Routledge, 1966), 121–45.

7. Compare Alain Badiou, *Saint Paul—La fondation de l'universalisme* (Paris: PUF, 1997).

8. Compare Everett Ferguson, *Backgrounds of Early Christianity* (Grand Rapids, MI: William B. Eerdmans, 2003), 368.

9. The quintessential articulation of Stoic indifference to things beyond one's power or control can be found in the *Enchiridion* of Epictetus. Epictetus wrote: "If [something] concerns anything beyond our power, be prepared to say that it is nothing to you." For this quotation and its source, compare Ferguson, *Backgrounds of Early Christianity,* 366.

10. Villey, *La Formation de la Pensée Juridique Moderne,* 84–85.

11. H. L. A. Hart, *The Concept of Law* (Oxford: Clarendon Press, 1961), 189–95.

12. Compare Macintyre, *A Short History of Ethics,* 121–45; Quentin Skinner, *The Foundations of Modern Political Thought,* 2 vols. (Cambridge: Cambridge University Press, 1978), II, 18.

13. Compare St. Augustine, *The City of God against the Pagans,* 7 vols., Loeb Classics (Cambridge: Harvard University Press, 1960), VI, 253–58, 265–75 (Book XX, paras. 2 and 5). Compare esp. 267 (referring to the "intermingling of good men and wicked men, and

of their separation hereafter, which will certainly take place on the day of judgement"); 271 (referring to Matthew's invocation of the "separation of the good and the wicked by the most immediate and final judgment of Christ . . . [w]hen the Son of Man shall come in his glory . . . and all the angels with him, then shall he sit upon the throne of his glory, and before him shall be gathered all nations, and he shall separate them from one another, as a shepherd divides the sheep from the goats"; and 253–57 ("Meanwhile, however, we are learning both to bear with equanimity the evils that good men also suffer and not to make too much of the good things that wicked men also acquire. . . . For we know not by what judgement of God this good man is poor and that the wicked man is rich . . . why an innocent man leaves the court room not merely unavenged but actually condemned, to a mass of false evidence, while conversely his guilty adversary goes not merely unpunished but even adds insults to injury by his vindication. . . . [We] know not by what judgment all these things are brought to pass or permitted to come to pass by God, in whom there is the highest virtue, the highest wisdom, the highest justice. . . . But when we shall have arrived at that judgement of God the time of which is in a special sense called the day of judgement, and sometimes the day of the Lord, then it will be seen that God's judgements are utterly righteous, not only judgements as shall then be pronounced, but also judgements as have been pronounced from the beginning or are hereafter to be pronounced from now till doomsday."

14. Jacob Taubes, *Abendländische Eschatologie* (Bern: A. Francke Ag. Verlag, 1947), 149–91, esp. 184 ("Das gesamte sozialökonomische Inventar der Analysen von Karl Marx instrumentiert nur das Thema der Selbstentfremdung, den Fall in die Fremde und den Weg zur Erlösung"); Karl Löwith, *Weltgeschichte und Heilsgeschehen—Die Theologische Voraussetzungen der Geschichtsphilosophie* (Stuttgart: J. B. Metzler, 1983), 42–68, esp. 47 ("Diese Philosophie des Proletariats als eines auserwählten Volkes"), 51 ("Das Proletariat rettet die ganze menschliche Gesellschaft"), and esp. 55 ("der kommunistische Glaube [ist] eine Pseudomorphose des jüdisch-christlichen Messianismus"). For further insightful discussions of these sources, compare Reinhart Koselleck, *Vergangene Zukunft* (Frankfurt a. M: Suhrkamp Verlag, 1979), 77; and Odo Marquard, *Schwierigkeiten mit der Geschichtsphilosophie* (Frankfurt a. M: Suhrkamp, 1973), 13–33.

15. Koselleck, *Vergangene Zukunft*, 38–67.

16. St. Augustine, *The City of God against the Pagans*, II, 243, 249–53 (Book V, paras. 19, 21). Compare also Koselleck, *Vergangene Zukunft*, 211–58, regarding the two worlds conception of history from St. Augustine to Schmitt.

17. Giorgio Agamben, *The Time That Remains* (Stanford: Stanford University Press, 2005), 33–43.

18. For a further discussion of this *as if not* existence of the Christian community, compare Johan van der Walt, "The Shadow and Its Shade," *South African Public Law* 24 (2009): 269–96.

19. William of Ockham, *Opus Nonaginta Dierum,* in *Guilelmi de Ockham Opera Politica*, ed. H. S. Offler (Manchester: Manchester University Press, 1974), 306; Villey, *La Formation de la Pensée Juridique Moderne,* 202–68.

20. Compare Karl Marx, "The German Ideology," in *Karl Marx: Selected Writings,* ed. David McLellan (Oxford: Oxford University Press, 1977), 168–71.

21. Compare G. W. F. Hegel, "Grundlinien der Philosophie des Rechts," in *Hegel, Werke in 20 Bänden* (Frankfurt a. M: Suhrkamp Verlag, 1970), VII, 26–27: "Die Vernunft als die Rose im Kreuze der Gegenwart zu erkennen und damit dieser sich zu erfreuen, diese vernünftige Einsicht ist die *Versöhnung* mit der Wirklichkeit." The emphasis on *Versöhnung* ("reconciliation") is Hegel's own.

22. Jean-Francois Lyotard, *La Condition Postmoderne, Rapport sur le Savoir* (Paris: Les Éditions de Minuit, 1979), 7 ("on décide d'appeler 'modern' la science qui [se réfère] . . . à tel ou tel grand recit, comme le dialectique de l'Esprit, l'herméneutique du sens, l'emancipation du sujet raisonnable ou travailleur, le development de la richesse . . ."; "on tient pour 'postmoderne' l'incrédulite à l'égard des métarécits . . . qui implique une philosophie de l'histoire": this citation scrambles Lyotard's text somewhat for the sake of conciseness). Odo Marquard's *Schwierigkeiten mit der Geschichtsphilosophie,* published seven years earlier (see Note 14, above), addresses the same "taking-leave of the philosophy of history" (*Abschied von der Geschichtsphilosophie*—compare 20–23) with cutting wit and insight.

23. Compare Wootton's observation in his introduction to More, *Utopia*, 11.

24. Friedrich Nietzsche, "Zur Genealogie der Moral," in *Kritische Studienausgabe*, ed. Giorgio Colli and Mazzino Montinari, 14 vols. (Berlin: Walter de Gruyter, 1990), V.

25. Michel Foucault, *Madness and Civilisation* (London: Tavistock Publications, 1971), 280.

26. Ibid., 286–89.

27. Karl Marx, "Critique of the Gotha Programme," in Marx/Engels Collected Works, 50 vols. (Moscow: Progress Publishers, 1989), XXIV, 86–87. Also available at www.marxists.org/archive/marx/works/1875/gotha/index.htm, accessed July 20, 2013. The original German text reads: "Das Recht kann seiner Natur nach nur in Anwendung von gleichem Maasstab [*sic*] bestehn; aber die ungleichen Individuen (und sie wären nicht verschiedne Individuen, wenn sie nicht Ungleiche wären) sind nur an gleichem Massstab messbar, so weit man sie unter einen gleichen Gesichtspunkt bringt, sie nur von einer *bestimmter* Seite fasst, z.B. im gegebnen Fall sie *nur als Arbeiter* betrachtet, und weiter nichts in ihnen sieht, von allem andern absieht." Compare Karl Marx, "Kritik des Gothaer Programms," in Karl Marx and Friedrich Engels, *Gesamtausgabe* (Berlin: Dietz Verlag, 1985), XXV, 14.

28. Translated from Theodor W. Adorno *Negative Dialektik* (Frankfurt a. M: Suhrkamp Taschenbuch, 1975), 304: "Recht is das Urphänomen irrationaler Rationalität.

In ihm wird das formale Äquivalenzprinzip zur Norm, alle schlägt es über denselben Leisten. Solche Gleichheit, in der die Differenzen untergehen, leistet geheim der Ungleichheit Vorschub."

29. Scott Veitch, "A Very Unique Case: Reflections on Neil MacCormick's Theory of Universalization in Practical Reasoning," in *The Universal and the Particular in Legal Reasoning*, ed. Zenon Bankovski and James Maclean (Aldershot: Ashgate, 2006), 143–58.

30. Compare Jean-Luc Nancy, *La communauté désœuvrée* (Paris: Christian Bourgois, 1999), 184, in which Nancy comments on a passage in which Marx rather romantically exults the particularity (as opposed to the generality or generic nature) of work in traditional communities: "La communauté signifie ici la *particularité* socialement exposée, et s'oppose à la généralité socialement implosée qui est celle du capitalisme. S'il y a eu un événement de la pensée marxienne, et si nous n'en avons pas fini avec lui, il a lieu dans l'ouverture de cette pensée.... Dans le mythe, ou dans la littérature mythique, les existences ne sont pas offertes dans leur singularité: mais les traits de la particularité contribuent au système d'une 'vie exemplaire' d'ou rien ne se retire, où rien ne demeure en decà d'une limite singulière, où tout se communiqué, au contraire, et s'impose à l'identification" (emphasis added).

31. Compare Adorno, *Negative Dialektik,* 398.

32. Italo Calvino, *If on a Winter's Night a Traveller* (London: Vintage Paperback, 1988), 72.

33. I have no training let alone expertise in physics or astrophysics and am relying for these basic references to the big bang theory on the scientific journalism published in *GEOkompakt* 29: "Der Urknall . . . und wie die Welt entstand," December 2012. The editors of this magazine nevertheless assert that all the articles in this fascinating edition that were not themselves written by practicing scientists were thoroughly checked by experts. It is also doubtful whether the minimal references to and assertions with regard to the big bang theory in this essay allow any scope for significant error. Apart from the brief invocation of one detail of the theory right at the end of the essay, I am only relying on the basic hypothesis that the matter and eventual order of the universe emerged from a gigantic explosion of sorts.

34. One can refer here to countless titles from the vast oeuvres of these thinkers, but quintessential engagements with the event among them would be Martin Heidegger, *Zur Sache des Denkens* (Tübingen: Max Niemeyer Verlag, 1976); Jean-Luc Nancy, *Une pensée finie* (Paris: Galilée, 1990); Nancy, *Le Sens du monde* (Paris: Galilée, 1993); Nancy, *Être singulier pluriel* (Paris: Galilée, 1996); Jacques Derrida, *Donner Le Temps 1: La Fausse Monnaie* (Galilée: Paris, 1991); Derrida, *Spectres de Marx* (Paris: Éditions Galilée, 1993); Hannah Arendt, *The Human Condition* (Chicago: University of Chicago Press, 1989); Arendt, *On Revolution* (London: Penguin Books, 1999). This essay does not claim to be exegetically faithful to any of these texts. The description of the event that it ventures

will surely not be found in any of them. It only claims to have been inspired and informed by them and wishes to recognize its debt to them.

35. Jean-Francois Lyotard, *The Differend* (Minneapolis: University of Minnesota Press, 1988). Compare also Giorgio Agamben, *Remnants of Auschwitz* (New York: Zone Books, 1999), 15–39.

36. Compare Jacques Derrida and Giovanna Borradori, "9/11 and Global Terrorism: A Dialogue with Jacques Derrida," at www.press.uchicago.edu/books/derrida/derrida911.html, accessed July 20, 2013: "But this very thing, the place and meaning of this 'event,' remains ineffable, like an intuition without concept . . . . We do not in fact know what we are saying or naming in this way: September 11, *le* 11 septembre, September 11."

37. Compare Nancy, *Une pensée finie.*

38. Compare Foucault, *Histoire de la folie à l'age classique* (Paris: Gallimard, 1972), 556: "[P]ar la folie qui l'interrompt, une œvre ouvre un vide, un temps de silence, une question sans réponse, elle provoque un déchirement sans reconciliation où le monde est bien contraint de s'interroger."

39. Compare ibid., 557: "Il n'y a de folie que comme instant dernier de l' œuvre—celle-ci la repousse indéfiniment à ses confins . . . . [La] folie est contemporarine de l'œuvre, puisqu'elle inaugure le temps de sa vérité. L'instant où, ensemble, naissent et s'accomplissent l'œuvre et la folie, c'est le début du temps où le monde se trouve assigné par cette œuvre, et responsible de ce qu'il est devant elle."

40. Compare ibid., 555, 557: "La folie d'Artaud ne se glisse pas dans les interstices de l'œuvre; elle est précisément *l'absence d'œuvre . . . . là où il y a œuvre, il n'y a pas folie*" (original italics).

41. Celan, "Der Meridian," 199: "Ich spreche ja von dem Gedicht, das es nicht gibt! Das absolute Gedicht—nein, das gibt es gewiß nicht, das kann es nicht geben!"

42. Celan, "Der Meridian," 195, referring to the darkness of poetry as "ein vielleicht selbstentworfenen Ferne oder Fremde zugeordnete Dunkelheit."

43. Foucault, *Madness and Civilisation,* 281. Compare Foucault, *Histoire de la folie,* 551: "*l'Idiot* qui crie et tord son épaule pour échapper au néant qui l'emprisonne, est-ce la naissance du premier homme et son premier mouvement vers la liberté."

44. Agamben, *The Time That Remains,* 75, 77.

45. The common sense objection may want to insist that the novel only gives a partial *sense* and *experience* of living through, a partial sense or experience of living through that is accompanied and complemented by an additional awareness of not really living through. This additional sense is marked, for instance, by the awareness of the familiar room in which the reading takes place, an awareness that takes the reader miles away from the imaginary reality evoked by the text. The partial sense of *living through* that reading produces, the objection may continue, is accordingly always checked by this additional sense. It is always checked by the sense that we are not *really*

*living through* but *only reading*. And this recollection that one is *only reading* shows up the experience of reading as merely an "as if" experience. This common sense objection, however, is informed by the experience that ensues when reading is interrupted, not by the experience of reading. It is informed by what happens when the novel or text momentarily fails to give the sense of living through for reasons of failing to fascinate and grab the reader completely. The common sense assessment of reading as an *as if* experience thus relies rather peculiarly on this *nonreading experience* or lapse in the reading experience to make its point. The sustained reading experience, however, is a real experience, a really *sensed* instance of living through. It is thus not an *as if* experience, but an *as if not* experience—as if we are not in the room, as if we are not on this side of the film of language.

46. Calvino, *If on a Winter's Night a Traveller*, 192.

47. Compare Celan, "Der Meridian," 201: "Und vor einem Jahr, in Errinnerung an eine versäumnte Begegnung im Engadin, brachte ich eine kleine Geschichte zu Papier, in der ich einen Menschen 'wie Lenz' durchs Gebirg gehen ließ. Ich hatte mich, das eine wie der andere Mal, von einem '20. Jänner', hergeschrieben." Compare also Derrida, *Schibboleth* (Paris: Galilée, 1986), 11–28.

48. Hans Kelsen, *Reine Rechtslehre* (Aalen: Scientia Verlag, 1994), 66–67.

49. Hart, *The Concept of Law*, 88–89. Hart's "internal aspect" is of course narrower than the broad description of legitimacy elaborated above.

50. René Girard, *La Violence et Le Sacré* (Paris: Editions Bernard Grasset, 1972), 38–40.

51. Martha Nussbaum, *Upheavals of Thought* (Cambridge: Cambridge University Press, 2003), 4: "The view that emerges may justly be called neo-Stoic, and I shall often use this term."

52. Compare ibid., esp. ch. VII.

53. Compare ibid., 16.

54. Consider in this regard the connection that Freud observed between literature and hysteria. Hysteria, Freud first believed, is a symptomatic return to an early experience that in most cases occurred during childhood, whereas the enjoyment of literature concerns a nonsymptomatic and sublimated equivalent of this return. Compare Sigmund Freud, "Der Dichter und das Phantasieren," in *Gesammelte Werke*, 18 vols. (Frankfurt a. M: Fischer Verlag, 1999), VII, 213–23, esp. at 221. It is important to note here Freud's invocation of an experience that *mostly* belongs to childhood—"ein meist der Kindheit angehöriges Erlebnis." This *mostly* surely implies a "not only" that allows one to read "childhood experiences" broadly, so as to include all eventful or life-changing experiences that disrupt mature and settled worlds and expose them to the infancy or nascence that marks all new beginnings. To the extent that Freud also took leave of the seduction theory of hysteria (analyses of many cases moved him to

recognize that the traumatic event most often never took place in fact) and moved toward a pathoanalytic (instead of a psychogenetic) theory that found the cause of hysteria to inhere in libidinal energies that the individual fails to integrate into an equilibrium of mature and settled sexuality, one can interpret hysteria as a symptomatic instance of the utopian resistance to mature and settled worlds and an obsessive return to the upheaval of awakening or unsettled sexuality. Hysterical individuals continue to live in the event or the infantile emergence from the event and fail or refuse to arrive in established worlds of mature and settled sexualities in which perversities are not repressed, but either do not exist or become well accommodated as part of the healthy sexual self. And should one under this postseduction theory of hysteria continue to maintain Freud's earlier link between hysteria and literature, the constellation that emerges is one in which literature is an engagement, not with a specific or nameable past event but with the interminable and unnameable upheaval of unsettled sexuality that vaults individuals into existence. Unsettled sexuality is of course not the only primordial *aboutness* that energizes the human individual, but only one of many strong emotional or libidinal responses that beckon individuals away from the established worlds of settled and transparent legal and moral normativity and toward unsettled and troubled (preworldly) regions of existence. But it remains one of the more forceful unsettling energies in human existence; hence also its prominence in probing utopian literature. Compare in this regard Milan Kundera's observations in the interview with Philip Roth published as an afterword to Kundera, *The Book of Laughter and Forgetting* (London: Penguin Books, 1983), 236–37. Compare further the illuminating discussion of Freud's observations regarding hysteria and literature in Philippe Van Haute and Tomas Geyskens, *A Non-Oedipal Psychoanalysis?* (Leuven: Leuven University Press, 2012), 11–72, to which this footnote is much indebted.

55. Compare Martha Nussbaum, "Equity and Mercy," in *Punishment: A Philosophy and Public Affairs Reader*, ed. Alan John Simmons et al. (Princeton: Princeton University Press, 1994), 167, 172–75, 180–81. For two previous engagements with Nussbaum on this count, compare Johan van der Walt, "Law and the Space of Appearance in Arendt's Thought," in *Hannah Arendt and the Law*, ed. M. Goldini and C. McCorkindale (Oxford: Hart Publishing, 2012), 63–88; and van der Walt, "Agaat's Law: Reflections on Law and Literature with Reference to Marlene van Niekerk's Novel *Agaat*," *South African Law Journal* 126 (2009): 695–739.

56. This also explains the way Nussbaum shares Ismene's assessment of Antigone ("You have a warm heart for the cold"). Compare Martha Nussbaum, *The Fragility of Goodness: Luck and Ethics in Greek Tragedy and Philosophy* (Cambridge: Cambridge University Press, 1986), 64–67. For Nussbaum Antigone does not have eros because of her "single minded identification with duties to the dead." But "we admire Antigone, nonetheless, in a way that we do not admire Creon," argues Nussbaum, because there

is some complexity and conflict in her single-mindedness when, before the moment of her death, she recognizes her loss and compares herself to Niobe ("wasted away by nature's snow and rain"). In other words, it is Antigone's brief moment of sanity (when she experiences conflict as others would) that redeems her for Nussbaum, not her mad obsession with burying Polinices. In terms of the radical literary turn in the utopian imagination described in this essay, Antigone's mad obsession with the singularity of her dead brother (she can have children again, she can have another husband, but she cannot have another brother—compare Sophocles, *Antigone* [Cambridge: Harvard University Press, 1994], 87, lines 905–10) makes her the archetypal utopian heroine.

57. Compare again Note 9, above.

58. John Rawls, *Political Liberalism* (New York: Columbia University Press, 1996), 243.

59. All comprehensive worldviews are plainly "utopian" in some respects. They are patently counterfactual and never correspond with the world as we know it.

60. Compare in this regard the poignant discussion between Jürgen Habermas and Hans Ulrich Reck in "Konservative Politik, Arbeit, Sozialismus und Utopie heute," in Jürgen Habermas, *Die Neue Unübersichtlichkeit* (Frankfurt a. M: Suhrkamp, 1985), 73–76.

61. Such an inquiry could begin with the explorations of the role of literature in the formation of human rights cultures that eventually result in the development of law in Lynn Hunt, *Inventing Human Rights* (New York: W. W. Norton, 2008); and Richard Rorty, "Human Rights, Rationality and Sentimentality," in *On Human Rights: The Oxford Amnesty Lectures,* ed. Stephen Shute and Susan Hurley (New York: Basic Books, 1993). Rorty writes: "Like everyone else, I too should prefer a bottom-up way of achieving utopia, a quick reversal of fortune which will make the last first. But I do not think this is how utopia will in fact come into being . . . . A better sort of answer is the sort of long, sad, sentimental story which begins 'Because this is what it is like to be in her situation—to be far from home, among strangers . . . .'" (I relied on web1.uct.usm.maine.edu/~bcj/issues/three/rorty.html for this quotation, and I am indebted to discussions with Sibylle van der Walt for this point and these references.) That literary accounts of suffering can change social sentiments that lead to positive social developments such as the rise of human rights cultures is plausible. It is also plausible that the literature that brings about such transformations may have a real utopian thrust before the normative sedimentation sets in that may lead to the establishment of positive normative cultures. It is nevertheless important not to confuse the subsequent formation of normative cultures such as a human rights culture with utopian imaginations, as Rorty appears to be doing here, and as Habermas surely does when he refers to the "realistic utopia of human rights." Compare Habermas, *Zur Verfassung Europas—Ein Essay* (Frankfurt a. M: Suhrkamp, 2011), 13–38. Human rights cultures

and law may indeed be the result of social upheavals precipitated by literary utopian explorations, but they largely serve to settle these upheavals and lay them to rest. It is up to significantly probing and experimental literature to sustain these upheavals and to resist the generic cultural and legal norms that ultimately curtail and even suppress rather than promote the singularity of human dignity, integrity, and autonomy that is supposedly promised, for instance, by the notion of human rights. The notion of a "realistic utopia" (Habermas) makes no good sense, nor does the notion of "utopia . . . [coming] into being" (Rorty), at least not from the perspective of the radical literary understanding of the concept of utopia that has been developed in this essay.

62. For this reference to the discourse of physics on matter and antimatter I rely on Martin Paetsch, "Das Rätsel der zwei mächtigsten Kräfte im All," *GEOkompakt* 29 (2011): 74–81. The metaphor of the "careening mud ball" is pinched from the epigraph in Ted Leason, *The Habit of Rivers* (New York: Lyons and Burford, 1994).

# "What about Peace?": Cotton Mather's Millennium and the Rise of International Law

NAN GOODMAN

So we are at war, aren't we? Fine. But then three questions can finally be raised: Who is involved? What are their war aims? And finally, the most important one: what about peace?
—Bruno Latour, *War of the Worlds, or What about Peace?*

The relationship between the law and utopia is varied and often fraught, as many of the essays in this volume attest, but for the purposes of the present essay one feature stands out above all others: the law and utopia inform each other. The reciprocity that exists between the law and utopia works on many levels, but I invoke it here to show how fundamental it has been to our understanding of the shape utopias have taken as a literary genre, as well as of the social purpose they have served over time. Of the mutual impact suggested by the concept of reciprocity—of utopia on the law and of the law on utopia—the former is perhaps the more familiar, as it is the subject of scholarly work that has long considered utopias—those imaginings of better and usually future worlds—as critiques of current events, shedding light on and in some cases leading to modifications of the political, legal, and social institutions of their day.[1] From Plato's *Republic* to Thomas More's *Utopia* to Edward Bellamy's *Looking Backward* and beyond, utopias have long been thought to carry the seeds of what utopian theorist Karl Mannheim referred to as ideological change.[2]

Even as they critique their existing worlds, however, utopias have also emerged as reflections of them, inevitably thinking through their alternative visions in contemporary terms. The imagined alternatives to the present, in other words, are shaped by present social, legal, and political institutions, which operate in turn as sources for the varied visions of peace utopias promote. In the *Republic*, for example, the impact of the Peloponnesian Wars and contemporary ideas of perfection find expression in Plato's vision of peace as a military virtue, whereas in *Utopia*, the impact of Renaissance humanism finds expression in More's vision of peace as the total absence of war.[3] Admittedly, for Frederic Jameson, whose work on utopia has been crucial to utopian studies, the reciprocity between utopias and their sources reduces their potential to serve as vehicles for social change. For our purposes, however, it provides a vital pathway for understanding how the language of the law is not only reflected in but also helps to shape utopic imaginations.[4] "Law," as Paul Berman writes, "is not merely the coercive command of a sovereign power, but a language for imagining alternative future worlds."[5]

Obvious perhaps from one standpoint, the significance of the reciprocity between utopia and the law comes into sharper relief when we consider the one rather large exception to the rule: the religious utopia. In religious writings, particularly Christian millennialist writings, the central features of utopia seem to vary little from place to place or year to year, taking their impetus from the celebrated passage in *Revelation* in which an angel, "having the key of the bottomless pit and a great chain in his hand," descends from heaven.[6] "And he laid hold on the dragon, that old serpent," the verse goes on, "which is the Devil, and Satan, and bound him a thousand years. And cast him into the bottomless pit, and shut him up, and set a seal upon him, that he should deceive the nations no more, till the thousand years should be fulfilled."[7] With Satan bound, it would seem, peace is secured, and little else needs to be known about it. Indeed the image of peace that emerges in the countless sermons and pamphlets about the millennium tends to be tied to this event and otherwise circumscribed, rendered in conspicuously vacant terms. In one popular account, for example, the millennium is described as having "no Temple," "no need of the Sun, neither of the Moon to shine in it, for the glory of God doth lighten it." In another, it is rendered as tautology: it is peace because "it is full of peace," or as another writer put it even more vaguely, "'Tis peace round about on every side."[8]

There are of course good reasons why religious utopias, unlike other utopias, might be devoid of full or familiar description. For one, the supernatural vision of apocalypse at the heart of the millennium is often difficult to reconcile with mechanisms that operate by means of human agency and that, like visions of advanced technology, typically find a place in utopic imaginations.[9] For another, religious utopias are often grounded in systems of thought that offer complete and universalizing alternatives to the world as we know it and that are sometimes even considered antithetical to it. Indeed certain theologians have gone so far as to consider all utopian thought heretical on the grounds that it is of and for this world and not, as religious thought is said to be, for the next.[10] Thus what we know about the peace of the millennium in the vast majority of sermons and pamphlets on the subject can be boiled down to three very otherworldly things: it is perpetual—lasting a thousand years, conveniently followed by an eternity; it is inevitable—waiting only for the proper sequence of *Revelation*-related, Satan-binding events to occur; and it is rooted in the past—predetermined by the signs of millennial expectation as set forth in the Bible.[11]

There have, however, been exceptions to this rule, places where the image of the millennium has given way to more descriptive detail and proved a sensitive register of changes in legal, social, and political thought. We can look to these as indices of how inextricably bound even the most severely circumscribed religious utopias are with the worlds in which they find expression and take root. One such example, Cotton Mather's book-length sermon *Things to be Look'd For,* delivered to the Artillery Corps of the Massachusetts Bay Colony in 1691, serves as my proof text here and demonstrates what the reciprocity between the law and utopia in a millennialist context looked like at a particularly transformative period of the law.[12] The law in question, moreover, was not domestic law, like that reflected in Plato or More. The law that finds a home in Mather's sermon was the law of nations, or international law, which turned Mather's millennialist vision, as we will see, into a text that speaks of peace not only at home but also in and for the world. Far from interfering with the supernatural or universalizing features of his religious expression, the law in Mather's hands helps him to describe a millennialist future that has, perhaps for the first time, reached its full potential.

First articulated by the Spanish scholastic Francisco de Vitoria in the context of the sixteenth-century Spanish conquests in the New World, the law of nations came to be, in the hands of subsequent thinkers such as the Italian civil law theorist Alberico Gentili and the Dutch political theorist Hugo Grotius, a way of regulating noncommercial relations between nations in Europe and beyond. As it continued to develop and find expression in the dozens of peace treaties that dominated the international scene in Mather's day, it addressed itself to more and more varied situations—piracy and diplomacy, preeminent among them—but its greatest innovation was to replace the traditional moral standards for assessing the justness of war (about which no one could agree) with neutral and objective ones (about which, at least in theory, all could agree).[13]

Three features of the law of nations followed in the wake of this innovation, and all three replace the more traditional features of the millennial peace in Mather's sermon: first, where the old peace of the millennium was perpetual, the new peace is contingent and limited; second, where the old peace was inevitable, the new one stems from hard work and labored negotiation; and third, where the old peace was devoid of detail, the new one provides a visible, detail-laden sense of a future world. What follows examines each of these alterations in turn, but to appreciate their scope, we begin with a brief account of the old millennialism so we can see just how different Mather's legally informed millennialism really was.

## Utopia and the Law, Old New England Style

To assess the extent to which Mather departed from a traditional millennialist hermeneutic in which legal and political phenomena were subordinated to a reading of prophetic history, we need first to set his project against the background of Christian utopian thought in general and the Puritans' approach to it in particular. A central part of Christianity from its inception, utopian thought proved to be especially popular with Protestants. Never burdened with the suspicion prevalent among Catholic thinkers that it might itself be a form of heresy, many Protestant works—Milton's *Paradise Lost* and *Paradise Regained*, to name just two—revolved around religiously inspired utopias. Indeed as James Holstun notes, there was an uptick in the writing of utopias during the Interregnum when many Puritans, with their coreligionist Cromwell in charge, believed they had realized a form of heaven on earth. There were also many Puritan pamphlets and sermons that ascribed utopian characteristics to their New World home, including John Cotton's "God's Promise to his Plantations," Edward Johnson's *Wonder Working Providence*, William Wood's *New England's Prospect*, and John Winthrop's "Model of Christian Charity," to name just a few.[14]

Of particular interest to the Puritans in New England, who conceived of themselves as newly refigured Jews, however, was the millennialist strand of utopia, for it offered the perfect opportunity to read themselves back into a prophetic history. Indeed millennialist thought provided the Puritans with the perfect platform not only for retracing their religious reformism back to the Hebrew Scriptures but also for redeploying that origin story for reformist political ends. Competing with many of the Old World visions, however, this New World vision of the millennium did not go unchallenged. Many Englishmen, including the well-known biblical scholars Joseph Mede and Nicholas Fuller, voiced their hostility to the association of the New World with the millennium, noting that the American colonies were the "Gog and Magog" of the early modern world, so far from utopic that they were the last place a Christian utopia would ever take root. "These nations & c.," Mede wrote, "which are spiritually called Gog and Magog [the mythical enemies of God first mentioned in the *Book of Ezekiel*] live in the Hemisphere opposite to us, which God had excluded from the call of the Christian Gospel."[15] Understandably, these critics from the Old World were troubling to the Puritans, but more troubling still were the growing number of critics from the New World who complained that the Puritans' own legal and social order fell far short of what a Christian utopia should be.[16] As the legal historian David Konig notes, there were many from the first generation of settlers who held the second and third generations responsible for "undermining the utopia [they] envisioned."[17]

Regardless of whether one sees Puritan society as having fulfilled its utopian vision or not, many agreed then as now that their hopes for identifying the New World with that utopia were dashed by the early 1680s when Charles II, moved by rumors that the Puritans were violating conditions of the Navigation Act, finally sent an agent to revoke their charter and divest them of their ability to govern themselves. Not surprisingly, as the fortunes of the Puritan commonwealth fell, the fortunes of the more traditional model of the Christian millennium rose, creating a resurgence of the more traditional type of millennialist thinking among New England's Puritans.[18] With publications like Increase Mather's "The Doctrine of Divine Providence" (1684), Samuel Sewall's *Phaenomena Quaedam Apolyptica* (1697), Nicholas Noyes's "New-England's Duty and Interest" (1698), and Cotton Mather's "The Present State of New England" (1690), *Things to be Look'd For* (1691), *Problema Theologicum* (1703), and *Triparadisus* (1713), millennialist fervor—the hope for a future peace and paradise—seemed to reach new heights.

Following the critical convention, these late-century aspirations are typically read as a symptom of the Puritans' disappointment with New England's mission. The millenarian disappointments of the mid seventeenth century, as N. H. Keeble writes, "paved the way for the timidity of restoration non-conformity."[19] In addition, the two most prominent Mather biographers, Robert Middlekauf and Kenneth Silverman, tie the millennialism of both Mathers, father and son, not only to a disappointment with New England but also to the increasing isolation the Puritans felt as both God and England seemed to have abandoned them.[20] Accurate as far as it goes, however, this view of the Puritans' approach to the millennium at the end of the seventeenth century overlooks the extent to which these newly enthusiastic millennialists were registering not their disappointment with New England but their excitement about finding another avenue for utopian thought in a reciprocity with the law of nations.

Deprived of their ability to appoint their own magistrates and representatives, the Puritans, I argue here, turned to the one remaining area of lawmaking—international lawmaking—that remained open to them at the time. The rise of international law in the West, of course, had a profound and well-documented effect on many Western nations, including England. Among other things, it raised questions about incipient social contract theory and the extent to which humans were inherently sociable; it caused people to question the place of natural law in the creation of communities, and it ushered in a discourse among nations that for the first time rivaled that of trade. But its main virtue was that it helped to end wars and to inaugurate new regimes of peace. Surfacing in the writings of many Englishmen who had taken up residence on the far side of the Atlantic, it also offered a way to restore their agency as lawmakers and to reintegrate those lawmaking powers into their utopian aspirations once again.

## Utopia and the Law, New England Style

The law of nations offered a vision of peace that differed from both the religious and secular visions of the past. Under the law of nations, states both inside and outside of Christendom could for the first time appeal to a set of agreed upon rules in a newly established international arena to verify the justness of their wars and to position themselves as peacemakers. Grotius's vision of an international legal arena got its first real trial in the peace treaties that concluded the Thirty Years' War, known as the Peace of Westphalia. Often heralded as the opening salvo in what became a dominant theory of nationalism in the nineteenth century, the Peace of Westphalia probably reinforced the idea of internationalism more than that of nationalism by opening up a space for communication between sovereign entities no longer dominated by states more sovereign than they. The principles articulated in Westphalia, moreover, were followed in countless subsequent treaties, including the Treaty of Breda in 1650 between Charles II and the Scottish Covenanters, the Treaty of Westminster in 1654 that ended the First Anglo-Dutch War, the Treaty of Paris in 1657 that brought England and France together to work against Spain, numerous treaties during the 1650s and 1660s between parties to the Northern War, including Poland, Prussia, and Sweden, and from the 1660s to the 1680s dozens of treaties between Austria, Venice, and the Ottoman Empire. In every case, the concept of peace that was advanced was increasingly malleable, established by negotiation and compromise, dependent on time and the fulfillment of conditions, and, perhaps most significantly, informed by a vision of the future that took a particular and legible shape, changing though it might from case to case. Informed by this secular peace, Mather's religious vision, as we shall see, followed suit.

## A Negotiated Peace

The first feature of peace under the law of nations that was markedly different from peace under the older regimes was its emphasis on negotiation. To the extent that it was reached and implemented, peace in the past was undeniably the product of negotiation as well, but the law of nations made negotiation its centerpiece. Indeed after Westphalia, news of diplomatic efforts flooded the printing presses and newspapers of Europe and negotiations were on everyone's mind, including in the far-flung American colonies. Some years after his sermon to the Artillery Corps, during the peace negotiations at Utrecht in 1712, Mather characteristically revealed both the scope of his knowledge about national difference and his personal engagement in international affairs in a letter to his friend and regular correspondent, Samuel Penhallow. The letter is worth quoting at some length to provide a sense not only of how extensive Mather's concerns were, but also how interested he was in the details of negotiation. "The Negotiation of Peace, is going on," he begins:

> and all Things conspire to give us a strong Expectation, that it will speedily be accomplished. . . . The French King makes an Explanation of his offers for a general peace; wherein he acknowledges the Q[ueen] of Great Britain, and the Succession according to the present Settlement. He demolishes Dunkirk, for an Equivalent that will not be much disputed about. . . . He consents to a Treaty of Commerce on the most agreeable Terms. He allowes the Dutch, the Barrier they desire in the Netherlands. He brings the Spanish Indies, into the Condition wherein it was before the Death of Charles II. . . . He consents to have things in Portugal and Germany, as they were before the War, and Contents the Duke of Savoy.[21]

Concise though it is, there is a distinct emphasis in this passage on the logistics of negotiation. Mather is attentive to the myriad ways in which peace can be brought about and resorts to an extraordinary variety of verbal expressions to articulate his new consciousness of these terms. Peace in this passage is variously "accomplished," "offered," "acknowledged," "agreed upon," "settled," "consented to," "allowed," and finally, "not much disputed about." Indeed similar ways of talking about peace are visible in *Things to be Look'd For,* in which Mather makes it clear that the peace he now associates with the millennium is neither abstract nor individual, as it had been in the past, but the product of a political process. "There is," he writes in the section reserved for the doctrine, "a Wonderful STATE of PEACE, which the God of Heaven will make His people upon Earth, to be the Joyful Partakers of."[22] "Now this we are to know," he explains:

> [External peace] lyes not merely in the Blessed Settlement and Composure of the Spirit, which Believers in all Ages, are the Subjects of. When our Lord Jesus went away to Heaven, He left us that legacy, peace I leave you with you, my Peace I give unto you . . . . [But] such a spiritual peace is not that we are to Be Looking for . . . . The Peace promised unto us, is that External, as well as Internal, harmony, Amity & Unity."[23]

No longer a peace of the individual soul, Mather's peace will bring external harmony, or a peace among people within communities. The phrase "Amity & Unity," moreover, extends this sense to imply a peace that is not simply imposed upon a community but arrived at between communities through negotiation. As such, this peace begins to resemble the terms of a treaty far more than those of a proclamation or papal bull. Indeed as Kalevi Holsti notes, diplomatic documents of the era speak of peace in just these terms, not as commands but as compromises that are taken for "the tranquility of Europe" or the "repose of Europe or peace of Christendom."[24] Lest there be any doubt about the need for compromise within the context of the millennium, however, Mather draws the point out, explaining that the millennium he envisions explicitly concerns the official acts of sovereign nations. "It is foretold concerning this [millennial] Time . . ," he writes, "[that] the wolf shall dwell with the Lamb. Which whether or not it shall . . . be fulfill'd in a Natural Sense, will doubtless be fulfill'd in a Political Sense."[25] In addition to revealing his concern with the acts of governmental entities as opposed to those of individuals, Mather's insistence here on the greater probability that the wolf will dwell with the lamb in a political rather than a natural sense sheds light on the kind of negotiation he has in mind. Indeed his reference to "a Political Sense," rather than to a military one, suggests an accommodation of difference, a model of coexistence with rather than assimilation to or obliteration of one's enemies.

This accommodation of difference was key to the internationalism Mather and Grotius imagined, and the first real evidence of this in Mather's sermon is in his mixed vision of the Turk, the figure at the heart of international law. According to some theorists, international law or the law of nations was originally intended to bring nations that were explicitly outside the bounds of any previous understanding of universalism or peace under a "more convenient arrangement" as Grotius put it.[26] For most people these other nations were the ones that lay beyond the borders of Christendom and were best exemplified by the Ottoman Empire, with which all commerce and negotiation had previously been forbidden in theory at least, if not in practice. Indeed Grotius referred to the Ottomans explicitly in his treatise on the law of nations in order to upend the previous understanding of peace, which before the law of nations excluded the infidel. To the question: "Do we perhaps believe that we have nothing in common with persons who have not accepted the Christian faith?" Grotius offered a resounding and somewhat lengthy "no." He wrote:

> Such a belief would be very far removed from the pious doctrine of Augustine, who declares (in his interpretation of the precept . . . whereby we are bidden to love

> our neighbours) that the term "neighbours" obviously includes *every human being*. . . . Accordingly, not only is it universally admitted that protection of infidels from injury (even from injury by Christians) is never unjust, but it is furthermore maintained . . . that alliances and treaties with infidels may in many cases be justly contracted for the purpose of defending one's own rights, too.[27]

The prospect of making peace with the infidel who inhabited the Ottoman Empire, long prohibited by Christian doctrine, became not only possible but also desirable for the first time under the terms of international law—terms that stressed not morality but legality and that provided guidelines for simultaneously making war just and peace lasting.

Most scholarship on Mather, the millennium, and the Puritans has not taken international law's turn to nations beyond Christendom into account. According to most accounts, the Puritans thought about the Ottomans and the Eastern world the way most Christians did, as a threat to be contained. Even Ottomanists like Nabil Matar, Daniel Goffman, and Daniel Vitkus, who have enriched our understanding of how the figure of the Turk functioned in this period, generally confirm the rise of an anti-Muslim rhetoric overall. Indeed anti-Muslim sentiment gained in strength after a series of Ottoman military victories over Belgrade and parts of Hungary and reached new heights when their presence at the gates of Vienna, leading to the siege in 1683, could no longer be ignored. For religious writers in particular, the threat posed by the Turk was easily accommodated by the story of the opening of the sixth vial from *Revelation*, which foretold the drying up of the Euphrates, a geographical indicator that was taken to refer to the Ottoman world. Occupying a position formerly held by the pope, the Turk in these sermons is typically figured as the new Antichrist, leading an Eastern enemy to ultimate destruction by Christianity.

Tucked neatly into the millennialist paradigm, the destruction of the Eastern Antichrist was generally acknowledged to be a sign of the millennium. It thus worked, as Timothy Marr explains, to "contain the transgressive threat of Islam within a comforting realm."[28] Marr points to the work of several Puritans, including John Cotton and both Mathers, to lend support to this belief.[29] On the strength of this conviction, Marr contends that "[e]arly American understandings of Islam emerged . . . neither from substantial comparative dialogue with Muslims nor from engaged scholarly study of Islamic texts, but largely from investigation into what the Bible seemed to reveal prophetically about its existence and duration as a worldly challenge to the Christian Church."[30] Other scholars, including scholars of Puritan millennialist texts, have made similar claims.[31] For Reiner Smolinski, for example, Cotton Mather's interest in the figure of the Turk as the eastern Antichrist was both obsessive and unchanging.[32] Yet to argue this point, which admittedly helps us identify the roots of America's antipathy toward Islam, nevertheless overlooks a substantial part of the literary output and reading matter of early modern Americans, including memoirs written by captives of Barbary Coast pirates as well as reports written primarily by English and Italian diplomats familiar with the Ottomans that do not abrogate the image of the heinous Turk but offer a convincing alternative to it.[33]

Scholars have mined the Barbary Coast captivity narratives for their mixed portraits of the Turks, who generally emerge as barbarians with a largely unexplained tolerance for cultural and religious difference.[34] Few, however, have paid attention to the numerous histories and diplomatic reports that spanned the length of the seventeenth century and proved extremely popular with the reading public all over Europe and North America—in France, in the Hapsburg Empire, in England, and in the English colonies. What these reports suggest helps us account for the figure of the Turk as it emerges in Mather's sermon, for as Daniel Goffman points out, it was within the precincts of the Ottoman Empire that the idea of negotiation and diplomacy in the form of the resident ambassador first took hold. The "Ottoman state was much more than an outside threat," he explains. It was the instigator of what he calls "the new diplomacy."[35]

Starting with Richard Knolles's *History of the Turkes*, published in 1603, these reports provided knowledge of secular Turkish history and government, which had the effect of putting the Ottomans, formerly thought to be barbaric and ungovernable, on a par with many Western nations. Knolles's *History*, which went through several editions, was followed by more subtle portraits of the Turks penned not by historians from afar, like Knolles, but by diplomats like Paul Rycaut, who served in Smyrna (present day Izmir) as English consul from 1667 to 1678. It was in works like Rycaut's *The Present State of the Ottoman Empire* in 1665 and his *General Historie of the Turks* in 1687 that we can identify a fundamental shift in the idea of the Turks that turns away from Knolles's defensive attitude—in which information is presented as a subset of espionage—to a more neutral posture in which information is presented for future diplomatic use. Turks in Rycaut's work and later in the work of William Trumbull, who served as English ambassador to the Sublime Porte from 1687 to 1691, are both the subjects and objects of study, receiving as much information about the English as the English received about them.

To be sure, Mather associates the Turk with the Antichrist in *Things to be Look'd For* more than once, and in one particular passage explicitly holds out the hope that the Turk's destruction will bring on the millennium. "There seem to be some Symptoms upon the Turkish Empire," he writes, "that speak hopefully about our Blessed State of Peace, and say, it will come quickly."[36] In the admission that follows this statement, however—"Well, you cannot but allow me, with all sensible Interpreters that the second Trumpet is the Turkish Empire"—we can begin to sense his discomfort with the notion of the Turkish Antichrist, for Mather rarely if ever felt the need to bolster his own readings with those of other "sensible interpreters." In fact in his reference to other "interpreters," Mather seems to reserve rather than to confirm his earlier judgment about the Turk and thus paves the way for the somewhat different view of the Turk that lies ahead.

If Mather drew on prophetic history to castigate the Turk on the one hand, he seemed to draw equally on secular history and diplomacy for rendering the Turk in more even handed and legally relevant terms on the other. Indeed so focused is Mather's sermon on the currency and immediacy of diplomatic negotiation that it seems to be in dialogue with the diplomatic negotiations that were being conducted with the Ottomans at the time of the sermon's delivery. Driven by the balance of power principle at the heart of international law, King William was preoccupied with brokering a peace between the Hapsburg Emperor, Leopold, and the Sublime Porte, so that Leopold would be free to help England defeat France, a goal close to William's heart. Since 1689, in fact, England's ambassador to the Porte, William Trumbull, had been working toward this end. Nor was this attempt at pacification, as one historian explains, a "mere bid for prestige or popularity at the Porte, but a vital object of William's policy, the consummation of which would have reacted throughout Europe—as Louis XIV fully recognized—to the detriment of France."[37]

Never quite imagining the Turk as anything other than a foe, Mather nevertheless gives voice to a more nuanced vision in which the Turk is the kind of foe with whom peace negotiations could be conducted and to whom one therefore owed a grudging respect. There is, for example, a long passage about the Turks in *Things to be Look'd For* that, while couched in the terms of their eventual destruction, offers a detailed and historically accurate narrative of their history that seems indebted to Knolles and Rycaut. "There were four Sultanies, or Kingdoms of Turks," Mather writes, "hovering about the River Euphrates, until they all united in the one Ottoman family, under which, by the Year Thirteen hundred, they were making themselves a formidable Wo to the Roman Empire."[38] Replete with an account of the Turks' origins, this passage is also noteworthy for the hint it holds of Mather's admiration for the Turkish attacks on the Roman Empire, which he loathed.

The history of the Turkish "Wo," however, as Mather goes on to note, is no longer a concern for the Romans but for Europe as a whole, and thus he turns in his thoughts about the Turks from the context of history to that of diplomacy. Giving an uncharacteristic nod to the mathematical prognostications about the millennium that he later parodies, he now estimates that within seven years "the Turk should be under such Humiliations, as might Obstruct his ever giving Europe Trouble any more." In the meantime, diplomacy appears to be Mather's medium of choice. Working it into his millennialist vision, he writes, "If we should shortly hear of a general Peace or Truce with him [the Ottomans], it would add unto our probabilities."[39] The probabilities to which Mather refers of course are those of the coming millennium, but the fact that he includes the possibility of a peace with the Ottomans among the signs of those probabilities suggests how altered his sense of the millennium has become. "A general Peace or truce with the Ottomans" is a feature of international law that in Mather's hands becomes a prophetic sign on a par with the vials and trumpets of *Revelation*.

This in itself suggests a major alteration in Mather's millennium, but the transformation of a millennialist peace goes beyond the incorporation of diplomatic efforts into a prophetic history. Indeed for Mather, the prospect of a negotiated peace seems to lie on a spectrum with the peace of the final days as he moves through the sermon using language that slips repeatedly between the peace of the world and the peace of the millennium. At one point, Mather deliberately pulls back from the traditional understanding of the relationship between peace and the destruction of the Antichrist when he cautions against thinking of peace as coming on suddenly in the wake of it. "Tis not unlikely," he writes, "that after the next fatal Blowes upon Antichrist the Perfect peace of the Church may Require some Time for the settling of it. But yet, be of Good Cheer, It comes on apace," where "apace" seems to hint at the kind of progress made by diplomats, not by soldiers.[40] The negotiations required to make the peace of the millennium, it would appear, like those of the peace of nations, depended on time, and unlike the time of *Revelation* so often rendered in precise temporal projections, this time, captured by the word "apace," seems gradual and at the same time incalculable.

## A Contingent Peace

Mather's emphasis on negotiation, or what he calls a "Time for the settling of it," seems to have informed his approach not only to the figure of the Turk but also to his understanding of when peace might come and how long it might endure. In place of a millennialist projection that encouraged readers to assume peace's perpetuity or precise moment of arrival, Mather offers a vision of temporal contingency that borrows from the language of the law of nations and the peace treaties of his day. Indeed treaties from this period which, according to Holsti, outlined the specific outcomes of war and tried to resolve many of the issues that led to war, did so with an eye less toward preventing war in the future than toward cementing admittedly fragile and time-limited bonds for the present.[41] Of course, the idea of a perpetual peace was often reaffirmed in the preambles to treaties, many of which specified a peace that would be "perpetual and universal," but the detailed provisions of these same treaties—ranging from new arrangements about border patrols, the repatriation of goods and territory, or the order of succession within a royal house—made a literal interpretation of such terms impossible.[42] In addition, conditions in these treaties often provided for a limited number of years of peace or set out exactly what should happen if the peace were violated. Any one treaty, moreover, might be subject to the fulfillment of peace terms in another, creating a cascade of treaties that reaffirmed the contingency of any one treaty in the process. The treaty of Ryswick, for instance, concluded between England and France in 1697, was described in the treaty itself as being contingent on the Articles of the Treaties of Nimmeguen (between France and Holland in 1678) and Westphalia (between France and the Holy Roman Empire in 1648).[43]

Mather gives voice to these and other forms of contingency throughout

*Things to be Look'd For*. In many places in the sermon, for example, he inserts a crucial sense of the unknown into the continuum between the fall of the Antichrist and the rise of the millennium, imbuing the timing of millennial peace with a rare uncertainty. "The Pagan Historian," he writes, "related concerning the Time of our Lords First coming, that there was then, Totius Orbis aut Pax aut pacis; a Peace, or at least a Truce among all the nations; but a far greater thing of the kind will be brought about, at the day."[44] In this passage, peace, which is admittedly the peace of Christ's "first" coming and so not necessarily akin to the peace of the millennium, is figured as a truce, a short-lived but nevertheless promising interruption of hostilities. To be sure, truces had been in constant use since the Middle Ages, but its invocation here, in order to define the millennial peace that will be like it but "far greater," could not have failed to put Mather's audience in mind of the frequent truces then being made between the European and Ottoman powers, among others.

The idea, moreover, implicit in a truce, that war might bring on peace not immediately but incrementally, could be traced directly to the rule of international law, which did not, as its many detractors liked to point out, move the world closer toward pacifism. "For tho' the Law of Nations do not authorize Wars not solemn," Grotius wrote, "yet it does not condemn them."[45] The real significance of the truce, however, lies not in Mather's imagination of war's legitimacy, but in the idea of a peace that could and eventually would be broken, leading to more war on the other end. Indeed Grotius paid almost as much attention to how peace might be broken as to how it might be made. "There are three ways," he wrote, "in which a peace may be broken—either by doing something contrary to the very essence of all peace—or something in violation of the express terms of a particular peace—or something contrary to the effects, which are intended to arise from every peace."[46] The peace, in other words, that issued from the midst of war rested on terms specified by the parties. It was not a general peace; nor did it apply to vast populations. As the product of an agreement between at least two partners, moreover, it was subject to a variety of conditions any one of which, if mismanaged, could make it fail.

Insofar as it implied that peace had to be managed in the first place, the concept of a broken peace had an additional significance for Mather and for international law. "Who are they that breake the Peace of the World," Mather asks, "more than the bad Rulers of it, they are the Jeroboams of the world, that corrupt and poison their Subjects with such evil manners as bring the Vengeance of War upon them."[47] One of the kings of Israel in the tenth century B.C.E., Jeroboam was a biblical figure of ill repute, known largely for leading the ten northern tribes of Israelites into unnecessary war with the remaining two tribes of the southern Kingdom of Judah. For making war—but, more important, for driving a wedge between people of the same nation—Jeroboam has been widely reviled by Jewish and Christian interpreters alike, but Mather's use of him here is notable not for its excoriation but for the distinction he draws between run-of-the-mill bad rulers and extraordinarily bad rulers like Jeroboam, who in his words "corrupt and poison their Subjects." For Mather bad rulers were not optimal, but unlike Jeroboam, they could still make and keep the peace, a vision sustained arguably for the first time by the formalism of the just war introduced by the law of nations. Put another way, having arrived under the law of nations at a point where the justness of war and the viability of peace were matters not of judgment but of empirical inquiry, peace was no longer the sole province of good rulers, and war no longer the sole province of the bad. Peace and war were inextricable.

In sharing his newly altered vision of the millennium with the Artillery Corps of the Massachusetts Bay Colony, this was a lesson Mather seemed to take to heart. As the literal embodiment of the inter-relatedness of war and peace, this elite arm of the militia would have been the perfect audience for Mather's emerging view of the millennium as less of a guarantee or inheritance than a popular asset in need of military protection. It was not the audience itself, however, that accounted for Mather's altered outlook, for just a few years earlier, in addressing the Artillery Company at Charlestown, he had demonstrated a military aggressiveness that rivaled that of many militia leaders themselves. In this address, entitled "Military Duties, Recommended to an Artillery Company," delivered in 1686, Mather had no trouble praising the soldiers for their "[a]dmirable *Strength* of BODY," on the basis of which he urged them into battle. The best soldiers, he wrote, "are like fiery metalsome *War-Horses* clothed with *Thunder,* they go on to meet *Armed men,* they laugh at *Fear,* and are not *affrighed,* neither turn they back from the *Sword.*"[48]

In *Things to be Look'd For,* by contrast, it is "miracles, not swords" that do the work of "our daily preservation." When swords are invoked, moreover, it is not as tools for aggression but rather for protection. "I pray, what Warrant have we to expect Miracles," Mather asks, ". . . when in our swords we may have the Means by which the Church of God has been hitherto protected?"[49] Speaking to the soldiers of the 1691 Artillery Corps directly, Mather continues to stress their role as protectors. "Tis to you under God, that we owe the many Comforts of our Lives. We should soon be Rob'd of all that is dear unto us, in the World. If it were not known that there were such as You to set the Price of all."[50] It is not merely personal comforts that the soldiers protect, moreover. The sermon goes on to suggest that the very essence of peace—the "Lives, Liberties, [and] Properties" that make life worth living—is to be "maintain[ed] by stronger Arms against all Foreign Injuries."[51]

In putting his trust in the Artillery Corps and by extension in the colonial militia, Mather solidifies his vision of a peace that has far more in common with the principles of international law than with Scripture. To make peace, provisional or permanent, Mather suggests, the soldiers need to do more than wield their swords; they need to cultivate relations within the domestic sphere in order to project a different, more global identity abroad. "There is like to be much occasion yet," Mather wrote, "for men to Learn war"—a statement in which the novel emphasis is on learning, not war.[52] For Mather, in other words, war was not simply a prelude to peace, as it had been before the law of nations and as it often was in traditional millennialism, but rather a complicated and unpredictable means to it.[53] No longer confined to a series of victories on the ground, war more specifically was now a way of understanding the world and the mixed approaches to peace among the nations. So it is not to war, Mather cautions, but to the "*Learning of War*, to which I must now for a while Encourage you," for there were many unpredictable things about war that needed now to be studied in order to bring peace about.

## A Legible Peace

The final way in which Mather's sermon gives voice to a sense of peace altered by the terms of the law of nations is in his conviction that regardless of what the peace of the millennium might be, it would be far less indebted to past events, of which the binding of Satan was pre-eminent, than to future expectations that were related to his focus on the learning, rather than the waging, of war. Learning war for Mather was not a matter of studying the signs of the past, as it was for so many millennialist theologians, but of preparing for the future in specific and substantive ways. Indeed in the beginning of *Things to be Look'd For,* Mather specifically rejects the millennialist hermeneutic that had for so long kept the millennium a prisoner of *Revelation* and other prophetic readings. Specifically targeting the many millennialist readings that traced contemporary events back to biblical forecasts of the Apocalypse, Mather notes that "you may almost everywhere, after some digging, throw up some unsuspected Intimations of this kind, whereas you will find impossible to forbear crying out, with some Transport of Soul, I have found! I have found!"[54] To read in this way, however, as Mather explains, is to engage in "very unsafe computations to which and by which many have expos'd themselves. It ha's been Ridiculous to see," he writes, "by what Chronology, by what Cabala, and with what Temerity, some have Steered, in Fixing, the end of the world."[55]

Mather, of course, was not alone in critiquing the millennialists who predicted the millennium's arrival down to the last day, hour, or minute. Many people, including one of Mather's contemporaries, James Franklin, Benjamin Franklin's older brother and the publisher of the influential *New England Courant*, were known to deride this kind of millennialism. Such "misguided prognostications," Franklin wrote, ". . . may serve to remind them [people who predicted the millennium with precision], that it is not for them to know the Times and Seasons, which the ETERNAL has reserv'd in his own Power."[56] Yet for Mather, whose powerful father, Increase, was among the "misguided" to whom Franklin referred, the turn away from the traditional hermeneutic was a posture not entered into lightly and did not signal, as it almost certainly did for Franklin, a turn away from religion as a whole. Rather for Mather, this altered approach made room for a rereading of the millennium as a mode of thinking about the future by way of forgetting the past. Indeed some of the most fundamental changes wrought by the law of nations on lawmaking in general was an emphasis on peace as a form of "oblivion": a forgetting of past events in order to secure tranquility for the future. The treaty between France and the Holy Roman Empire that formed a part of the treaty of Westphalia, for example, stipulated that "there shall be on the one side and the other a Perpetual Oblivion, Amnesty, or Pardon of all that has been committed since the beginning of these Troubles."[57]

That the past would become less relevant to lawmaking than the future, as

David B. Goldman suggests, also seems to have opened up some space for imagining the millennium in more detailed terms than in the past.[58] Still figured in the abstract, the peace of the millennium nevertheless emerges in Mather not as the absence of familiar things but as a possible location for unfamiliar ones. Here as elsewhere, Mather incorporates lessons from international law, especially those learned in the context of the new resident diplomacy, which favored ambassadors who knew more about peace than they did about war. As Jeremy Black argues, as international agreements became routine, the importance of sending a negotiator who understood the culture in question and who could speak the language became more pressing.[59] This facility with the language and familiarity with the culture would naturally have led in turn to fuller and more detailed descriptions of what a peace, potentially agreeable to all parties, might have looked like.

The description of the peace of the millennium, even in Mather's hands, scarcely reached a full three dimensions. Nevertheless it received a moderate amount of detail and specificity, and more significantly, perhaps, was figured in terms of human rather than divine thought—an alteration mirrored by the language of numerous peace treaties. Peace is achieved in the treaty of Westphalia, for example, as a result not of legislatures declaring peace but of people forming thoughts of it. "It has at last happened," the treaty reads, ". . . so that on the side, and the other, they have form'd Thoughts of an Universal peace. And for this purpose, by a mutual Agreement and Covenant of both Partys, in the Year of our Lord, 1641."[60] Even in the absence of much detail, then, the peace of the millennium yields to the descriptive power of the human imagination and holds out the promise of being fully described at some point. No longer bound simply by peace as an abstraction or as the consequence of Satan's capture in chains, peace under the law of nations can apparently be produced by human agency and thought. Taking another cue from the law of nations, Mather accordingly encouraged people to "form Thoughts of peace," based on a program of learning. The soldier, he wrote, "should wake up and study," not simply war, but a wide variety of other things as well. Indeed Mather suggests a broad, interdisciplinary program of study that includes not just military training but also the humanities.[61] The soldier "should indeed have some Insight into all the Liberal Arts," he noted. "They that Learn War, had need Learn something else, and they that handle Swords & Spears ought at the same time to be furnished with Qualifications that shall be truly Extraordinary."[62] Driving this point home is his use of the metaphor of a school to describe the Artillery Corps. "If you meet with any persons that causelessly refuse to come into your Company," he writes, "pray, ask them, why they play the Truant so. But, now that you may be, Apt Scholars, I am to lay before you, a few Considerations which may close the Exercise that we are now upon."[63]

## Conclusion

Turning soldiers into students of course may sound suspiciously like beating swords into plowshares, a traditional Christian exhortation. Even as we note the similarities between the two directives, however, we cannot help but see their differences as well. Peace, even the ostensibly immutable peace of the millennium, becomes under the rubric of education a process with uncertain results. To beat a sword into a plowshare is to turn war into domestic productivity and to work toward that certain end; to turn a solider into a student is to do the opposite, to labor toward an uncertain end and yet to reconcile oneself to the fruits, whatever they might be, of that labor. We recall the principles of the emerging global order under the law of nations: negotiation, contingency, and a future that while tethered to the past was not determined by it. To find an image of the millennium as negotiation and contingency in Mather's work reminds us just how deeply intertwined the worlds of utopian religious and legal thought were in late seventeenth-century New England.

That Mather emerges as the source for the expression of such a reciprocally legal and religious utopia, however, may strike some as something less than reliable. After all, the Mather of *Things to be Look'd For,* with its image of a millennial peace in many ways freed from the strictures of traditional theology, was also the Mather who just one year later spearheaded a campaign to hang nineteen "witches" on the basis of evidence that remained unseen. How to reconcile these two Mathers? In the Mather of the 1691 sermon, we see a learned and forward-looking man, given to contemplating world affairs, while in the Mather of the witchcraft trials, we see a holdover from some earlier time, a man given to magical thinking. Yet the visions of both Mathers are not that far apart. What the millennialist vision in *Things to be Look'd For* suggests is how Mather could bring the religiously and legally inspired parts of his mental universe together, or, put another way, how he could give voice to a utopian peace that was at the same time no less real than the peace being ushered in on the ground under the rules of the new law of nations. No doubt Mather worked hard to bring these two parts of his world together, but it was precisely this effort—this making—that ultimately informed his idea of millennial peace and of his colony's place in the larger world. Peace, as Bruno Latour notes in his pamphlet "War of the Worlds," is a "unity [that] has to be made; it is not simply observed." What we have seen here of course is that Mather had the same insight long before him. In a sermon whose title we can now read ironically, peace is finally not to be "Look'd for" at all, but to be taught, learned and negotiated.[64]

## Notes

1. Lyman Sargent puts it simply: "Most utopias compare life in the present and life in the utopia and point out what is wrong with the way we now live, thus suggesting what needs to be done to improve things." See Lyman Tower Sargent, *Utopianism: A Very Short Introduction* (Oxford: Oxford University Press, 2010), 5.

2. See Karl Mannheim, *Ideology and Utopia: An Introduction to the Sociology of Knowledge*, trans. Louis Wirth and Edward Shils (New York: Harcourt, Brace, 1936).

3. For more on Plato's utopia and peace in the ancient world in general, see Gerardo Zampaglione, *The Idea of Peace in Antiquity*, trans. Richard Dunn (Notre Dame, IN: University of Notre Dame Press, 1973), 54.

4. On the limitations of utopia specifically, see Frederic Jameson, "Utopia and Failure," *Politics and Culture* 2 (2000).

5. Paul Schiff Berman, "From International Law to Law and Globalization," *Columbia Journal of Transnational Law* 43, no. 2 (2005): 485–56, 534.

6. Of course, students of millennialist writing will note that the millennium, imagistically impoverished though it may have been, has often been endowed with the ideological power of more secular utopias. Most famously Eric Hobsbawm and Christopher Hill have described millennialist movements as avenues for social protest, or ways for the underclasses to advance the image of a future world that would attend to their needs over those of others. This understanding of millennialism, however, revolves around its role as an historical phenomenon and so remains distinct from my own, more literary concern. See Eric J. Hobsbawm, *Primitive Rebels: Studies in Archaic Forms of Social Movement in the 19th and 20th Centuries* (New York: W. W. Norton, 1965); and Christopher Hill, *Antichrist in Seventeenth-Century England* (Oxford: Oxford University Press, 1971).

7. *Revelation* 20:1–3.

8. James Warner, "Derekh Leshalom Shalom Betsok Ha-Etim, Or, The Surest Way To The Safest Peace, In Troublous Times Delivered In A Sermon Preached Before The Right Honourable Sr. John Eyles, Kt." (London, 1688), 11; William Dewsbury, "A True Prophecie of the Mighty Day of the Lord" (London, 1655), 1; Joan. Henr. Alstedius, "The Beloved City or, The Saints Reign on Earth a Thousand Yeares" (London, 1643), 21.

9. This divide, between a human and a supernatural means of ushering in the millennium, was especially fraught during the rise of the Fifth Monarchy Men. J. F. Maclear notes that of all the Christian utopists of the early modern period, it was the expectations of the Fifth Monarchy Men that came the closest to bridging this divide in suggesting that soldiers might work together with God to usher in the millennium. "These vivid expectations of the latter-day glory," he writes, "must have suggested to some colonists the prospect of doing more than awaiting God's providence." See J. F. Maclear, "New England and the Fifth Monarchy: The Quest for the Millennium in Early American Puritanism," *William and Mary Quarterly* 32, no. 2 (1975): 223–60, 237.

10. See Sargent, *Utopianism*, 98.

11. To speak of the millennium in general of course is to gloss over some important distinctions in millennialist visions themselves. There were millennial, protomillennial, and amillennial themes, as Dwight Bozeman reminds us, including distinctions made between Christ's three comings, his earliest coming in biblical times, his second coming at the start of the thousand years of peace, and his middle or penultimate coming, which was often the one the Puritans had in mind. For our purposes here, however, it will suffice to speak of a millennium, since the focus is on the nature of the peace that was said to accompany it in all cases. See Dwight Bozeman, *To Live Ancient Lives: The Primitivist Dimension in Puritanism* (Chapel Hill: University of North Carolina Press, 1988), 232–33.

12. Many have said that when it came to the millennium, Mather was a literalist, and it is not my intention to dispute that claim here. Certainly there are references to the millennium throughout Mather's work and suggestions that he continued to think about its imminence long after the Artillery sermon. Rather, what I have tried to show here is how malleable the concept of the millennium became for Mather and how informed it was by a number of critical concepts of peace drawn from the treaties of his day and from the law of nations.

13. On the origins of international law, see Stephen C. Neff, *War and the Law of Nations: A General History* (New York: Cambridge University Press, 2005); and Olaf Asbach and Peter Schröder eds., *War, State, and International Law in Seventeenth-Century Europe* (Burlington, VT: Ashgate), 2010.

14. These utopian characteristics, however, were not necessarily millennialist. Indeed there is some question as to exactly how millennialist the early Puritans were. See Bozeman, *To Live Ancient Lives*, 193–236, for a reading that argues that the millennialist strains have been exaggerated.

15. Quoted in Reiner Smolinski, ed., *The Kingdom, the Power & The Glory: The Millennial Impulse in Early American Literature* (Dubuque, IA: Kendall/Hunt Publishing, 1998), x.

16. Even William Nelson, the only legal historian who has, to my knowledge, explicitly written about Puritan law in utopic terms, acknowledges its unusual rigor. For Nelson, Puritan law, though rigorous, was restrained, a compromise vision that, according to Nelson, may have led scholars like Konig to see the "utopian glass of the founding generation emptied . . . half way," but leads him to see it as "half full." See William Nelson, "The Utopian Legal Order of the Massachusetts Bay Colony, 1630–1686," *American Journal of Legal History* 47, no. 2 (2005): 183–230, 189.

17. Quoted in ibid., 185.

18. On the fortunes of the millennium in this period, see Hill, *Antichrist in Seventeenth-Century England.* See also James Holstun, *A Rational Millennium: Puritan Utopias of Seventeenth-Century England and America* (New York: Oxford University Press, 1987).

19. N. H. Keeble, *The Literary Culture of Non-Conformity in Later Seventeenth-Century England* (Athens: University of Georgia Press, 1987), 11.

20. See Kenneth Silverman, *The Life and Times of Cotton Mather* (New York: HarperCollins, 1984), 323–33. See also Robert Middlekauf, *The Mathers: Three Generations of Puritan Intellectuals, 1596–1728* (New York: Oxford University Press, 1971), 328–29.

21. Cotton Mather, *Selected Letters of Cotton Mather*, ed. Kenneth Silverman (Baton Rouge: Louisiana State University Press, 1971), *Diary*, 100.

22. Cotton Mather, *Things to be Look'd For: Discourses on the glorious characters, with conjectures on the speedy approaches of that state, which is reserved for the church of God in the latter dayes: together with an inculcation of several duties, which the undoubted characters and approaches of that state, invite us unto: delivered unto the artillery company of the Massachusets colony, New England, at their election of officers, for the year 1691*, 5. Cited hereafter as *Things to be Look'd For*.

23. Ibid., 7–8.

24. Kalevi J. Holsti, *Peace and War: Armed Conflicts and International Order, 1648–1989* (Cambridge: Cambridge University Press, 1991), 45.

25. Mather, *Things to be Look'd For*, 14.

26. Hugo Grotius, *Commentary on the Law of Prize and Booty* (Indianapolis, IN: Liberty Fund, 2006), 35.

27. Ibid., 434.

28. Timothy Marr, *The Cultural Roots of American Islamicism* (Cambridge: Cambridge University Press, 2006), 89.

29. Ibid., 8.

30. Ibid., 93.

31. See, for example, Andrea Brady and Emily Butterworth, eds., *The Uses of the Future in Early Modern Europe* (New York: Routledge, 2010).

32. Reiner Smolinski, *The Threefold Paradise of Cotton Mather: An Edition of Triparadisus* (Athens: University of Georgia Press, 1995), 21–37.

33. See, esp., William Oakley, "Eben-ezer, or, A Small Monument of Great Mercy" (London: Printed for Nat. Ponder, 1675), in which the figure of the Turk is given very favorable treatment.

34. These include Adrian Tinniswood, *Pirates of Barbary: Corsairs, Conquests and Captivity in the Seventeenth-Century Mediterranean* (New York: Riverhead, 2010); Daniel Vitkus, ed., *Piracy, Slavery, and Redemption* (New York: Columbia University, 2001); and Paul Baepler, "The Barbary Captivity Narrative in Early America," *Early American Literature* 30, no. 2 (1995): 95–120.

35. Daniel Goffman, *The Ottoman Empire and Early Modern Europe* (Cambridge: Cambridge University Press, 2002), 61–62.

36. Mather, *Things to be Look'd For*, 31.

37. C. Wood, "The English Embassy at Constantinople, 1660–1762," *English Historical Review* 40, no. 160 (1925): 533–61, 545.

38. Mather, *Things to be Look'd For*, 32.

39. Ibid., 32.

40. Ibid., 31.

41. Holsti, *Peace and War*, 145.

42. There were admittedly several utopian theories during the second half of the seventeenth and into the early eighteenth century that contemplated the kind of peace that presupposed a cosmopolis or virtual world community, including those by William Penn in 1693 and Charles Francois Irénée Castel de Saint-Pierre in 1713, but it wasn't until the Peace of Utrecht in 1712 that an interest emerged in thinking through a peace that might prevent the recurrence of war. See, generally, F. H. Hinsley, *Power and the Pursuit of Peace: Theory and Practice in the History of Relations between States* (Cambridge: Cambridge University Press, 1963).

43. See the texts of Westphalia, Nimmeguen, and Ryswick in Fred L. Israel, ed., *Major Peace Treaties of Modern History*, vol. 1 (New York: Chelsea House Publishers, 2002).

44. Mather, *Things to be Look'd For*, 15.

45. Grotius, *The Rights of War and Peace, Book I* (Indianapolis, IN: Liberty Fund, 2005), 189.

46. Ibid., 1568.

47. Mather, *Things to be Look'd For*, 22.

48. Cotton Mather, *Military Duties, recommended to an artillery company; at their election of officers, in charls-town* (Boston, 1686), 10, 12.

49. Mather, *Things to be Look'd For*, 75.

50. Ibid., 80.

51. Ibid., 75.

52. Ibid., 72.

53. In this, moreover, he deliberately turns away from the recommendations of earlier millennialists, specifically the Fifth Monarchy Men.

54. Mather, *Things to be Look'd For*, 46.

55. Ibid.

56. James Franklin, *New-England Courant*, no. 8, September 18–25, 1721, cols. 1–2, 1.

57. Israel, ed., *Major Peace Treaties of Modern History*, 9.

58. David B. Goldman, *Globalisation and the Western Legal Tradition: Recurring Patterns of Law and Authority* (Cambridge: Cambridge University Press, 2007), 160–61.

59. Jeremy Black, *A History of Diplomacy* (London: Reaktion Books, 2010), 72–79.

60. Israel, ed., *Major Peace Treaties of Modern History*, 8.

61. Mather, *Things to be Look'd For*, 49.

62. Ibid., 77.

63. Ibid., 71–72.

64. Ibid., 3.

# *Globus terraqueus:* Cosmopolitan Law and "Fluid Geography" in the Utopian Thinking of Immanuel Kant and Joseph-Pierre Proudhon

DIANE MORGAN

## Introduction: Kant and the Utopian Imagination

Kant's contribution to utopian thinking has been occluded by the stereotypical portrayal of him as a rather forbidding, dry, and mechanical thinker, a promulgator of instrumental reason whose monotonous private life left much to be desired.[1] This misrepresentation is regrettable, as it has meant that a major philosophical resource for thinking and expressing the hopeful and inspiring "desire for a better way of living" has been neglected.[2]

Even the most cursory of evocations of some of his works conjure up their largely untapped potential for the utopian imagination. For example, in The *Critique of Judgement,* the aesthetic idea of the beautiful is presented as giving us a powerful and empowering sense of unity, of the interconnectedness of things in the world, and of the association of our faculties working together harmoniously. We become aware of our not yet actualized potential when the beautiful inspires us with the aesthetic idea of "an integral whole of an ineffable wealth of thought."[3] We venture to presuppose a "common sense" *(sensus communis)* that binds us together in a disinterested, noninstrumentalizing way. This creative and reflective "experience" can open the prospect of another type of society (more open to exchange, sharing, and debate) to come. In *The Conflict of the Faculties,* Kant introduces the idea of a "sign of history" [a *Geschichtszeichen, signum rememorativum, demonstrativum, prognosticon*] to indicate a "moral disposition" in the human race;[4] it demonstrates that a general striving for a constitution that would "by its very nature avoid wars of aggression" is potentially at work.[5] Peace is often dismissed as "utopian": the term is used in a loose, but evidently derogatory, way to indicate an idea that is not realistic, not of this earth. Despite such adverse odds stacked against its eventual realization, Kant nevertheless makes a strong bid for a more pacific future. Indeed, as Otfried Höffe points out, Kant was the "first thinker, and to date the only great thinker, to have elevated the concept of peace to the status of a foundation concept of philosophy."[6] In *Idea for a Universal History with a Cosmopolitan Purpose,* Kant deliberates about whether we are justified in understanding events as ultimately amounting to an overall "universal history," or whether they are merely more or less chaotic, and in the long term lamentably insignificant happenings, which mainly just befall us. If some teleological direction can be gleaned from what happens to and around us, our hope for eventual "progress" is encouraged.[7] This "utopian" prospect for a substantially better future is predicated on the cultivation of a less limited and egotistical, more "multiperspectival" thinking of ourselves in terms of a global situation.[8] In *Critique of Practical Reason,* Kant defines "hope" as an important "spur to action" toward changing the world into a better place; as such it encourages an actively moral engagement in this world.[9]

Kant also reveals himself to be a defender of utopian visions in the *Critique of Pure Reason.*[10] Referring to Plato's *Republic,* he discusses the idea of a perfect constitution that permits "the greatest possible human freedom in accordance with laws by which the freedom of each is made to be consistent with that of all others."[11] He defends Plato's proposal that in a perfect society "no punishments whatsoever would be required," and that, as a consequence, legislation and government should be brought more and more into harmony with this idea.[12] In effect rejecting the commonplace definition of "utopian" as that which is unrealistic, improbable, or fanciful, he calls the republican "dream of perfection" an idea that is "pure" and "necessary" if politics is to be, and is to have, a project, one that is open to future possibilities. That is to say, it is crucial to have and promote such ideas so that political life does not foreclose possible change as a result of preconceived notions of what is, and what is not, possible. Kant writes:

> For at the start we are required to abstract from the actually existing hindrances, which, it may be, do not arise unavoidably out of human nature, but rather are due to a quite remediable cause, the neglect of the pure ideas in the making of the laws [*nicht sowohl aus der menschlichen Natur unvermeidlich entspringen mögen, als vielmehr aus der Vernachlässigung der echten Ideen bei der Gesetzgebung*].[13]

An appeal to "adverse experience" in the guise of set ideas about, for instance, human nature ("Something—for example, world peace—will never work as human nature is such and such") or drawing on historical experience for proof that something would never work (for example, "World peace has never existed before and therefore it never will") is deemed by Kant to be "vulgar," most "damaging and not worthy of a philosopher."[14] The reduction of political vision to *Realpolitik*, and the exclusion of "pure ideas"—what "should be done" or what "should be brought about"—on the basis that experience has revealed what works and what does not [*was getan wird*], amounts to a renegation of the task of thinking and of political responsibility.[15] Kant states that:

> Such [so-called] experience would never have existed at all, if at the proper time those institutions had been established in accordance with ideas, and if ideas had not been displaced by crude conceptions which just because they have been derived from experience, have thwarted [*vereitelt*] all good intentions.[16]

The destruction of those hopeful prospects which might allow a future to emerge, one which is not entirely preconditioned by past events, just reinforces the depressing effect of so-called adverse experience; the failure to consider political questions as projects for the future according to pure ideas becomes a self-fulfilling prophesy whereby humans are caught within known limitations as fatalities that disable creative thinking and acting.[17] When evoking Plato's idea of a perfect state wherein there is no need for punishment, as goodness reigns, Kant comments:

> This perfect state may never indeed come into being; none the less this does not affect the rightfulness of the idea. This pure idea presents us with an archetype [*Urbild*] to which we can aspire when passing constitutional legislation in the hope of gradually getting closer to its perfection. No one should or can determine how wide the gap is between the idea and its practical execution, nor should or can they determine how set in their ways humans are, i.e. where the human limits for adapting to change actually lie, as Freedom has the capacity to overcome every imposed boundary.[18]

According to Kant, such "concepts of reason" or "mere ideas" can have "veritable causality" [*wahrhafte Kausalität*]; they can have or produce effects in the realm of morality, but also in relation to nature. Indeed, nature has its origin in ideas ("nature" otherwise does not exist as an entity as such). He writes:

> A plant [*Gewächs*], an animal, the regular order of the universe (and probably the whole order of nature)—these clearly show that they are only possible according to ideas, that no single creature, considered in the individual conditions of its existence, is congruent with the idea of the completeness of its species (just as little as any individual human fulfils the idea of humanity that he bears in his soul as an archetype [*Urbild*] of his actions).[19]

Only the "whole" is entirely adequate to the idea, whether this whole be "the animal kingdom," "humanity," "the universe," or "the earth," and these ideas have an important "regulative" use as *foci imaginarius.*[20] Our understanding is directed by them toward a particular goal, all lines of direction [*Richtungslinien*]—whether these be understood as various standpoints, opinions, fantasies, particularities, instances, or individual specimens—converge with this point as a *focus imaginarius.* This *focus imaginarius* is a point from which the concepts of the understanding do not proceed, as it lies outside the bounds of our possible experience. However, this point nevertheless serves to produce the greatest unity alongside the "greatest extension" for the understanding. *A focus imaginarius* does entail the deceptive illusion [*Täuschung*] that these converging directional lines actually "shoot out" from an object that exists out there. This illusion is analogous to the optical effect produced by looking in a mirror; one seems to see objects in front of one that would be situated through the looking glass. This optical illusion is a necessary and unavoidable one, Kant tells us, when we wish to see, not only those objects that are actually there before our eyes but also those that are behind us. When we wish to expand understanding beyond given experience (that is, beyond the small part of the whole possible experience that presents itself to us in an unassisted way) to its "greatest possible and uttermost extension," we have recourse to such useful, but illusory, devices. Likewise a *focus imaginarius* can also lead us astray: we can end up really believing that, for example, world peace is on the moon or in the universe, if only we were able to get there.[21] However, this deception can be corrected by refracting our vision back to more down-to-earth preoccupations so as to consider how less bellicose international relations could be generated around us, on this planet, using the fragile "purity" of the moon as an analogy or model to guide us.[22] Thereby the *focus imaginarius* might function as a productive, heuristic device for developing a globally shared interest in "maintaining the whole."[23] The sense of "the whole" (the "whole earth," "humanity" as a whole) given to us by *focus imaginarius* is a necessary condition, or rather, a necessary hypothesis for (thinking and doing) cosmopolitan law. Thus, by rejecting a passive and fatalistic acceptance of a "way things are," and concomitantly opening out a field of possible action and positive change before our eyes, the *Critique of Pure Reason* in effect makes a bid for "utopian" political ideas.

Having presented Kant as a promulgator of a form of utopian thinking, I now want to consider more specifically his ideas about cosmopolitan law, whose concern is described as being "the welfare of the human race as a whole."[24] "Cosmopolitan law" thereby also further contributes to "utopian" thought and practice; it can address what Levitas has identified as the salient concerns of utopianism: "the need for social transformation, the need to cultivate imaginative and visionary thinking, as well as dialogue, towards that end."[25]

If cosmopolitan law can be proven to be not impossible, it could be regarded as a creative and productive act of the imagination, instead of being dismissed as visionary in the sense of being *schwärmerisch*.[26] For William Morris this is the difference between a powerful vision and a mere dream:[27] "Yes surely! And if others can see it as I have seen it, then it may be called a vision rather than a dream."[28]

## Cosmopolitan Law and Its Utopian Differences

The dynamic and creative aspects of utopias have often suffered when the law has been laid down about how things should be done, and for whom. Once established, the letter of the law tends to impose itself inflexibly; it therefore reveals itself to be unaccommodating to change. Utopias then rapidly tend to lose their spontaneity, sometimes becoming petrified, defensive, repressive, dystopian.[29] As a consequence, utopian theory and practice have tried to move away from the "blueprint" model of legislation as a means of implementing social progress, instead seeking more innovative and generative ways of avoiding and settling conflicts, and setting and managing limits. In line with this tendency, I wish to explore "cosmopolitan" law as a different form of justice, more evolutive and explorative than other forms of legislation. My point of departure will be that the cosmopolitan existence evoked by Kant, in *Idea for a Universal History*, is "the matrix within which all the original capacities of the human race may develop":[30] this proposition already alerts us to how cosmopolitan thinking and doing for him are not predicated on a fixed notion of "human nature," in whose name one could ever lay down the law with certainty. A law is required that adapts to, interacts with, and even helps to foster the *yet-to-be activated potentiality* of "the human race" *as a whole.* All too often utopian projects are doomed before they even get off the ground because of preconceptions about "human nature."

### *Alas, Human Matter/The Matter with Humans . . .*

> "No doubt you were right," rejoined Doctor Leete, but all that is changed now. We have no parties or politicians, and as for demagoguery and corruption, they are words having only an historical significance.
>
> "Human nature must have changed very much," I said.
>
> "Not at all," was Doctor Leete's reply, "but the conditions of human life have changed and with them the motives of human action . . . ."
>
> ". . . By what title does the individual claim his particular share? What is the basis of allotment?" "His title," replied Doctor Leete, "is his humanity. The basis of his claim is the fact that he is a man."
>
> "The fact that he is a man!" I repeated, incredulously.
>
> Bellamy *Looking Backward* (1982, 68, 87).

> Being alone in the wilderness, [his soul] had looked within itself, and, by heavens! I tell you it had gone mad. I had—for my sins, I suppose—to go through the ordeal of looking into it myself. No eloquence could have been so withering to one's belief in mankind as his final burst of sincerity ["The horror! The Horror!"]. He struggled with himself, too. I saw it, heard it. I saw the inconceivable mystery of a soul that knew no restraint, no faith, and no fear, yet struggling blindly with itself."
>
> Conrad *Heart of Darkness* (1981, 95–96)

> As hard as it may sound, the problem of setting up a state can be solved even by a nation of devils (so long as they possess understanding).
>
> Kant "Towards Perpetual Peace" (1994, 112; see Note 12)

In order to entice the "legal imagination" back from its repelled retrenchment against utopian thought's apparent promise of, and reliance on, "moral perfection" (see the remit for this series), I would like to briefly analyze how Kant conceives "human nature." I have already stated that Kant is not working with a fixed model of "human nature," and how cosmopolitanism as a world view with its own—more evolutive and explorative—laws is seen to promote the *potential* characteristics of "humanity" (itself an "utopian" Idea).[31] In order to have a framework for thinking how utopias generally aim to form human matter, it is informative to refer to Edward Bellamy's *Looking Backward.* In this classic "utopian" text, Doctor Leete states that past societies placed a "premium on dishonesty," encouraging egocentric and brutal "competition."[32] By contrast, his more enlightened social organization is founded on associative "concert"; it appeals to the "self-interest of a rational unselfishness" and to "the social and generous instincts of men." He claims that it is "not necessary to suppose a moral new birth of humanity, or a wholesale destruction of the wicked and survival of the good."[33] It is sufficient to change the environment for the good and to offer various inducements, in order to foster the positive potentials already within human nature. Apparently there has been a complete turnabout in thinking about what makes a society work well as a cohesive whole:

> It was the sincere belief of even the best of men at that epoch that the only stable elements in human nature, on which a social system could be safely founded, were its worst propensities. They had been taught and believed that greed and self-seeking were all that held mankind together, and that all human associations would fall to pieces if anything were done to blunt the edge of these motives or curb their operation. In a word, they believed—even those who longed to believe otherwise—the exact reverse of what seems to us self-evident; they believed, that is, that the antisocial qualities of men, and not their social qualities, were what furnished the cohesive force of society. It seemed reasonable to them that men lived together solely for the purpose of overreaching and oppressing one another, and of being overreached and oppressed, and that while a society that gave full scope to these propensities could stand, there would be little chance for one based on the idea of cooperation for the benefit of all.[34]

Leete's world has given cooperation a chance and thereby permitted "human nature" to express itself freely and positively.

In bleak contrast, Mister Kurtz has also discovered the ideal environment for giving free play to "human nature." The abysmal negativity of human matter is able to express itself "freely" in the world of the *Heart of Darkness,* but what comes to the surface is akin to the "emancipation" of the black slaves left to die by the roadside, "whose moribund shapes were as free as air—and nearly as thin."[35] Reflecting on the meaning of Kurtz's dying words, "the horror, the horror," Marlowe muses:

> Droll thing life is—that mysterious arrangement of merciless logic for a futile purpose. The most you can hope from it is some knowledge of yourself—that comes too late—a crop of unextinguishable regrets.[36]

As a study of "human nature," the world unveiled in *Heart of Darkness* does not leave much hope for utopian thinking or doing.

Kant's position on "human nature" can be situated between the optimism of Bellamy and the pessimism of Conrad. He writes:

> There is only one rational way in which rational states coexisting with other states can emerge from the lawless condition of pure warfare. Just like individual men, they must renounce their savage and lawless freedom, adapt themselves to public coercive laws, and thus form an *international state* [*civitas gentium*] which would necessarily continue to grow until it embraced all the peoples of the earth. But since this is not the will of the nations, according to their present conception of international right (so that they reject *in hypothesi* what is true *in thesi*), the positive idea of a *world republic* cannot be realized. If all is not to be lost, this can at best find a negative substitute in the shape of an enduring and gradually expanding *federation* likely to prevent war. The latter may check the current of man's inclination to defy the law and antagonize his fellows, although there will always be a risk of it bursting forth anew. *Furor impius intus-fremit horridus ore cruento* (Virgil) ["Wicked frenzy rages savagely with blood-stained mouth"].[37]

For Kant the transitional phase of an international federation involves a mechanism of checks and balances that work both with and against the "unsociable sociability" of humans, their constitutional ambivalence, their internal and external contradictions, in the fragile hope of betterment. For Kant the "evil that men do" is not a symptom of sensual weakness but a "positive act freely carried out."[38] This freedom makes us responsible for our acts but evidently does not prevent us from carrying out evil ones, quite the contrary. A transitional federation of republics would have to work even with and for a "nation of devils," while also providing a "precinct" for a possible moving toward the ultimate "matrix" [*Schoss*] of cosmopolitanism.[39]

### *Peace Promotion and the Cosmopolitan Law*

In *Metaphysics of Morals* "the Idea of a *Right of all nations* [*ius gentium*] or *cosmopolitan* Right [*ius cosmopoliticum*]" is presented as one of the three possible forms of juridical condition, together with *constitutional* (*public*) and *in-*

*ter-national right* (*Right of Nations*).[40] All three aspects are structurally required to limit external freedom. If one form is missing, the others ultimately collapse engendering violence.[41] However, enduring peace—which presumably is generated most through the establishment of cosmopolitan right—is not merely *an* aspect or *one* part of the doctrine of right; rather it is also posited as its "entire final end," being the "highest political good" [*höchsten politischen Gut*].[42] As we have seen, before this "entire final end" of perpetual peace is reached, a lengthy period of transition is envisaged:[43] International right is a compromise compared with cosmopolitan right; ideally the latter, as a supranational formation, should supersede the former. The international federation shored up by international right is a mere "negative substitute" for the larger global organization, which is the only one that holds out prospects for a sustainable peace.[44]

Perpetual peace is the most compelling instance of what Kant calls a "metaphysical sublimation":

> [T]he condition of peace is the only condition in which what is "mine" and "thine" is secured under *laws* for a multitude of men living in proximity to one another [*eine Menge einander benachbarter Menschen*] and therefore under a constitution . . . . [T]he rule of this constitution . . . must, rather, be derived a priori by reason from the ideal of a rightful association of men under public laws as such. For all examples (which only illustrate but cannot prove anything) are treacherous. Even those who ridicule admit its necessity, though carelessly, when they say, for example, as they often do, "The best constitution is that in which power belongs not to men but to the laws." For what can be more *metaphysically sublimated* than this very Idea . . .?[45]

As we have seen, cosmopolitan law is not anchored in preconceived notions of the "human" based on "experience." It cannot be because cosmopolitanism, as a way of life, is the "matrix" [*Scho* ] within which not-yet activated human capacities may develop.[46] Kant's cosmopolitan vision gives positive change a real chance, while also clearly seeing that it often dematerializes like a mirage. Dutch innkeepers have a point when they bluntly state that perpetual peace is found only in graveyards.[47]

Be this as it may, rights should not be sought through warfare. In any case only peace provides the conditions for sustainably ensuring respect for what is "mine and thine."[48] We are, or at least should be, forced to "respect" others. Owing to the spherical shape of the globe—that is, to the fact that "nature has enclosed [us] all together within determinate limits"—any claim that might be made on a particular part of the land as property (for private use) has to be moderated by the original right we all have to the "determinate whole." It therefore should follow that

> all peoples [*Völker*] . . . stand in a community of possible physical interaction [*Wechselwirkung*] [*commercium*], that is, in a thoroughgoing relation of each to all the others of offering to engage in commerce [*Verkehr*] with any other, and each has a right to make this attempt without the other being authorized to behave toward it as an enemy because it has made this attempt. This right, since it has to do with the possible union of all peoples [*Völker*] with a view to certain universal laws for their possible commerce [*Verkehrs*], can be called *cosmopolitan right* [*ius cosmopoliticum*].[49]

In this article my suggestion will be that, as a "fluid geographer,"[50] Kant would necessarily have to adopt a mereological argument which as a consequence means that particular claims to parts of the land's surface as "private property" have to be reassessed, even temporarily suspended, in terms of others' more universal, and rightful, claims to access to this planet and its resources *as a whole*. Such an argument may well speak to us forcefully now given the ever-increasing privatization and monopolization of natural resources and concomitant ecological concerns.[51] However, much—everything!—would depend on the imperative strength of Kant's ethicopolitical argument: what does it mean to say that particular claims to parts of the land's surface as "private property" are to be—that is, *should be* and *have to be*—reassessed, even temporarily suspended, in terms of others' more universal, and rightful, claims to access to this planet and its resources *as a whole?* Where would the force for enforcing this injunction come from?[52] Is this ultimately just politically naive and therefore impotent social dreaming? Is this just pure theory that is totally unrelated to the hard realities of the practice? Is the vision of a "peaceful, even if not friendly, thoroughgoing community of all nations on the earth" realizable at all?[53]

### *The Not-impossibility of Peaceful Cosmopolitan Law, Its Disjunctive Judgments, and the Utopian Impulse behind Its Potential Seriality*

In "On the Common Saying: 'This May Be True in Theory, but It Does Not Apply in Practice,'" Kant rebukes cynics who refuse to entertain alternatives to the supposed *status quo* because of lack of empirical proof that things can be changed.[54] He laments the "sententious, inactive times" [*spruchreichen und tatleeren Zeiten*] in which he lived. By demonstrating that theory can be put into practice, that we "should assume" that what "ought to be" is "possible (in praxis)," he wants to reenergize our sense of agency so that the ills of fatalism, apathy, complicity with the dominant ideology, can be shaken off.[55] For Kant these are critical times and maybe the times should always be especially critical. He writes that "[our] epoch is in especial degree, the epoch of critique, and to critique everything must submit." Not only religion and law-giving but also reason itself must be subjected to critique. Kant proclaims: "The matured judgement of the epoch issues a call to reason to undertake anew the most difficult of all its tasks, that of self-knowledge."[56] If reason does not examine itself, it is in a "state of nature, and can establish and secure its assertions and claims only through war."[57] It could be what most strenuously tests the "tribunal" of reason are those claiming cosmopolitical rights.

As Kant reminds us in the "Towards Perpetual Peace" essay, the earth is indeed a more or less hospitable globe.[58] This geographical fact of globality inevitably puts the squeeze on resources.[59] Nevertheless, despite the planet's sphericity, we still cannot be certain that the "world as a whole" [*Weltganzen*] exists as such; indeed we might well not experience it at all as one entity. We likewise might not be completely convinced that "humanity" exists as a whole. These wholes, composed of all the world and/or all humans, are, and maybe should remain, debatable.[60] Similarly, the claims of human rights oblige debate. They force us, implicitly or explicitly, to find responses to probing existential and essential questions about human nature, values, needs, rights, duties, and responsibilities.[61] These questions are raised not only in relation to an abstract notion of Humanity (the postulated All of humans out of time), but also in relation to The Human as historically contextualized (that is, through time) *and* to the particular instances of humans in their individual, maybe most precariously particularized, situations. These demands are concerned with crucial life issues about how to coexist on a finite planet and whether the exchanges that are carried out on, above, and below its surface are equitably reciprocal or not.[62] Kant describes the judgments which bear on these relational categories of community [*Gemeinschaft*] as "disjunctive."[63] "Disjunctive judgments" negotiate between relations of "logical oppositions" between two or more propositions. Each standpoint or case is a "sphere" that excludes the other, but each part (or partial view) forms a "certain community of the known constituents"; despite their mutual exclusivity, they form the whole; they "constitute the whole content of one given knowledge."[64] In an ongoing fashion they have to negotiate and coordinate between the many different parties that form the complex aggregate; they cannot operate unilaterally as one can with a series where it is possible to start with a hypothetical cause and follow on through its supposed effects.[65] The disjunctive claims of humans for their rights to be judged by cosmopolitan law push to the limit reason's critical attempts to act purely in accordance "with its own eternal and unalterable laws."[66]

The cosmopolitan point of view generally takes us beyond egotism, just thinking in our own terms, toward pluralism—that is, to "a way of thinking which considers itself and behaves not as a world unto itself but as a simple citizen of the world [*sondern als einen blossen Weltbürger*]."[67] Such "pluralism" can take the form of a synchronic dialogue with others.[68] In "On the Common Saying: 'This May Be True in Theory, but It Does Not Apply in Practice'" (1793), the cosmopolitan sphere is also presented as a diachronic engagement with humanity as an evolving species. Kant writes:

> I am a member of a series of human generations [(*ein*) *Glied der Reihe der Zeugungen*], and as such, I am not as good as I ought to be or could be according to the moral requirements of my nature. I base my argument upon my inborn duty of influencing posterity in such a way that it will make constant progress (and I must thus assume that progress is possible—it can be interrupted [*unterbrochen*] not broken off [*abgebrochen*] and that this duty must be rightfully handed down from one member of the series to the next [*von einem Gliede der Zeugungen zum andern*].[69]

The getting beyond our partial and finite perspective,[70] the mobilization of a dynamic sense of humanity as a whole, constantly emerging in and through time, is brought about by a dutiful and responsible engagement with our seriality: I am indeed "a member of a series of human generations."

"Seriality" (or "seriation") was a key term for Pierre-Joseph Proudhon.[71] For him "seriality" was a way of understanding the world around us and a method of engaging with those within it. He identified the operations of "seriality" in Kant's table of categories. In the *Critique of Pure Reason,* Kant describes this table as containing "nifty observations" ["*artige Betrachtungen*"] that helpfully provide:

> the complete plan of a whole science, so far as that science rests on a priori concepts, and [divides] it systematically *according to determinate principles* . . . the table con-

> tains all the elementary concepts of the understanding in their completeness, nay, even the form of a system of them in the human understanding, and accordingly indicates all the *momenta* of a projected speculative science, and even their *order*.[72]

In *La création de l'ordre dans l'humanité* (1843), Proudhon highlights the importance of Kant's table of categories for serial theory and practice: they are "twelve types (genres), or points of view, which are preformed in understanding. [Every series is necessarily constructed under] these general points of view."[73] Proudhon describes Kant's serial procedure as follows:

> [H]aving divided the concepts into four families, each composed of three categories, Kant had demonstrated that these categories engendered themselves so to speak; the one producing the other, the second always being the antithesis or opposite of the first and the third proceeding from the two others by way of a sort of composition."[74]

According to Proudhon, Kant's aim was to show that "the fundamental law of reasoning consists above all things in not at all concluding from one category to another [*à ne point conclure d'une catégorie à une autre*]." He therefore ingeniously established "the very principle of serial dialectics" that other dialecticians, including Hegel, just went on to generalize.[75]

As the series is a fluid process, it is "the antithesis of unity; it forms itself through repetition, from positions and diverse combinations of unity."[76] The serial dialectic is an "unfolding" [*déroulement*], "a transformation of terms," a "perpetual equation." It is the "art of composing and decomposing our ideas" in a manner that engages with the world reflectively, dialogically, and creatively.[77] Proudhon maintains that seriality continuously gives form to nature, to life itself:

> Everything in nature produces itself and develops itself by series. The series is the supreme condition of life, duration, beauty, as well as of science and reason. Every manifestation of substance and force which does not contain within itself its own law, i.e. the mode of seriation which makes it what it is, is anormal, subversive and transitory.[78]

If they are sensitively interpreted, social phenomena can also express a natural seriality. This prospect of a possible compatibility between the various constructs and elements of society, including a way of laying down of the law within society which is not coercive, as it is somehow "natural," is an essential aspect of any utopian project. The seriality that, as we have seen, Proudhon locates in Kant but which he then substantially elaborates upon, has an energy that takes us along with it. We end up having to leave aspects of existing social structures, which we would otherwise just continue to accept as necessary and unavoidable, far behind us. As Proudhon points out, once we are engaged with, or rather when we actually *see* that we are already engaged in, seriality, it becomes clear to us that heavy-handed normativity, the forceful imposition of sameness upon differences which characterizes so many aspects of our contemporary world, is incompatible with its utopian impulse:[79]

> To discover a series is to perceive unity in multiplicity. It is not about using one's mental predisposition to create an order but about putting oneself into the presence of order. When one uses one's awakened intelligence, one perceives its image.[80]

The replication of seriality within cultural, socioeconomic, legal, and political systems can create "order in humanity." This "order" has incessantly to negotiate with, counterbalance, work with and against what Kant identifies as the contradictory and disjunctive "unsocial sociability" of human relations.[81] For Kant, the possibility of this cosmopolitan "order" is enforced by a moral injunction: it is a duty to contribute to the creation of such an "order" for humanity as a whole in time.[82] Duty is one of the prime examples, if not *the* prime example, of a theory that cannot be considered to be an "empty ideality" by fault of supporting evidence in the form of practice. He writes:

> For it would not be a duty to strive after a certain effect of our will if this effect were impossible in experience (whether we envisage the experience as complete or as progressively approximately to completion).[83]

All moral aims "as long as it is not demonstrably impossible to fulfil them, amount to duties."[84] The repeated rejection of "theories," such as that of our having "duties," by recourse to an argument about their being "invalid in practice," is deemed by him to be an "illusory wisdom." In a delusory fashion one "imagines [one] can see further and more clearly with [a] mole-like gaze fixed on experience than with the eyes which were bestowed on a being designed to stand upright and to scan the heavens [*den Himmel anzuschauen*]."[85] Rather than grounding those theories which "ought to be" practiced in this world by presupposing adverse experience, there is more mileage, more vision, in looking beyond what is imminently here and now so as to actualize what "should be." In becoming responsible we take upon ourselves the duty of contributing positively to the future for posterity. By thus seeing oneself in relation with serial others to come, the joyful and invigorating "hope" that progress is possible is bolstered.[86] Hopes nevertheless remain fragile. However, even if they do evaporate, Kant claims that duty still has a "force of certainty" that can resist "a rule of expediency which says that I ought not to attempt the impracticable (i.e. an *illiquidium* [something uncertain]), since it is purely hypothetical."[87] According to Kant, given one knows a duty, it cannot be definitively proven that to carry it out is "impractical."

Proudhon also considers our implication in seriality in terms of duties and rights, but he extrapolates these from needs that Kant would not permit.[88] As we have seen, for Kant cosmopolitan law refuses to be based on the evidence of "experience," and we can be said to experience needs. We tend to resort needily to our experience as a means of judging the world, which often leads us to exclude as not-possible that which has not existed to date. Cosmopolitan law has therefore to resist the empirical, so as to draw its force from its being able *not to be disproved as impossible.*[89] Nevertheless, despite this substantial difference between Kant and Proudhon when considering how the evolving cosmopolitan law relates to our empirical senses, there is a consequential and forceful logic to Proudhon's need-right-duty series of which the former might well have approved. The powerful potential of the series for bringing about social awareness and requiring societal transformation pulsates through the following passage:

> *Duty* and *right* are born of *need*, which when considered in connection with others is a *right*, and in connection with ourselves, a *duty*. We have a *need* to eat and sleep; we have a *right* to procure those things which are necessary for rest and nourishment; we have a *duty* to use them when nature requires it. We have a *need* to labour in order to live; it is also our *right* and *duty* . . . . We have a *need* to exchange our products for other products; we have a *right* for this exchange to be one of equivalents, and since we consume before we produce, it would be our *duty*, if it depended on us, to see to it that our last product should follow our last consumption.[90]

Our *need* to consume and produce gives us *rights* and in turn implicates us in *duties* toward others, here and now, and in the future.

Proudhon considers that the unnatural suspension of "seriation" has a detrimental impact on human intelligence, spirit, and conscience, as, for him, the human is naturally the producer and contemplator of a series. Regardless of whether the human creates or imitates, acts or reflects, the series naturally informs him, and he also forms or deforms it. Proudhon elaborates on how a whole series can emerge from partial acts as follows:

> When humans make the most ingenuous and complex of things, those things which are multiple yet unified, they are necessarily made by him in infinitely small parts. These parts are linked by a relation of progression. At the end they produce an assemblage, a whole, a composition, a series. The immobilization of the worker in one of these infinitesimal parts of production constitutes fragmented work [*travail parcellaire*]. This immobility is a factor of disorder, a consequence of the simplistic and subversive organisation of the right to property that everything is working toward abolishing.[91]

While the mobilization of the need-right-duty series can creatively affect our world, its interruption can have negative consequences. The "immobilization" of the series can be politically, economically, socially, and indeed ecologically catastrophic. To take just the example of ecology: the natural resources of this planet, which should remain a serial possession, are increasingly converted into controlled and frozen private property. This contracosmopolitan development has already aggravated conflict.

As temporal and spatial immobility is anathema to seriality, its full expression requires the overthrowing of any centralizing, governing, institutionalizing, hierarchizing structure that imposes a simplistic unity and stultifying uniformity on its members. We can be considered members of a series according to the three categories of sociality and well-being identified by Kant in "On the Common Saying: 'This May Be True in Theory, but It Does Not Apply in Practice'": as a private individual or business person [*Privat-* or *Geschäftsmann*]; as citizens within the state [*Staatsmann*], where we are concerned with political relations regarding the well-being of the state;[92] and from a "cosmopolitical point of view," where the concern lies with "the well being [*Wohl*] of the human species [*Gattung*] as a whole, in so far as the welfare of humankind is increasing within a series of developments extending in all future ages [*in der Reihe der Zeugungen aller künftigen Zeiten begriffen ist*]." At this level of international or even better, transnational right, as cosmopolitically aware citizens of the world as a whole, the redistribution of the limited land and sea mass on our *globus terraqueus* in the light of current overall needs should ensue both as a right and as a duty.

### *Grounding the Idea of Cosmopolitan Law: Reminding Ourselves of Globus Terraqueus*

As we have seen, Kant asserts that it is the physico-geographical fact of the earth's sphericity and the limitations of its various watery and earthy surfaces that grounds "cosmopolitan law." The facticity of "globality" should prevent cosmopolitan law from being a mere "castle in the sky." The different parts "can only be thought of" as continuously communicating with, interacting with, the whole across its differential surfaces in ways nonapplicable to a flat plane. It follows that a claim to a part of this finite planet (finite for us) is made on the back of the "original right" that everyone has to "the whole." Therefore the Idea of an "original community of land [*communio fundi originaria*], [*ursprüngliche Gemeinschaft des Bodens*]" or "original possession in common" [*communio possessionis originaria*] [*ein ursprünglicher Gesamtbesitz*] is necessarily posited.[93] This Idea has "objective practical reality": it has to secure "what is mine and thine" equitably, and thereby peacefully, according to principles of distributive justice, whereby the allocated parts are bestowed in reference to the Idea of a whole. Kant explains:

> Original possession in common is [instead of being empirical and dependent on temporal conditions] rather a practical rational concept which contains a priori the principle in accordance with which alone men can use a place on the earth in accordance with principles of Right [*nach welchem allein die Menschen den Platz auf Erden nach Rechtsgesetzten gebrauchen können*].[94]

I have suggested earlier that, as a cosmopolitan thinker, Kant is obliged to adopt a mereological argument whereby particular claims to parts of the land's surface as "private property" are to be reassessed, even temporarily suspended, in terms of others' needs for, and rights to, the resources of this planet *as a whole*. Proudhon's distinction between "possession" [*possession, Besitz*] and "property" [*propriété, Eigentum*] has to come into operation for serial theory and practice to work. "Possession" indicates a temporary occupation whose territorial claim is up for regular reassessment, particularly in times when primary resources are scarce and the needs are not commonly satisfied.[95] "Property" aims permanently to fix the terrain to ownership; its absolutist claims are undermined by the claims of original possession. As is well known, for Proudhon "property is theft."[96] However, possession can also protect "property" when its legal claims are made in the name of a responsible stewardship of collective resources that benefits all. After all, for Proudhon property is not always just "theft" but also "liberty."[97] Such an ecologically informed cosmopolitics would respond to Kant's concern for the respect of other economically "minor" cultures' property, which is vulnerable to imperialist (and nowadays multinational) domination, inasmuch as biodiversity is (should be recognized as!) crucial for the future sustainability of the globe, for the liberty of all to live well.[98] Ecological concerns correspond to the seriality of needs-duties-rights expounded by Proudhon. They recognize in a responsible way that we are mere "member[s] of a series of human generations," of a species whose potential for bringing about positive change can be awakened by the challenge that is cosmopolitan existence.[99] In the name of future generations, a scorched-earth politicoeconomics should be scrapped in favor of a different approach to the three walks of life and their corresponding categories of well-being [*Wohl*] already indicated by Kant—the *Privat-* or *Geschäftsmann,* the *Staatsmann,* and the cosmopolitan citizen of the world who is an instantiation of "the human species as a whole" [*der Menschengattung im Ganzen*"]. Proudhon's conclusion, which in effect reiterates Kant's "utopian" argument for the adoption of a cosmopolitan existence and the implementation of a cosmopolitan law, is that

> [t]here is a place for everyone under the sun. Each one may tie his goat to the hedge, lead his cow to pasture, sow a corner of a field, and bake his bread by his own fireside.[100]

## Notes

1. Perhaps Pierre-Joseph Proudhon requires less introduction as a "utopian" thinker, though everything depends on how this term is employed. For analyses that place Proudhon alongside the other, most prominent French "utopian" socialists, Claude-Henri de Saint-Simon and Charles Fourier, see F. Dagognet, *Trois philosophes revisités: Saint-Simon, Proudhon, Fourier* (Hildesheim: Georg Olm, 1997); and D. Morgan, *Saint-Simon, Fourier and Proudhon: "Utopian" French Socialism in the History of Continental Philosophy,* vol. 1, general ed., A. Schrift; vol. ed., T. Nenon (Durham: Acumen, 2011).

2. R. Levitas, in *Imagining and Making the World: Reconsidering Architecture and Utopia*, ed. N. Coleman (Oxford, Bern: Peter Lang, 2011), 302.

3. Kant, *Critique of Judgement,* trans. J. C. Meredith (Oxford: Oxford University Press, 1988), 194 §53.

4. Kant, *Political Writings,* ed. and intro. H. Reiss, trans. H. B. Nisbet (Cambridge: Cambridge University Press, 1994), 181.

5. Ibid., 182.

6. O. Höffe, *Kant's Cosmopolitan Theory of Law and Peace* (Cambridge: Cambridge University Press, 2006), xv.

7. Kant, *Political Writings,* 41.

8. For more analysis of how Kant's fostering of "multiperspectival thinking" can contribute to "cosmopolitics," see D. Morgan, "Kant, Cosmopolitics, Multiperspectival Thinking and Technology," *Angelaki* 12, no. 2 (2007): 35–46.

9. Kant, *Critique of Practical Reason,* trans. L. W. Beck (New York: Macmillan, 1956), 152. For the importance of "hope" as something to be both taught and learned, see E. Bloch, *The Principle of Hope* (Cambridge: MIT Press, 1986), 3: "The emotion of hope goes out of itself [*geht aus sich heraus*], makes people broad instead of confining them, cannot know nearly enough of what it is that makes them inwardly aimed [*inwendig gezielt*], of what may be allied to them outwardly [*auswendig verbündet*]. The work of this emotion requires people who throw themselves actively into what is becoming, to which they themselves belong [*die sich ins Werdende tätig hineinwerfen, zu dem sie selber gehören*]. It will not tolerate a dog's life which feels itself only passively thrown into What Is, which is not seen through, even wretchedly recognized." Cosmopolitanism, a key aspect of Kant's "utopianism," has long been associated with becoming a "citizen of the world" for which "breadth" of mind, an openness toward others, an active engagement with worldly affairs as well as self-knowledge are desirable. Bloch is in effect suggesting that "hope" can help us acquire these attributes. As Adam Sitze has helpfully pointed out to me, more would need to be said about the tendency of Kant's hope to veer toward the providential—not to say toward theodicy and its justification of warfare—which would give a more restricted, less excessive conception of hope than Bloch's. However, as Sitze has also suggested, Bloch's rendition of hope could equally function as a means of releasing otherwise untapped utopian potential within the limitations of Kant's own thought. Indeed, in this article I will be exploring Kant's "categories of relation" of inherence and subsistence [*substantia et accidens*], of causality and dependence (*cause and effect*), of community (reciprocity between agent [*Handelnden*] and patient [*Leidenden*]) through Pierre-Joseph Proudhon's hopeful understanding of "seriality." For Proudhon, the "seriality" that he detects at work within Kant's First Critique can substantially contribute to the production of cosmopolitan law. In anticipation of this later argument, I give the corresponding reading of Kant's "categories of relation"—that is, of inherence and subsistence [*substantia et accidens*]; of causality and dependence (*cause and effect*); of community (reciprocity between agent and patient): we must try to know our "inherent and substantial" selves (our "human nature") so as to become responsible subjects, as well as consider ourselves as agents producing and creating

a series of effects in the world, and as coexisting members of a system, engaged in reciprocal relations with others. For the "categories of relation," see I. Kant, *Critique of Pure Reason*, trans. N. K. Smith (London and Basingstoke: Macmillan, 1983), 113, B106.

10. The following analysis of *focus imagarius* as a demonstration of how Kant can be styled as a utopian thinker is also to be found in D. Morgan, "'The Camel (Ship of the Desert)': 'Fluid Geography,' 'Globality,' and 'Cosmopolitics' in the Work of Immanuel Kant," in *The Epistemology of Utopia: Rhetoric, Theory and Imagination*, ed. Jorge Bastos da Silva (Cambridge: Cambridge Scholars Publishing, 2013).

11. Kant, *Critique of Pure Reason*, 312, B373.

12. In the remit for the seminar series on "Law and the Utopian Imagination" organized by the Department of Law, Jurisprudence and Social Thought at Amherst (2011–12), it was suggested that the "legal imagination" is both "allured by the vision of complete justice" and "repelled by the utopian promise of moral perfection." Bearing this latter reservation in mind, one should remind oneself that Kant also recognized, most pragmatically, that: "[the] real morality of actions, their merit or guilt, even that of our own conduct, thus remains entirely hidden from us. Our imputations [*Zurechnungen*] can refer only to the empirical character. How much of this character is ascribable to the pure effect of freedom, how much to mere nature—that is, to faults of temperament for which there is no responsibility—or to its happy constitution [*merito fortunae*] can never be determined; and upon it therefore no perfectly just judgments can be passed. However, when someone lies, "in the moment when he utters the lie, the guilt is entirely his" (Kant, *Critique of Pure Reason*, 475, B579; 477, B583). This initial judgment is possible as pure reason is out of time ("it is not subject to the form of time"); it is therefore to be seen as determining, and not determinable by, any series of events in the world. Any circumstances arising from the "empirical character" of the subject which can mitigate this original attribution of full responsibility for one's action intervene only subsequently. The question of human nature and the degree of moral rectitude required for the pacific federation of peoples envisaged by Kant in the "Towards Perpetual Peace: A Philosophical Sketch" essay (*Political Writings*, 93–130) has to be addressed, as will indeed be the case later on in this article, when considering Kant's cosmopolitan law and the "utopian imagination."

13. Kant, *Critique of Pure Reason*, 312, B373.

14. Ibid.

15. Such a foreclosure of possibilities also underestimates human agency and the cumulative force of "universal history." As Stephen Coleman writes in relation to the work of William Morris: "The enemy of the dreamer of better times to come is the ideologist of the present, armed in defense of the existing miseries with the claim that the prevailing relationships are immutable." And yet "[history] can explode. And when it does it is ignited by those who have dared to dream, who have the courage to take

on seemingly unbeatable odds, who are brave enough the demand the impossible" (Coleman, cited in W. Morris, *News from Nowhere and Other Writings*, ed. and intro. C. Wilmer [London: Penguin, 2004], xxxix). There would be much to say about Kant's differing views on revolution and historical processes in the context of these comments regarding Morris. However, Coleman's signaling of the reactionary and paralyzing effect of basing one's view of the future merely on what one thinks one is seeing in the present, does nevertheless echo Kant's analysis as outlined above. Indeed, one of the main enemies of the *Critique of Pure Reason* is the bigoted dogmatist who does not think critically about the ground he stands on; see Kant, *Critique of Pure Reason*, 32, BXXXV; 620, B809.

16. Ibid.

17. Hence Kant's critical project wishes to map out reasonable limits [*Grenzen*] that permit facultative energies to be channeled in productive directions, instead of their being wastefully dispersed. See Note 18, below.

18. Kant, *Critique of Pure Reason*, 312, B374, *translation modified*. Freedom's capacity for overcoming "every imposed boundary" can be both productive and counterproductive. It encourages us to surmount limitations [*Schranken*] that thwart our becoming autonomous beings. It can also encourage us to develop ourselves in directions that lead to the fruitless dissipation of our energies, hence a degree of limitation is of critical importance. Some boundaries [*Grenzen*] need to be set. But, as Kant makes clear in this passage, no one "can or ought to" set in stone the boundaries [*Grenzen*] determining human nature.

19. Ibid. See D. Morgan, "Goethe's 'Enhanced Praxis' and the Emergence of a Cosmopolitical Future," in *Cosmopolitics and the Emergence of a Future*, ed. Gary Banham and Diane Morgan (Basingstoke: Palgrave Macmillan, 2007), 245–46, 253, for a discussion of the complexity of archetypes as understood by Kant and Goethe; for Lacoste's definition of them as "synthetic global models"; and for the suggestion that they are akin to what the scientist Ian Stewart calls "phase space," the "space of the adjacent possible." For Wells modern utopia is exactly that, a "phase space": it is not an entirely other world, difficult to attain, at least for the time being if we make the decision to opt for change right now; see H. G. Wells, *A Modern Utopia* (London: Everyman Dent, 1998), 16.

20. Kant, *Critique of Pure Reason*, 533–34, B672–73.

21. The moon as an obscurely elusive, and probably illusory, object of desire is evoked in William Blake's 1793 drawing "I want, I want." For the moon as a focus for and symbol of world peace, see the UN "Agreement Governing the Activities of States on the Moon and Other Celestial Bodies" (1979) and my discussion of this shining example of lunar utopianism in Morgan, "The Camel (Ship of the Desert)."

22. For an analysis of how "analogy" and/or "model" function in Kant's work, see

Joseph A. May, *Kant's Concept of Geography and Its Relation to Recent Geographical Thought* (Toronto: University of Toronto Press, 1970), 127. Edgar Mitchell (one of the Apollo 14 astronauts) also indicates how looking back upon the Earth from another planet could propagate a more cosmopolitically inclined way of thinking (and behaving). He states: "We've got to sort the problems out on this planet; then we're more ready to go. We can take something good with us, instead of our brand of insanity. When I go to Mars and look back at this tiny little dot, it's utterly stupid to say, 'I came from the United States. Or France. Or the Republic of China.' And we're not ready to do that yet" (cited in Andrew Smith, *Moon Dust* [London: Bloomsbury, 2005], 74). For the importance of space travel for Kant and cosmopolitics, see Morgan in da Silva, *The Epistemology of Utopia.*

23. Kant, *Political Writings*, 51. For how "concepts of reasons" function as heuristic fictions and how they have to be thought problematically so as to serve as a base for the "regulative principles of the systematic employment of the understanding," see Kant, *Critique of Pure Reason*, 600, B799; just because we have invented them, we cannot assume them to be possible, but also *cannot presume them to be impossible.* They do not serve as hypotheses, inasmuch as they cannot be employed as "explanations of actual appearances," but they could be similarly useful "weapons of war" for the purpose of "defending a right, not in order to establish it" [*nicht um darauf ein Recht zu gründen, sondern nur es zu verteidigen*]; see ibid., 617, B805. Kant goes on to describe a most surprising form of attack, that of giving the opponent one's weapons so as to "grant him the most favourable position he would possibly desire." Thus unarmed—but thereby radically disarming—we could hope to accompany that which would be a "possession which can never again be contested": that is to say, "perpetual peace" [*ewigen Frieden*] (ibid., B806, B805). For unarmed accompaniment as a new tactic in conflict resolution and the attempt to enforce human rights, see L. Maguren and L. E. Eguren, *Unarmed Bodyguards: International Accompaniment for the Protection of Human Rights* (Sterling, VA: Kumarian Press, 1997).

24. Kant, *Political Writings*, 63.

25. Levitas, *Imagining and Making the World*, 322.

26. See Note 23, above, for how "heuristic fictions" can give a sense of the not-impossibility of cosmopolitan law. This not-impossibility could challenge dominant ideas regarding, not only "The Law," but also "The Utopian Imagination." For example, when discussing how the tradition of political novels, such as More's, "open the floodgates to the social and political imagination in *voyages imaginaries*" [*sic*], Höffe writes: "Contrary to this tradition, Kant understands his aim of a federation of peoples to be a product not of the imagination but of legal morals and of practical 'reason'" (Höffe, *Kant's Cosmopolitan Theory of Law and Peace*, 165). While not only acknowledging that Kant's idea of the cosmopolitan federation of people is indeed a

legal project that is charged with a moral categorical imperative, but also presenting it as an act of the imagination, we would in effect be breaking down the divide between the Law and the Imagination that Höffe presupposes: the legal imagination can be utopian, but, as we should know, utopia is not just a no-place, it is also a good place that we should at least strive to reach (T. More, *Utopia,* trans. and ed. R. Adams (New York: Norton Critical Editions, 1975), 3.

27. "Mere" dreams are impotent and therefore maybe a waste of time and energy; for these reasons they could be considered to be, not only counterproductive but also dangerous, undermining any real possibilities for effective change. Morris's distinction between "dreams" and "visions" can be compared to that of Kant between imaginative acts which can create or compose [*dichten*], and those that just "enthuse" [*schwärmen*]; see Kant, *Critique of Pure Reason*, 613, B797.

28. Morris, *News from Nowhere and Other Writings,* 228.

29. One of the most helpful, because most succinct, explanations of this weakness of utopias remains the wonderful opening chapter of Wells's *A Modern Utopia.* For Wells modern utopias, cognizant of Darwinian evolution, can only be conceived as dynamic and therefore imperfect; there would therefore be no initial blueprint to be implemented.

30. Kant, *Political Writings,* 51.

31. See my "Kant, Cosmogony and the Interplanetary Perspective," in *Kant, Cosmopolitics and Globality* (Palgrave/Macmillan, forthcoming 2014), for the important function the term "rational beings" plays throughout Kant's writings in keeping the "nature" of humans open to questioning and to exploration.

32. E. Bellamy, *Looking Backward* (London: Penguin 1982), 68.

33. Ibid., 196.

34. Ibid., 200.

35. J. Conrad, *Heart of Darkness* (London: Penguin, 1981), 24. Incidentally, Conrad also gives us a very different account of the geography of most seamen, very different from the "fluid" one described by Buckminster Fuller and drawn on below (see Note 50, below): "[M]ost seamen lead . . . a sedentary life. Their minds are of the stay-at-home order and their home is always with them—the ship; and so is their country—the sea. One ship is very much like another, and the sea is always the same" (ibid., 8). But then Marlowe was a completely different sort of traveler.

36. Ibid., 100.

37. Kant, *Political Writings,* 105.

38. J. Copjec, ed., *Radical Evil* (London: Verso, 1996), xi. See also D. Morgan, *Kant Trouble: The Obscurities of the Enlightened* (London and New York: Routledge/Taylor and Francis, 2000), 159–200).

39. "Precinct," which has become a rather debased term as a result of today's

intensified mania for shopping, is Nisbet's translation for Kant's *Gehege* (Kant, *Political Writings,* 46). The verb *hegen* is associated with protecting and conserving, hence *Gehege* can evoke a sanctuary—though it also refers to a segregated zone for the purposes of hunting! The fragility of the cosmopolitan project is neatly captured in this linguistic ambiguity.

40. A "Right of all nations" supersedes national differences, establishes principles of commonality, and is thereby cosmopolitan.

41. Kant, *The Metaphysics of Morals,* trans. M. Gregor (Cambridge: Cambridge University Press, 1991), 123–24, §43–44.

42. Ibid., 161. Boldly I suggest that cosmopolitan law and morality are ultimately the same thing.

43. Cosmopolitan law could be seen as persuasively powerful, as it is "interesting" for us. It is interesting for us because it invests in peace. As stated here, peace is the "entire final end" of the doctrine of right. Even if its nonimpossibility cannot be proven, its "interest" still might be: "If someone cannot prove that a thing is, he can try to prove that it is not. If (as often happens) he cannot succeed in either, he can still ask whether he has any *interest* in assuming one or the other (as a hypothesis), either from a theoretical or from a practical point of view [*ob es ihn interessierte, das eine oder das andere* (*durch eine Hypothese anzunehmen*] (ibid., 160). Cosmopolitan law is ultimately predicated on the pleonasm "perpetual peace"; see Kant, *Political Writings,* 93; and Morgan, "Why 'Perpetual Peace' Is Almost a Pleonasm," *Peace Review: A Journal of Social Justice* 25, no. 1 (January–March 2013): 9–16. This hypothetical state of affairs should nevertheless be categorically binding for us; we should act as if it were not impossible. If we cannot, perpetual peace can still be "interesting" to us, as only it—and not war—opens hopeful prospects for a sustainable future.

44. Kant, *Political Writings,* 105.

45. Kant, *The Metaphysics of Morals,* 161 (author's italics). The complicated concatenation that is the globe's population might be best rendered by translating "*eine Menge einander benachbarter Menschen*" more literally than Gregor does—that is, as "a multitude of one-another beneighboured humans."

46. Kant, *Political Writings,* 51.

47. Ibid., 93. Holland is undeniably watery, but also very flat. This geographical particularity is perhaps why Dutch innkeepers apparently have problems engaging with the vital issues of what I will be calling, following Buckminster Fuller, "fluid geography" (see Note 50, below)—that is, why, unlike Kant, they do not entertain a more expanded and creative notion of "peace" given the relative insignificance of our spherical planet within the wider scheme of things and our inevitable, but also rather wonderful, interconnectivity as dependent and finite creatures.

48. Kant, *The Metaphysics of Morals,* 161, cited above.

49. Ibid., 158 §62 (translation modified). I have adapted Mary Gregor's translation as she translates Kant's "Völker" with "nations." I consider that this choice of term reductively ties Kant's idea of a cosmopolitical future down to international relations. It is also debatable to what extent people/peoples are to be equated with the nation state, and whether it might even be desirable that the former remains always in excess of what the latter tries to express. See S. Benhabib et al., *Another Cosmopolitanism* (Oxford: Oxford University Press, 2006), 16–67, in which she also addresses the problems attending a conflation of nationality and peoplehood. See J. Derrida, *On Cosmopolitanism and Forgiveness,* trans. M. Dooley (London and New York: Routledge/Taylor and Francis, 2000), for "unconditional hospitality" as a reserve or remainder which always already challenges a restricted economy of identity and belonging.

50. The term "fluid geography" is borrowed from the eponymous essay by Buckminster Fuller in *Buckminster Fuller Reader,* ed. J. Mellor (Worcester/London: Trinity Press, 1970), 128–47. Fuller gives us a beautiful analysis of how sailors, unlike landlubbers, necessarily deal "directly and daily with the mechanics of the stars" as they circumnavigate the globe. He evocatively states that "without thinking of themselves as cosmogonists, sailors naturally develop a spontaneous cosmic viewpoint. They view the world from outside; they 'come upon' the land" (ibid., 133). For Fuller, terrestrially bounded inhabitants carve the surface of the earth up into immobilized places located in the East or West, North or South. By contrast, sailors have a more dynamic sensibility of space. Riding the waves, negotiating the currents, they "see everything in motion" (ibid., 134). They keenly experience the interconnectedness and variability of the globe's earthy-watery surface. For sailors directionality is paramount; their experience of the earth's sphericity is continually informed by the direction they set out from and where they head to. For them all placing is transitional, temporary, temporalized and relative. By presenting Kant also as a "fluid geographer," I am going against the rather stereotypical portrait of him as a "static" thinker of space. For one such analysis, see D. Harvey, *Cosmopolitanism and the Geographies of Freedom* (New York: Columbia University Press, 2009), 212, who suggests that Kantian spatiality is "fixed," "dead," "undialectical." See also D. Morgan, "La terre est une sphère: la 'globalité' et les sciences de la terre chez Kant," in *Kant, la science et les sciences,* ed. M. Lequan et al. (Paris: Vrin, 2011), 191–202, for a different reading.

51. As we know, wars will be increasingly fought over basic natural resources essential to survival. For the essential and existential importance of water, see V. Strang, *The Meaning of Water* (Oxford, New York: Berg, 2004).

52. I allude to the well-known and most pertinent words of Hannah Arendt about the relative impotence of the "right to have rights"—that is, the right to be "a legal person"—in *The Origins of Totalitarianism* (San Diego, London: Harcourt Brace, 1975), 298: "[H]umanity which for the eighteenth century, in Kantian terminology, was no more than a regulative idea, has today become an inescapable fact. This new situation,

in which humanity has in effect assumed the role formerly ascribed to nature or history, would mean in this context that the right to have rights, or the right of every individual to belong to humanity, should be guaranteed by humanity itself. It is by no means certain whether this is possible. For, contrary to the best-intentioned humanitarian attempts to obtain new declarations of human rights from international organisations, it should be understood that this idea transcends the present sphere of international law which still operates in terms of reciprocal agreements and treaties between sovereign states; and for the time being, a sphere that is above the nations does not exist." Evidently what is debated nowadays is the extent, and the legislative capacity, of emerging transnational governing bodies and whether these ensue from a "taming" or "transcending" of "liberal nationhood" (see Kymlicka, in Benhabib et al., *Another Cosmopolitanism*, 130–31; see also S. Benhabib, *The Rights of Others* (Cambridge: Cambridge University Press, 2004), 3. For Kantian critique as a utopia (good/no—place) wherein supranational disputes could be neutrally settled, see Kant, *Critique of Pure Reason*, 601, B779.

53. Kant, *The Metaphysics of Morals*, 158.

54. Kant states that often projects "which are founded only on hope" are rejected from the start just because they do not as yet exist in world. This fatalistic doom would have precluded inventions such as "aerostatic balloons." However, he considers that such short-sighted objections, which aim to ground "utopian" projects before they are given a chance to take off, ultimately do not carry any weight. He adds that their irrelevance is especially evident when it comes to moral aims, "which, so long as it is not demonstrably impossible to fulfil them, amount to duties" (Kant, *Political Writings*, 89).

55. Ibid., 63, 92.

56. Kant, *Critique of Pure Reason*, 9, AXI.

57. Ibid., 601, B779.

58. Kant, *Political Writings*, 106.

59. Assuming that one accepts that it is indubitably true that the earth is round (that is, rather than insisting that it is evidently more or less flat), one then would need to decide what force this fact carries with it. As Benhabib points out, just because land surface is limited, it does not mean that anyone will recognize someone else's right to occupy a part of it (Benhabib, *The Rights of Others*, 33). Indeed the finite nature of resources might well be a very good reason for getting rid of them.

60. In her otherwise pessimistic analysis of human rights and their governing bodies, Arendt rather optimistically states outright that humanity is nowadays a "fact" (see Note 52, above). Along with Kant, I am suggesting that "humanity" is not a fact, but an Idea or even Ideal. The term gathers together essential qualities of humans' natures but it is not to be found as such in this world. The idea(l) of "humanity" nevertheless has "practical power"; it can "form the basis of the possible perfection of certain actions" (Kant, *Critique of Pure Reason*, 485–86, B596–97.

61. Kant suggests that cosmopolitan law cannot be instrumentalized: "[T]he rule

of this constitution, as a norm for others, cannot be derived from the experience of those who have hitherto found it most to their advantage; it must rather be derived a priori by reason from the Ideal of a rightful association of men under public laws as such" (Kant, *The Metaphysics of Morals*, 161). Unlike other normative programs that wield power so as to close down debate, the "normative" intentions of the cosmopolitan project would rather encourage creative, synchronic, but as we will see, also diachronic, dialogue with others. Indeed, what might "the Ideal of a rightful association of [all] humans under public laws as such" actually look like? This utopian projection provokes lively discussion.

62. As we will see later, "seriality," derived by Proudhon from Kant's table of categories, is equally concerned with the crucial life issues of needs, rights, and duties.

63. Kant, *Critique of Pure Reason*, 109–10, B99–100.

64. Ibid., 109, B99.

65. Later we will see that Proudhon gives a more creative reading of, what he sees as Kant's own idea of, the series than Kant himself does at this point. Here Kant seems to suggest that the series, even if its starting-point is a mere hypothesis, can nevertheless proceed to develop itself inexorably as if blindly programmed for self-production.

66. Kant, *Critique of Pure Reason*, 9, Axii.

67. Kant, *Anthropology from a Pragmatic Point of View*, trans. M. Gregor (The Hague: Martinus Nijhoff, 1974), 12. Kant states that the "constraints of law [limit] our freedom solely in order that it may be consistent with the freedom of others and with the common good of all." However, he continues: "This freedom will carry with it the right to submit openly for discussion [*öffentlich zur Beurteilung aufzustellen*] the thoughts and doubts with which we find ourselves unable to deal, and to do so without being decried as troublesome and dangerous citizens. This is one of the original rights of human reason in which everyone has his say." This right is therefore "sacred and must not be curtailed." However, in the name of human rights, what about hate speech? Is that also "free speech"? Is the dogmatism of a racist mere words, to be laughed at as "child's play," mere "ridicule," unlike "sticks and stones" that do really break bones? (Kant, *Critique of Pure Reason*, 596, B771). Again human rights challenge reason's founding principles as defined by Kant.

68. Hearing other voices and using them as a testing ground or touchstone [*Probierstein* or *criterium veritatis externum*] for our ideas is not only an antidote to egotism, but it is also the indication of a healthy, well-balanced mind for Kant. See Morgan, *Kant Trouble*, 176–77, for an analysis of whether this could also be a sign of madness.

69. Kant, *Political Writings*, 63.

70. Ibid., 90. For an analysis of Kant's mereological cosmopolitics, see D. Morgan "Introduction: Parts and Wholes—Kant, Communications, Communities and

Cosmopolitics," in *Cosmopolitics and the Emergence of a Future,* ed. Gary Banham and Diane Morgan (Basingstoke: Palgrave Macmillan, 2007), 1–11.

71. As well as adopting the idea of "seriality" from Kant, Proudhon also found it in the writings of Saint-Simon and, even more evidently, those of Charles Fourier. The latter had identified it as the way natural processes develop and as the manner in which societal relations should be likewise organized. According to Fourier, when enlightened philosophers appeal to an abstract, disembodied notion of reason that all humans are supposed to have in common, they are in effect thwarting qualitative social change as they stultify those very mechanisms, the passions, that exist to combine us into social harmony. A creatively dynamic social whole is produced, *not in spite of* the passions, *but* in a finely tuned concert *with* them as long as they are expansively developed in what he calls a "progressive series" that fosters not only variety and differentiation but also creative intersplicing and cross-fertilization (C. Fourier, *Theory of the Four Movements,* ed. G. Stedman Jones and I. Patterson [Cambridge: Cambridge University Press, 1996], 15). The enthusiastic adoption of seriality as a social practice would provide a solution to many current antisocial ills. For seriality in the work of the French utopian socialists, see Morgan, *Saint-Simon, Fourier and Proudhon,* 267, 276–80, 283–84, 293–94, 298. For the importance of seriality as a way of organizing work in a more productive and creative way than is currently the case, see D. Morgan, "Are You Working Enthusiastically? Fourier, Proudhon and the Serial Organisation of the Workplace," *Parallax* 59 (2011): 36–48; and "The Flat Management of 'Crises' on Our Spherical Planet: Anarchist Order for a Sustainable Future," in *Utopia/Dystopia,* ed. P. Gallardo and L. Russell (Cambridge Scholars Publishing, forthcoming 2014).

72. Kant, *Critique of Pure Reason,* 115–16, B109–10.

73. P.-J. Proudhon, *De la création de l'ordre dans l'humanité I* (Anthony: Editions Tops/H. Trinquier 2004) : 163.

74. Ibid., 164.

75. Ibid.

76. Ibid., 175.

77. Ibid., 189.

78. Ibid. II, 17.

79. For the cosmopolitan law as implying a different form of normativity, one that is not coercive, that doesn't smother differences, see Note 61, above.

80. Proudhon, *De la création de l'ordre dans l'humanité I,* 197.

81. Kant, *Political Writings,* 44. Proudhon also suggests that seriality can be a source of happiness for us. The ensuing sense of fulfillment we feel might even help us overcome our seemingly structural ambivalence. However these eventual results cannot be considered to be the designed end of seriality.

82. Proudhon is also an advocate for a form of order; it is just that, rather unlike

Kant, he suggests that "society seeks [it] in anarchy" (P.-J. Proudhon, *What Is Property?* ed. and trans. D. R. Kelly and B. G. Smith (Cambridge: Cambridge University Press, 2007), 209. A dialogue between Kant and Proudhon would have been interesting!

83. Kant, *Political Writings,* 62.

84. Ibid., 89.

85. Ibid., 63.

86. Ibid., 89.

87. Ibid.

88. For Kant the moral law is "independent of everything empirical"; it is "inexplicable from any data of the world of sense" (Kant, *Critique of Practical Reason,* 43–44. It is therefore not to be derived from needs, whether these be corporeal or psychological.

89. Kant, *The Metaphysics of Morals,* 160.

90. Proudhon, *What Is Property?* 213 (author's italics). I've edited out some of Proudhon's rather "unfortunate" remarks about wives. Feminism was not his strong point (unlike Fourier).

91. Proudhon, *De la création de l'ordre dans l'humanité I,* 57.

92. Regarding governmentality there are evidently many differences between Kant and Proudhon. However, the former does promulgate a federation of republics in the "Towards Perpetual Peace essay, a proposal that Proudhon would have approved of (Kant, *Political Writings,* 104.

93. Kant, *The Metaphysics of Morals,* 84 §14.

94. Ibid., 84.

95. Proudhon, *What Is Property?* 66.

96. Ibid., 14.

97. P.-J. Proudhon, *Théorie de la propriété* (Paris and Montréal: L'Harmattan, 1997), 37. For an account of Proudhon's paradoxical statement: "property is theft . . . liberty," see Morgan, *Saint-Simon, Fourier and Proudhon,* 299–300.

98. This concern about colonizing invaders is one of the reasons why hospitality has to be conditional; see Kant, *Political Writings,* 106; and D. Morgan, "Trading Hospitality: Kant, Cosmopolitics and *Commercium,*" *Paragraph* 32, no. 1 (2009): 116.

99. Kant, *Political Writings,* 51.

100. Proudhon, *What Is Property?* 69. Proudhon's statement invites a reflection about the relation between cosmopolitan law, hospitality, and temporality. How much time does it take to tie a goat to a hedge, lead a cow to pasture, sow a field, or bake bread? For the beginning of such an analysis, see my "Trading Hospitality," 117–18.

# Dystopian Narratives and Legal Imagination: Tales of Noir Cities and Dark Law

SHULAMIT ALMOG

## I. Introduction

Since compiling systemic sets of norms is at the center of both the utopian and the legal projects, there is an innate kinship between many legal and utopian expressions. The utopian mode was indeed characterized by "its pursuit of legal, institutional, bureaucratic and educational means of producing a harmonious society."[1]

Utopia, according to such perception, is a form of ideal society that imposes order through law.[2] As J. C. Davis put it: "The utopian mode is one which accepts deficiencies in men and nature and strives to contain and condition them through organizational controls and sanctions."[3]

This paper is based upon a complementing premise, maintaining that there is also a meaningful linkage between normative systems that are products of law, and speculative delineations of dystopias. This linkage derives from the duality pertaining to the utopian/dystopian notion. Many legal systems draw from utopian imagination, since utopian expressions are closely linked to law's purpose—creating norms that reflect a vision of optimal societal existence. At the same time, each normative system draws from imagining dystopias, which are visions of societies in which the quality of life is extremely undesirable.[4] According to such perception, the utopian imagination and the dystopian imagination are the opposite faces of one coin.[5]

Amid the aspiration for utopian future and the apprehension from a dystopian one, the present societal condition is located. Under the background of flawed reality, the utopian vision serves as an inspiration for achieving a better model of societal existence, and imagining the dystopian stimulates its pursuing.[6]

In the following, two dystopian articulations, Jean-Luc Godard's *Alphaville* (1965) and Ridley Scott's *Blade Runner* (1982), will be presented as offering a meaningful contribution to the legal imagination, by creating manifestations to law's potential function as both generator of highly undesirable future, and a means to resist it. In both, the dystopian elements are intermingled with imagery that evokes present-day patterns.[7] In both films, narratives that employ metropolitan settings create a similar cautionary tale, according to which the metropolis—the pillar of liberal and rational social existence—turns into a dystopia. In both cases, law is presented as taking an active role in enabling and facilitating the dystopian regime.

The following section will describe how dystopian tales are different from utopian models. The third section will deal with *Alphaville*, a depiction of a dystopian technocracy where the rule of law is replaced by the rule of logic, employing what is declared to be metarationalization. The next section will present *Blade Runner*, which manifests a dystopia established and maintained by employing secretive, brutal law. The following section will analyze the complementing vision of urban disaster facilitated by law that the two films create. The concluding section will describe how dystopian narratives augment the legal imagination by producing images of disastrous societal existence, while casting light on the role law can play in establishing it and resisting it.

## II. Utopian Schemes and Dystopian Tales

Although one of the main utopian modes is literary,[8] Fredric Jameson suggests that utopian text is typically non-narrative.[9] Even when it takes the form of prose fiction, like the originating text, Thomas More's *Utopia*,[10] or Edward Bellamy's seminal *Looking Backward*,[11] its core is not a story that relates to a subject; rather than that the typical utopian text describes a mechanism or a scheme.[12]

Dystopian text on the other hand, even when it gives account of a mechanism, is generally constructed as a narrative, which is a depiction of what happens to a specific subject or character.[13] Consequently, because of their storytelling form, dystopian texts produce a significant contribution for enriching and widening the scope and contents of the legal imagination. They challenge both the present and the imagined future, by reflecting and representing the fate of individuals.

This paper deals with narratives of dystopia that can be characterized by three elements. The first is that they relate to dystopias generated by human decision-making, and not by unavoidable catastrophes such as lethal epidemics, atomic or ecological disaster, hunger, or lack of resources; the second is that they reveal how law is a significant factor in constituting the dystopian situation; the third is that they illuminate the dystopia by focusing on the situation of a specific subject or character.

One of the oldest dystopian myths, the biblical story of Sodom and Gomorrah, aptly exemplifies the appearance of all the three elements in a dystopian tale. As Genesis tells us, the outcry against the grievous sins of Sodom and Gomorrah was so great that God decided to destroy the two cities.[14] According to Jewish legends, the governance of the cities was constituted and maintained by their laws and their judges. Here is one vignette, from the ancient Book of Jasher, expounding how legal mechanisms were employed in order to control the entry to the cities: "And by desire of their four judges the people of Sodom and Gomorrah had beds erected in the streets of the cities, and if a man came to these places . . . if the man was less than the bed . . . six men would stretch him at each end . . . . And if he was longer than the bed then they would draw together the two sides of the bed at each end until the man had reached the gates of death . . . . And when men heard all these . . . they refrained from coming there."[15]

The Talmud lists four judges who represent the evil traits of Sodom. Each judge is linked to a narrative relating to the specific injustice inflicted by him.[16] The Talmud and the Book of Jasher recount in detail several stories about Sodom and Gomorrah's abusive laws. According to one story a poor man came into Sodom to seek help and food. The Sodomite people's response was the enactment of a rule forbidding offering of food or drink to the poor man.[17] Two young women defied the law, and fed the man. When they were caught, they were brought before the local judges. One was sentenced to death and was burned alive. The other girl was smeared with honey and hung from the city wall until she was killed by bees. Her screams in particular, tells the Talmud, are alluded to in the term "outcry," mentioned in Genesis as the reason for God's decision to destroy the cities.[18]

This story, alongside other narratives in Jewish lore, translates the "great outcry" succinctly mentioned by the narrator of Genesis into tangible situations. The cluster of complementing stories transform the short biblical report about the evil cities that were destroyed by God's wrath into an elaborate cautionary tale, encapsulating the danger in erecting unjust regimes, supported by legal norms. They tell about a dystopia that was created by human governance; they present law—legislation and judging—as central in constituting the dystopian situation, and they manifest the dystopian character of the situation by relating the sufferance of individuals one can pity and identify with.

Moving to contemporary culture, innovative images of dystopia are abundant, and the warnings of "what will happen if . . ." seem more relevant than ever.[19] However, the platforms of dystopian narratives have dramatically changed. Since the turn of the previous century, dystopian images have figured notably in cinema, mainly in films that are linked to the science fiction genre.[20] As Chris Darke explains: "[T]he dystopian scenario need not be the exclusive preserve of science fiction, but, with the genre's propensity for speculation, allegory and straightforward prophecy, it appeared as its natural home."[21]

Indeed, as Jameson noted, the use of dichotomy between utopia and dystopia became salient since science fiction.[22] Science fiction films, observed Susan Sontag in her seminal essay (to which I will return later) "The Imagination of Disaster," serve to "reflect world-wide anxieties, and they serve to allay them."[23] The cinema, because of its capacity to charge the dystopian visions with evocative representational dimensions, became a natural habitat.

## III. *Alphaville*: The Capital of Pain

Alphaville is the capital city of a remote planet. Lemmy Caution (Eddi Constantine), an American secret agent, arrives to the city from the Outerlands, apparently planet Earth. His mission is to find out what happened to Henry Dixon, an agent who had been sent to Alphaville and disappeared. In order to do that, he must find Professor von Braun (Howard Vernon)—the mind behind Alpha 60, the city's omnipotent megacomputer, which is in complete control on all of Alphaville.

Disguised as Ivan Johnson, a reporter from the *Figaro-Pravda*, Lemmy gradually finds out Alphaville's ways and rules, with the help of Natasha (Anna Karina), von Braun's beautiful daughter, whom he falls in love with. Lemmy finds Dickson (Akim Tamiroff), who before dying tells him that the city is a technocracy, where citizens are governed by computerized dictates and are executed for acting illogically. Dickson instructs Lemmy to destroy the machine. Lemmy then attends a gala reception that includes, as entertainment, the execution of citizens who had displayed emotions. After being trapped by von Braun's bodyguards, Lemmy is interrogated by Alpha 60, and then senior team members accompany him in a guided tour around the computer's nerve center. Later Lemmy confronts von Braun, who offers him the opportunity to stay in Alphaville and enjoy power and wealth. Lemmy refuses, kills von Braun, and then damages Alpha 60's control panels. The city runs into havoc. Lemmy finds Natasha and they flee in his car, which he navigates toward the Outerlands. During the trip, Natasha, for the first time in her life, gains the ability to feel, and tells Lemmy: "I love you."

Lemmy Caution explains why and how Alphaville is a dystopian society:

> In the last four years, under the direction of von Braun and his assistants, Alphaville has developed itself at lightning speed, by following the orders of its electronic brains .... Outsiders have been assimilated wherever possible .... The others, who could not adapt, were simply put to death. I visited the execution theater where they were electrocuted in their seats while watching a show. The sits tipped up and deposited them into huge garbage cans, making way for the next to be executed.[24]

Several critics referred from different angles to the dystopian nature of *Alphaville*. Allan Wollfolk sets the film alongside a well-known literary tradition of dystopian novels, such as Yevgeny Zamyatin's *We* (1924), Aldus Huxley's *Brave New World* (1932), and George Orwell's *Nineteen Eighty-Four* (1949), all depicting political oppression destructive to individual life.[25] Godard's conception of Alphaville, he maintains, "draws upon this tradition of manipulation and coercion of the most private activities."[26] Chris Darke describes the dystopia in Alphaville as a technocracy,[27] "society in which *techné* has overwhelmed *demos*, a computer-controlled society ordered according to the dictates of 'prudence, control and security.'"[28] Clements maintains that the film presents "a dystopian nightmare world hostile to individuality, love and self-expression," warning against "computerized horrors of the city."[29] Lastly, Richard Roud sees the film as a study of the totalitarian state, and Alphaville as the Capital of Pain (*Capitale de la Douleur*),[30] where inhabitants have become the slaves of electronic probabilities.[31]

How was Alphaville constructed as "labyrinths of power, mazes at whose centre lies death"?[32] What transformed it into a Capital of Pain? Answers in the vein of "Artificial intelligence that has gone awry is responsible for all that misery" miss the gist of the matter: the machine is not accountable for the sufferance caused by its orders. As the plot gradually discloses, the dystopia is chiefly established and maintained by a regime that employs legal mechanisms that consist of two complementing elements.

The first is an intentional replacement of the rule of human law with what is perceived as the rule of logic; the second is the systematic tramping of individuality, emotions, and autonomy. These two complementing elements produce a social existence devoid of overt poverty, but at the same time devoid of creativity, self-fulfillment, and emotions that make life worth living.

It is somewhat vague how the rule of logic actually took control of Alphaville. In the original treatment of the film, the governing system of the city is described in the following: "In fact, the machine doesn't actually govern, but it amounts to the same thing, for the city obeys all its orders—that is to say, its logical conclusions."[33]

The narrative suggests that the rule of logic is an application of Professor von Braun's theory. The professor also works on further developments. During his last conversation with Lemmy, von Braun mentions that he and his associates are in the process of making themselves masters of new and fantastic technology. Yet it does not really matter if Alpha 60 is merely an avatar of von Braun, or if rather than being a master of his own creation, von Braun is entrapped by the rule of logic, like his daughter and all the rest of the citizens of Alphaville. The generators of the catastrophe are people; people that developed the Alpha system and maintain it, and people that shaped and honed the normative nature of Alphaville's rule of logic.

The application of the rule of logic in Alphaville is absolute yielding to a vision—or a nightmare—of outmost efficiency. It seems that the pragmatic meaning of efficiency is determined by the computer, as are the means for optimally achieving it.

The range of Alpha 60's rules is sweeping. It covers the most personal emotions and acts and the most imperative state acts. As explained to Lemmy by the chief engineer of the Alpha 60, "The function of Alpha 60 is the prediction of the data which Alphaville obeys. . . . Everything is determined by cause and effect."[34] Consequently, the desirability of every act is modeled, according to the parameter of efficiency.[35] Emotions interrupt the computerized modeling, and therefore forbidden in Alphaville. One is not allowed to feel fear, because "one must not be afraid of logic."[36] In fact, one is not allowed to have any other emotion, or to engage in artistic endeavors like writing or reading poetry, because Alpha 60 calculates such practices as lacking any value in promoting efficiency models.

As specified in the treatment, "[T]he city has developed in the last twenty years at an unheard-of rate, by following the orders of the machine."[37] Von Braun can boast the rule of logic's success in utilitarian terms, as he indeed does. Yet, interestingly, Alpha 60 also insists: "My judgment is just. I am working for the Universal Good."[38]

The rule of logic and alleged justice results in a society in which people are no more than "slaves to probability."[39] The citizens' status as mere computational objects transforms them into slaves. Their obedience is achieved by coerced indoctrination that goes on during their entire life, and by the ever-present inspecting gaze of Alpha 60.

*Alphaville*'s narrative highlights the systematic employment of legal mechanism that nullifies individuality. The nullification of individuality is constituted by controlling the creation and modification of social meaning.[40] A pivotal scene in this regard is the spectacular execution of dissidents. Citizens unable to adapt and restrain emotions are executed as part of a festive spectacle. Soldiers with submachine guns shoot them into a swimming pool, where bikini-clad girls, with knives in their hands, jump into the water and stab them while the audience applauds.

The shocking effect of this scene mainly derives not from the cruelty of the "artistic" killings but from the chilling reactions of the spectators. They experience the event not only as reflecting acceptable and logical normative order and punitive norms, but also as high-class entertainment, that deserves the repetitive clapping.

As the film reveals, the shaping of social meaning is achieved by brainwashing that goes on during the entire lifespan of each citizen. Alpha 60's doctrine and its orders are learned in schools. Educating the citizens never ceases. In a practice that brings to mind George Orwell's Newspeak, the authorities produce and supply to each citizen a "Bible," which is actually a *dictionary* of permissible vocabulary. It is ever-evolving, omitting daily words that are suspected of evoking emotion. Natasha explains the practice to Lemmy: "Well, nearly every day there are words which disappear because they are no longer allowed. In their place one must put new words to correspond to the new ideas. And you know . . . in the last few months . . . some words have disappeared that I liked very much." Lemmy asks: "Which words?" and Natasha offers some examples: robin redbreast, to weep, autumn light, tenderness.

A key scene takes place when four policemen barge into Lemmy's hotel room and interrupt his emotional and subtle conversation with Natasha. The policemen order Lemmy to come with them to the Residents Control, but before they take him, they order Natasha: "Mademoiselle, Story number 842." Natasha complies. She relates a short narrative, actually an elaborated joke, which is entirely out of any overt relevance to the situation at hand.

The order to tell a story identified by a number, obviously belonging to a limited repertoire of official and permissible stories, is highly revealing. As widely noticed and researched, creating narratives and listening to narratives created by others has a central role of producing meaningful concepts of self and society.[41] The forced story-telling, in front of the immobile and passionless faces of the cops, and without any comprehensible context, echoes not awareness of shared emotions but the opposite; it reflects social alienation and lack of self-awareness. The bizarre employment of narrative demonstrates the core of Alpha 60's failure. Its attempt to reduce the richness of human consciousness into binary terms of efficiency is doomed to fail, because of the inability of the machine to grasp the complex meaning of notions such as "story" or "joke."

This scene is important because it also echoes the liberating option, which is manifested by Lemmy's reaction to the story. Lemmy is the only free-thinking and free-feeling person in the scene. In spite of the ominous cops and in spite of the absurdity of the coerced story-telling, which he surely realizes, he can't help responding to the content of the narrative, and he does it full heartedly. The story is genuinely funny, and Lemmy doubles up laughing, demonstrating what a normal, natural human reaction to stories and to jokes looks like and feels like.

Lemmy is a private-eye in trench coat and ever-present cigarette, blending self-parody, poetry quotations, and half-chauvinistic half-chivalrous gestures. His intricate humanity is the source of his power and courage. He is the first in Alphaville to effectively defy the computer's authority. When Alpha 60 declares it is logical to condemn the insubordinate Lemmy to death, he simply retorts: "You can go and stuff yourself with your bloody logic!"[42] Then he shoots the computer's control panels. Lemmy's main achievement is metamorphosing Natasha from a passionless peon into a sentient human being. As Wollfolk maintains, the film implies "that it is the liberation of the individual from repressive social forms that permits the spontaneous expressions of the spirit. Pitting the individual against such an obviously oppressive regime affirms the right and the power of the individual."[43]

To conclude, *Alphaville* presents a civic world in which individual autonomy and freedom are forfeited by a political regime that perceives humans as disposables that are used for enhancing efficiency. The result is Capital of Pain, an existence characterized by sadness, isolation, and lack of solidarity and vitality.

*Alphaville*'s rule of logic bespeaks one of the darkest rules humanity has experienced, and indeed several critics have noted that the film is scattered with references to Nazi Germany.[44] Through the perspective gained by setting *Alphaville* alongside the Nazi regime, the role of technology as a generator of dystopia becomes ancillary. Using Alpha 60's term, the menace to the "universal good" is not the miscalculations or the obtuse nature of advanced technology. The menace is created by people who control technology. Technology, very much like law, is a mere mechanism given to human manipulation. The real threat lies in the seizure of such forceful mechanisms, in the name of some all-embracing ideology or worldview. Technology was abused in Alphaville by the state, in the battle it proclaimed against each and every individual. As with the practices of Nazi rule, Alphaville's regime also misused the machinery of law. A potential precaution against recurrences of "*Alphaville* scenarios" in reality is the maintenance of alert legal imagination. One of the most important ways of preserving such imagination is continuous engagement with narratives that conceptualize law's failures.[45] Godard's dystopian fable is a fine example of such a narrative.

## IV. *Blade Runner*: Where Law Is the Secret Maker

Ridley Scott's *Blade Runner* (1982)[46] resonates with *Alphaville* on several levels.[47] In stylistic terms, it is also a merger of science fiction and film noir, presenting an urban dystopia. Here again the dystopia is human made, and being preserved by legal tools.

*Blade Runner* gained much wider attention than *Alphaville*, and produced a rich body of diverse critique.[48] Some of it touched on issues relating to law. Attention was given, for example, to the definition of human implied by the film,[49] and to racism.[50] I will discuss the role of law in *Blade Runner* from a wider perspective, pointing to its position as a protagonist of a dystopia.

Let me start with telescoping the plot. Rick Deckard (Harrison Ford), a retired cop in 2019 Los Angeles, is forced back into active duty and ordered to capture several Replicants, humanlike androids with short life spans that have escaped space colonies and invaded Earth. Deckard finds and kills three Replicants. In the meantime, Roy Batty (Rutger Hauer), the leader of the fleeing group, reaches Eldon Tyrell (Joe Turkel), the head of the Tyrell Corporation that produced the Replicants, and kills him. Deckard falls in love with Rachael (Sean Young), Tyrell's assistant and a Replicant who was unaware of her true nature. Deckard confronts Batty, who almost overtakes him, but spares Deckard's life. In the last scene, Deckard and Rachel leave Deckard's apartment, probably to run away together.

Like *Alphaville, Blade Runner* is typically perceived to portray a dystopia,[51] and it has become an iconic representation of the nightmarish future city.[52] Yet, unlike *Alphaville*, where oppression and deep sadness are overt, a careful scrutiny is called for in order to determine what exactly renders the *Blade Runner*'s city a dystopia.

The central social institutions and conventions—such as marriage, employment, financial and leisure activities—exist in futuristic Los Angeles more or less according to well-known patterns. Familiar, even if notorious, sexist practices portrayed in the film echo existing ones. Male Replicants are designated to serve as warriors, and women are intended to provide sex. One female Replicant (Pris) is a "Basic pleasure model," and another (Zhora) is a striptease dancer. The first sexual contact between Deckard and Rachael has been interpreted as rape,[53] or as coerced sex "difficult to distinguish from rape."[54] These characteristics, alongside some other unpleasant factors, such as urban alienation and air pollution, do not turn the city into a future dystopia; though replete with similar problems, contemporary urban life is not generally viewed as dystopian.

More than that, the *Blade Runner* city is exciting, brimming with vitality, presenting a wide range of urban temptations and attractions. Restaurants, night clubs, sushi stands, ethnic quarters, technology experts' stalls as well as mobile and stationary giant screens producing an ever-changing buzz of images and sounds encapsulating consumers' temptations are just some of the attractions. The urban space is characterized by constant intermingling of races and languages.[55] Ethnic pluralisms seems to be the norm. The crowds are huge and the flood of sights and sounds is overwhelming, but these are not representations of dystopia; rather than that, they present metropolitan vibrancy. As Stephen Rowley has noted, the *Blade Runner* city has all that today's Los Angeles is missing and all that makes New York an attractive and exciting place to live: "If vibrancy and vitality are what we are after, there is a lot to like about this fictional Los Angeles of 2019. It has plenty of street-level convenience retailing and restaurants. The nightlife looks fantastic. There is either a good public transport system, or everything is pretty close together—civilians seem to get around okay on foot."[56]

A reference to the urban delights of *Blade Runner* is offered by Wong Kin Yuen, who describes the striking resemblance between the streets of *Blade Runner* and the Times Square quarter in Hong Kong. *Blade Runner*'s "Ridleyville" (as the city depicted in the film is coined by Yuen), as well as twenty-first century Hong Kong, represent the cityscape of the future, "that embraces racial and cultural differences"[57] and happily accommodates "shoppers, blue and white collar workers, tourists of all nationalities, and an ever-changing population of new immigrants (some of them illegal) . . . , rich and poor, young and old,"[58] all enjoying an "explosion of urbanism" in an "intercultural scenario."[59]

And yet, despite the exciting energy pulsing through it, *Blade Runner*'s city is, after all, an oppressive environment. According to the reading suggested here, the central factor that renders the city into a dystopia is its subordination to invisible and arbitrary law, serving unknown masters and unclear purposes. Los Angeles of *Blade Runner* is another variation on Kafka's dark vision, in the center of which is law as a constant menace. The following opening of the film captures the core of the narrative:

> *Early in the 21st Century, THE TYRELL CORPORATION advanced robot evolution into the NEXUS phase—a being virtually identical to a human—known as a Replicant. The NEXUS 6 Replicants were superior in strength and agility, and at least equal in intelligence, to the genetic engineers who created them. Replicants were used Off-World as slave labor, in the hazardous exploration and colonization of other planets. After a*

> *bloody mutiny by a NEXUS 6 combat team in an Off-World colony, Replicants were declared illegal on earth—under penalty of death. Special police squads—BLADE RUNNER UNITS—had orders to shoot to kill, upon detection, any trespassing Replicant, this was not called execution. It was called retirement.*

The celebratory and concise style of this text echoes a quasi-constitutional mode. It encapsulates the permissible and the forbidden. It commences with a festive mentioning of the invention of the Replicants by a corporation. The next sentences reveal what separates Replicants from humans.[60] The Replicants, even if more intelligent than their creators, are defined and perceived as property. They are used as slaves on other planets. When necessity demands, they are put to death without trial: "After a bloody mutiny . . . Replicants were declared illegal on earth—under penalty of death. Special police squads—BLADE RUNNER UNITS—had orders to shoot to kill, upon detection, any trespassing Replicant."[61]

Normally, declaration of individuals as "illegal," subjecting them to the death penalty as well as assigning and authorizing police units for their capture, is a prerogative of governmental and legal authorities, such as legislators, prosecutors, and judges. In *Blade Runner*, if such authorities exist, they operate sub rosa, and their procedures remain hidden. The Replicants are sentenced to death and being executed without having been tried. Kafka's Joseph K, who famously faced a verdict without knowing what he has been accused of, comes to mind: "[It] is an essential part of the justice dispensed here that you should be condemned not only in innocence but also in ignorance."[62]

Condemnation and execution without trial—the embodiment of injustice—is the primary element that overshadows the liveliness of the city and turns it into a dystopia.

Another element, that again intones the practices in *Alphaville*, is the forfeiture of the private sphere. Each individual is under surveillance, activated by moving light beams.[63] The permanent presence of the police and the enforcement authorities creates an ever-present externalization of policing and control.[64] The constant pursuit of data creates vulnerability, and the most vulnerable individuals are the Replicants.

If in *Alphaville* humans are transformed into slaves in order to fulfill the vision and instructions of the nonhuman computer, in *Blade Runner* nonhumans are created and molded in order to serve humans as slaves. In both cases, the result is a dystopia in which legal mechanism is employed in order to facilitate exploitation. In *Blade Runner*, the pseudo-legal procedure determining one's status (human or Replicant) is the "Voight-Kampff test." The law facilitates the implementation of the test and the immediate execution that follows failing it.

The enslavement and sometimes killing of the Replicants is represented not as defensive acts but as a plain manifestation of force, as crude violence backed by invisible law. Following Derrida, the Voight-Kampff procedure means employing the law as a system producing criteria that exclude some "subjects" from the protection of the law, or from the discourse related to justice, morality, and rights.[65] In his "Force of Law," Derrida analyzes the marking of certain subjects (such as animals) and pushing them outside the frameworks of the law: "There are still, many 'subjects' among mankind who are not recognized as subjects .... The opposition between just and unjust has no meaning in this case."[66] The Voight-Kampff procedure, and the immediate killing of those who fail it, are manifestations of the system Derrida describes, a system of setting criteria that exclude subjects from the protection of the law, or from the discourse related to justice, morality, and rights. Human history is abundant with examples of such oppressive practices, and indeed similarities between the exploitation and oppression of Replicants in *Blade Runner* and other forms of exploitation and oppression have been mentioned in a number of contexts.[67] More than that, the city is subjected to an all-encompassing and aggressive law. Human activity, on earth and outside of it, takes place within the boundaries it defines. Yet it is not disclosed how and by whom this law is enacted or determined. Again, the situation resonates Joseph K's suspicions in regard to the nature of the law he faces: "There can be no doubt that ... there is a great organization at work. An organization which ... has at its disposal a judicial hierarchy of high, indeed the highest rank, with an indispensable and numerous retinue of servants, clerks, police and other assistants, perhaps even hangmen."[68]

Individuals in the city of *Blade Runner*, whether defined and labeled as humans or Replicants, are, like Joseph K, subjected to a furtive "great organization" that has at its disposal legal and governmental mechanisms. Rules are imposed by unknown jurisdiction and activated by authorities that derive their mandate from yet another concealed source.

Roy Batty, assuming that Dr. Eldon Tyrell, the head of the corporation creating the Replicants, is empowered to turn him into a "human," entitled to a life span that is not predetermined, confronts Tyrell. "It's not an easy thing to meet your maker," he tells him. Tyrell refuses Roy. He tells him: "Death. Well, I'm afraid that's a little out of my jurisdiction." Tyrell's choice of the word "jurisdiction," which is taken from a legal semantic field, is loaded. Roy Batty's implied assumption is that the key to his salvation is in the hands of the one who is able to "make" Replicants. Nevertheless, Tyrell is not the real creator of Roy. The real maker is the one who has the power to allow the creation of life and to determine its length. The true maker is the one who grants the Tyrell Corporation the power and the authority to create.

The Tyrell Corporation is in fact authorized to act within a certain jurisdiction. Roy would have had a better chance of getting what he desperately seeks if he could have access to the authority that enabled Tyrell to create Replicants—but such access is unavailable. The identity and nature of the metamaker, who uses the law as a tool, remains elusive.

Roy Batty's situation is worse than that of the man who wishes to enter the law in Kafka's *The Trial*. The latter spends his life passively and futilely at the law's doorstep. However, during his life he is entertaining the hope of somehow, someday, entering the law.[69] Roy Batty has no such hope, since he is unaware of the link between his predicament and the hidden maker.

To reiterate, *Blade Runner* presents an urban dystopia chiefly established and maintained by legal mechanisms that operate along two axes.

The first is the rule of secret, brutal law, which is in constant pursuit of data regarding each individual, through the use of privacy-invading surveillance. Individuals, on the other hand, have no access to even the most basic information regarding the law. The other is employing the power of law, first in order to create exploitable beings, and then to mark them as nonhuman or nonbeing. *Blade Runner*, then, is an acute warning against institutional, violent employment of authorized power, and against abusing legal instruments by using them as tools for exclusion of certain subjects from the domain mastered by law.

## V. Urban Disasters Facilitated by Law

As has been noted by several scholars, *Alphaville* and *Blade Runner* reveal some apparent similarities.[70] In cinematic terms, both merge the aesthetics and mood of film noir with those of science fiction. The term "noir," while still denoting a cinematic genre, is now employed metaphorically, to signify a harsh human existence that takes place in a recognizable, mundane setting, usually urban.[71] As Prakash elaborates, "In these portrayals, the city often appears as dark, insurgent (or forced into total obedience), dysfunctional (or forced into machine-like functioning), engulfed in ecological and social crises, seduced by capitalist consumption, paralyzed by crime, wars, class, gender and racial conflicts, and subjected to excessive technological control."[72] The noir genre, whether by the black and white cinematography (which is used in *Alphaville*) or by employing stylistic measures that enhance the interplay between the seen and the unseen (as is done in *Blade Runner*), insinuates that what meets the eye is not necessarily a credible reflection of reality.[73] The human condition is depicted in film noir as something we can see and perceive only partially and dimly.[74]

The perception that what we see is always segmental, and that justice, fairness, and clear vision of reality are basically unattainable, are among the main properties of the genre. In this respect, the film noir is considered "realistic."[75]

Science fiction representations and ideas, on the other hand, are usually set in spaces that are clearly far beyond the contemporary, and are distinguishable by their highly futuristic characteristics. Consequently, the juxtaposition of science fiction and noir modes creates distinctive articulations. The noir atmosphere loads the science fiction dystopias with credibility, relevance, and depth. It transfers them from the domain of clichéd tropes like "Come quickly, there's a monster in my bathtub" or "They must be vulnerable or something"[76] into new fields of nuanced, multileveled evolving crises, attributable to human behavior and not to unavoidable calamities like earthquakes or floods. The noir mode leads toward a denser imagination of disaster, by adding themes and subtexts that link the depicted dystopias to political (in a wide sense) situations, choices, and decisions. Accordingly, the role of law, whether as a safeguard against dystopia or as instrumental in bringing it about, stands out, as it does in both *Alphaville* and *Blade Runner*.

Another important feature the two films share is their similar urban setting. In "The Work of Art in the Age of Mechanical Reproduction," Walter Benjamin famously alluded to the affinities between cinema and the modern city, and to the ways in which cinematic techniques illuminate certain facets of the metropolis. Benjamin wrote: "Our bars and city streets, our offices and furnished rooms, our railroad stations and our factories seemed to close relentlessly around us. Then came film and exploded this prison-world with the dynamite of the split second, so that now we can set off calmly on journeys of adventure among its far-flung debris."[77] Cinema acts as a mediator that recomposes the urban sights and experiences, and casts light on the city's hidden infrastructure. As both *Alphaville* and *Blade Runner* reveal, law is a central component of this infrastructure. Its presence looms in the bars, streets, offices, and roadways of the cities the films present. It is reflected in the daily life of the citizens of Alphaville, who are subjected to the rule of covert law, which constantly invades and manipulates their privacy and autonomy; and the presence of similarly oppressive law emerges from the urban darkness of *Blade Runner*, where legal instruments exclude some beings.

The breadth of the city facilitates the presentation of myriad persons and activities that together create a rich picture of political, social, and commercial life, presented through the urban perspective. The two films emphasize the force and validity of Benjamin's early intuition. The cinematic portrayals of dystopian cities create acute pictures of disturbed urban life, while offering sharp critiques that diagnose the roots of the city's maladies and catastrophes, and perhaps some remedies. Law is a fundamental factor in regard to both.

## VI. Conclusion: The Imagination of Disaster alongside the Imagination of Law

In "Imagination of Disaster" Susan Sontag argued that science fiction films are not really about science or technology; they are about disaster, which is one of the oldest subjects in art.[78] In many such films the calamity is depicted as "urban disaster on a colossally magnificent scale,"[79] originated by nonhuman forces such as gigantic robots or monsters invading from outer space. On a primary level of interpretation, such films produce fantasies about conducting a righteous "good war" that "poses no moral problems" and "admits no moral qualifications."[80] However, closer scrutiny reveals that the deeper roots of the standard motifs used in the films are the primeval fear of depersonalization, of humanity's being "taken over" by arbitrary powers, and the dread of sinking into unstoppable catastrophe and unbearable dystopia. The heroic triumphs in science fiction, claims Sontag, hardly present satisfactory answers to such deep fears. The standard motifs of rescuing humanity by savior-scientists and their like typically lack meaningful cultural or social criticism, and thus cannot be linked easily to profound confrontation with the deep existential threats and dreads intoned by the narrative of imminent catastrophe. As she concludes, the imagery of disaster in science fiction film is above all the emblem of "the inadequacy of most people's response to the unassailable terrors that infect their consciousness."[81]

The reading suggested here delineates one way of addressing the ever-lurking fears of disaster. It juxtaposes the imagination of disaster with the legal imagination. The two narratives transcend the common patterns of science fiction cinema, and create a new trope that elucidates the nature of potential civic disaster and some feasible defenses. Reiterating the three elements that characterize dystopian narratives dealt with here is useful to explain how they manage to do that.

Firstly, both films describe dystopias that were created by human actions, decisions or choices, and not by circumstances beyond human control. *Alphaville* and *Blade Runner*'s Los Angeles are perceived as dystopias because they are subjected to all kinds of regulation, control, and surveillance that carry a dehumanizing effect.

Secondly, as was elaborated in the previous sections, the presence or absence of law is a primary factor that consolidates the dystopia. In Alphaville all that is not perceived as rational or efficient (such as display of emotions or creating art) is banned and punished. Human judgment is relinquished, and replaced by authorizing extralegal and extrahuman metarationalization, which is given unconditional discretion and power. In *Blade Runner* secret law subjects each individual to control and surveillance. The power of law is used first in order to facilitate the creation of exploitable beings, and then to define them as nonhuman or nonbeing. In both films, to use Jameson's description of the city in *Blade Runner*, which applies to *Alphaville* as well, the entry and exit to the dystopian territory is highly controlled by law: "all of it sealed into an inside without an outside."[82] Together the two representations produce a complementing caution against excessive and abusive use of law, and cast light on the essential role law can play in establishing a dystopia or preventing it.

Thirdly, both films exemplify the dystopian nature of the situation by narratives that focus on specific characters. As mentioned, the presence of stories differentiates utopian expressions from dystopian expressions. Utopian typical text, explains Jameson, "does not tell a story at all; it describes a mechanism or even a kind of machine, it furnishes a blueprint rather than lingering upon the kinds of human relations."[83] A dystopian text, on the other hand, is generally a narrative, often focusing on the fate of an individual and on human relations. Both films appositely demonstrate this point. They are not abstract models of "bad" societies, as opposed to utopian texts that are often models of ideal society. They derive their thrust from narratives about individuals. Both describe the dystopian condition by focusing on tales of men and women caught in almost impenetrable webs of power, with no access to legal remedies.

The nature of *Alphaville*'s dystopia becomes lucid through the exploits of its two central characters, Lemmy and Natasha, and their emerging love. Natasha's inability to experience emotions is symptomatic of *Alphaville*'s disaster. Lemmy's attempts and finally his success in waking her dormant emotional capacity are a response that through the personal alludes to the collective calamity. Lemmy's actions and choices, and mostly his blunt defying of the rule of logic, carry a redemptive quality. It is compelling enough not only to evoke humanity and love but also to subvert the foundations of *Alphaville*'s dystopia and redeem all.

A similar course takes place in *Blade Runner*. The nature of the dystopia becomes perceptible through Deckard, who proceeds from emotional alienation into regaining his ability to feel. The climax of the course is his reciprocal love of Rachel, an individual declared by law "illegal" and doomed to execution. As noted by David Ryan, in the dystopia of *Blade Runner*, Deckard's growth allows for the redemptive nature of all humans.[84] As in *Alphaville*, the redemption derives from defying the legal dictate.

To conclude, both films exhibit how dystopian imagination augments the legal imagination. The two narratives illustrate dystopia as an urban disaster, which is expressed as gradual abrasion of humanity. The abrasion is facilitated and supported by legal mechanisms, devoid of independent values or stable moral codes. Such law is used solely as a tool for translating the political will of its masters into normative language. As the cinematic tales suggest, if a chance of recovery looms, it is through the emergence of empathy that evokes dissidence.

## Notes

1. J. C. Davis, *Utopia and the Ideal Society: A Study of English Utopian Writing 1516–1700* (Cambridge: Cambridge University Press, 1981), 371.

2. Gregory Claeys and Lyman Tower Sargent, "Introduction," in *The Utopia Reader*, ed. Claeys and Sargent (New York: New York University Press, 1999), 1.

3. Davis, *Utopia and the Ideal Society*, 370. A different issue that is associated to this notion is the place of law in human utopia. According to one approach, utopia, by nature, is lawless, since in utopia human beings live in constant harmony and there are no conflicts that must be settled by using legal regime. Another variation of this approach contends that law inevitably restricts liberty because of its coercive nature. Consequently, law is incompatible with utopia because of law's inherently problematic attributes, and society is ideal if there are no laws. According to the differing approach, "The utopian mode is distinguished by its pursuit of legal, institutional, bureaucratic and educational means of producing a harmonious society" (ibid., 371 .(Utopia, according to such perception, is a form of ideal society that imposes order through law. For elaboration on this issue, through the perspective of literary expressions, see Shulamit Almog, "Literary Legal Utopias: Alexander's Visit to Kasiah and Law at the End of Days," *Utopian Studies* 12, no. 2 (2001): 164.

4. According to Lyman Tower Sargent's definition, dystopia is "a non-existing society described in considerable detail and normally located in time and space that the author intended a contemporaneous reader to view as considerably worse than the society in which the reader lived." See L. T. Sargent, "The Three Faces of Utopianism Revisited," *Utopian Studies* 5, no. 1 (1994): 1, 9. For elaboration on the history of the term, see C. Darke, *Alphaville* (Urbana: University of Illinois Press, 2005), 23–27.

5. Darke, *Alphaville*, 23.

6. Almog, "Literary Legal Utopias"; Miguel A. Ramiro Avilés, "On Law and Utopia: A Reply to Shulamit Almog," *Utopian Studies* 14, no. 1 (2003): 132; Shulamit Almog and Amnon Reichman, "On Law and Utopia: Rules vs. Principles?—A Comment on Ramiro Avilés's Reply," *Utopian Studies* 14, no. 1 (2003): 143. Be that as it may, even those who envisage utopian as lawless may find the utopian and the dystopian imagination a useful vehicle for improving the present law.

7. Interestingly, in both films aesthetics plays an important role in representing the dystopian condition. *Alphaville*, which was filmed in Paris during the mid-sixties, presented the urban sites as a fusion of science fiction and film noir signifiers. *Blade Runner* juxtaposed digital effects with metropolitan sites. See A. O. Scott, "The Way We Live Now—Metropolis Now," *New York Times*, August 6, 2008. Available at http://www.nytimes.com/2008/06/08/magazine/08wwln-lede-t.html?_r=0.

In a 2011 Victoria and Albert Museum exhibition titled "Postmodernism—Style and Subversion, 1970–1990," stills and scenes from *Blade Runner* were presented as characterizing different themes of postmodernism. As the exhibition's catalogue elaborates, the visuality of *Blade Runner* creates dystopian aesthetics by intertwining views of Western and Eastern megacities, science fiction icons, and forties aesthetics: *Postmodernism—Style and Subversion, 1970–1990*, ed. Glenn Adamson and Jane Pavitt (V&A Publishing, 2011), 38.

8. On utopian literature and its categorization, see Sargent, "The Three Faces of Utopianism Revisited."

9. F. Jameson, *The Seeds of Time* (New York: Columbia University Press, 1994), 55–56.

10. T. More, *Utopia* (London: Penguin Books, 1965).

11. E. Bellamy, *Looking Backward—2000 to 1887* (Bedford, MA: Applewood Books, 2000).

12. On utopian literature and its categorization, see Sargent, "The Three Faces of Utopianism Revisited."

13. Jameson, *The Seeds of Time*, 55–56.

14. Genesis 18:20–21.

15. *The Book of Yashar* (New York: Hermon Press, 1972), 51–52.

16. Sanhedrin, 109b.

17. *The Book of Yashar*, 52.

18. Sanhedrin, 109a. See also *The Book of Yashar*, 53–54.

19. R. Levitas, *The Concept Of Utopia* (New York: Philip Allan, 1990), 195.

20. For discussion of the links between science fiction and dystopia, see Raffaella Baccolini and Tom Moylan, eds., *Dark Horizons: Science Fiction and the Dystopian Imagination* (New York: Routledge, 2003).

21. Darke, *Alphaville*, 25.

22. Jameson, *The Seeds of Time*, 55.

23. S. Sontag, *Against Interpretation and Other Essays* (New York: Dell, 1967), 209.

24. J.-L. Godard, *Alphaville* (New York: Simon and Schuster, 1966), 53–54.

25. Allan Wollfolk, "Disenchantment and Rebellion in Alphaville," in *The Philosophy of Science Fiction Film*, ed. Steven M. Sanders (Lexington: University Press of Kentucky, 2008), 200–201.

26. Ibid., 202.

27. "Technocracy" is a term that evolved after World War I, denoting "rationalized, industrial democracy." See Darke, *Alphaville*, 70.

28. Ibid., 71.

29. David Clements, "From Dystopia to Myopia: Metropolis to Blade Runner," report from the "Future Vision: Future Cities" conference held December 6, 2003, in London. Available at http://hem.passagen.se/replikant/dystopia_myopia.htm.

30. *Capital de la Doleur* is the title of the poetry volume the dying Dickson gives Lemmy. Faux-quotations from the book are used in the film to represent the

transforming power of art and emotions. The original title belongs to Paul Eluard. See P. Eluard, *Capital of Pain* (Boston: Black Widow Press, 2007).

31. Godard, *Alphaville,* 10–11.

32. Ibid., 12.

33. Ibid., 93.

34. Ibid., 49.

35. In fact, such a model is suggested by the chief engineer of the Alpha 60, explaining how the orders of the machines are constituted: "An order is a logical conclusion. . . . We know nothing . . . we record... we calculate . . . and we draw conclusions." Ibid., 50.

36. Ibid.

37. Ibid., 93.

38. Ibid., 70.

39. Ibid., 33.

40. For analysis of the links between legal norms and the creation of social meaning, see Lawrence Lessig, "The Regulation of Social Meaning," *University of Chicago Law Review* 62 (1995): 943.

41. See, for example, Jonathan Culler, *Literary Theory: A Very Short Introduction* (Oxford: Oxford University Press, 1997), 83–94. See also Shulamit Almog, "From Sterne and Borges to Lost Storytellers: Cyberspace, Narrative, and Law," *Fordham Intellectual Property, Media and Entertainment Law Journal* 13 (2002): 1.

42. Godard, *Alphaville,* 70.

43. Wollfolk, "Disenchantment and Rebellion in Alphaville," 202.

44. Some examples are the numbers tattooed on the bodies of women and the name von Braun, which echoes the name of the German missile scientist Wernher von Braun. See: Darke, *Alphaville,* 76–77.

45. For an elaboration on the role of conceptualizing legal narratives, see Almog, "From Sterne and Borges to Lost Storytellers."

46. The central text discussed here is *Blade Runner—Director's Cut*. See *Blade Runner—Director's Cut* (Ridley Scott, 1992). It should be noted that *Blade Runner* has several versions. Two of the others are the 1982 version (Domestic Cut), and the 2007 version (Final Cut). For elaboration, see S. Bukatman, *Blade Runner* (London: British Film Institute, 1997), 33–40.

47. Several scholars have mentioned the kinship between the films. See, for example, Bukatman, *Blade Runner*; Clements, "From Dystopia to Myopia"; Scott, "The Way We Live Now—Metropolis Now."

48. For a short review of various critical comments, see David C. Ryan, "Dreams of Postmodernism and Thoughts of Mortality: A Twenty-Fifth Anniversary Retrospective of Blade Runner," *Senses of Cinema* 43 (2007). Available at http://sensesofcinema.com/2007/feature-articles/blade-runner/.

49. See, for example, Marilyn Gwaltney, "Androids as a Device for Reflection on

Personhood," in *Retrofitting Blade Runner: Issues in Ridley Scott's Blade Runner and Philip K. Dick's Do Androids Dream of Electric Sheep?* ed. Judith B. Kerman (Bowling Green, OH: Bowling Green State University Popular Press, 1991), 32.

50. See, for example, M. K. Booker, *Alternate Americas: Science Fiction Film and American Culture* (Westport, CT: Praeger, 2006), 183.

51. See, for example, Douglas E. Williams, "Ideology as Dystopia: An Interpretation of Blade Runner," *International Political Science Review* 9, no. 4 (1988): 381; Andrew Milner, "Darker Cities: Urban Dystopia and Science Fiction Cinema," *International Journal of Cultural Studies* 7 (2004): 259; and Michael Webb, "'Like Today, Only More So': The Credible Dystopia of Blade Runner," in *Film Architecture: Set Designs from Metropolis to Blade Runner,* ed. Dietrich Neumann (Munich: Prestel, 1996), 44–47.

52. Stephen Rowley, "False LA: Blade Runner and the Nightmare City," in *The Blade Runner Experience: The Legacy of a Science Fiction Classic,* ed. Will Brooker (London and New York: Wallflower Press, 2005), 203.

53. Lessig, "The Regulation of Social Meaning," 960.

54. Williams, "Ideology as Dystopia."

55. There are other approaches which indicate that *Blade Runner* manifests a racial problem. See R. Dyer, *White* (London: Routledge, 1997), 213; and Kaja Silverman, "Back to the Future," *Camera Obscura: A Journal of Feminism and Film Theory* 27 (1991): 109.

56. Rowley, "False LA," 21.

57. Wong Kin Yuen, "On the Edge of Spaces: Blade Runner, Ghost in the Shell and Hong Kong's Cityscape," *Science Fiction Studies* 27, no. 1 (2000): 80.

58. Ibid.

59. Ibid.

60. For elaboration, see Almog Shulamit, "When a Robot Can Love—Blade Runner as a Cautionary Tale on Law and Technology," in *Human Law and Computer Law: Comparative Perspectives,* ed. Mireille Hildebrandt and Jeanne Gaakeer (Dordrecht: Springer, 2013), 181.

61. See the screenplay: Hampton Fancher and David Peoples, *Blade Runner—Screenplay* (1981), 1. Available at http://www.dailyscript.com/scripts/blade-runner_shooting.html.

62. F. Kafka, *The Trial* (New York: Modern Library, 1961), 50.

63. Herb A. Lightman and Richard Patterson, "Blade Runner: Production Design and Photography," *American Cinematographer* 63, no. 7 (1982): 684, 723.

64. Judith B. Kerman, "Technology and Politics in the Blade Runner Dystopia," in *Retrofitting Blade Runner,* 18.

65. Jacques Derrida, "Force of Law: The Mystical Foundation of Authority," *Cardozo Law Review* 11 (1989–90): 920, 951.

66. Ibid.

67. Francavilla compares the oppression of Replicants to the exploitation of the

Aztec Indian, the American Indian, African Slaves, and Jews during World War II. See Joseph Francavilla, "The Android as Doppelganger," in *Retrofitting Blade Runner*, 9. Kerman sees parallels between the destruction of Replicants and the creation of concentration camps and the dropping of the atomic bomb during World War II. See Judith B. Kerman, "Introduction," in ibid., 1.

See also: Peter J. Hutching, "From Offworld Colonies to Migration Zones: Blade Runner and the Fractured Subject of Jurisprudence," Law Culture Humanities 3 (2007):381.

68. Kafka, *The Trial*, 51.

69. Ibid., 234–36.

70. See, for example, Clements, "From Dystopia to Myopia"; Scott, "The Way We Live Now—Metropolis Now." While Clements indicates the similarity between the films in suggesting a bleak view of the future, using what he describes as an 'imaginary future,' Scott emphasizes their functional use of the city as a "cautionary tale."

71. For elaboration, see Gyan Prakash, ed., *Noir Urbanisms: Dystopic Images of the Modern City* (Princeton: Princeton University Press, 2010), esp. Prakash, "Introduction: Imagining the Modern City, Darkly," 1.

72. Ibid.

73. For elaboration, see Shulamit Almog and Amnon Reichman, "Ethics, Aesthetics, and Law: The Third Man's Three Prongs," *Studies in Law, Politics, and Society* 46 (2008): 169.

74. See, in this regard, Bukatman's introduction on the role of seeing in *Blade Runner*: Bukatman, *Blade Runner*, "Introduction: On Seeing, Science Fictions and Cities," 7–12.

75. Realism in general is tightly connected to the film noir genre. See C. Richardson, *Autopsy: An Element of Realism in Film Noir* (Metuchen, NJ: Scarecrow Press, 1992), 2.

76. One of Sontag's examples in "The Imagination of Disaster." See Sontag, *Against Interpretation and Other Essays*, 209.

77. Walter Benjamin, "The Work of Art in the Age of Its Reproducibility," in *Walter Benjamin: Selected Writings*, ed. Michael Jennings (Cambridge: Belknap Press of Harvard University Press, 2002), 117. For a discussion of other thinkers who identified intricate links between films and metropolis, see Gilloch Graeme, "Urban Optics: Film, Phantasmagoria and the City in Benjamin and Kracauer," *New Formation* 61 (2007): 115. For other discussions of Benjamin's theorizing of the affinities between modern cities and cinema, see *The Cinematic City*, ed. David B. Clarke (New York: Routledge, 1997); James Donald, *"Light in Dark Spaces: Cinema and City" in Imagining the Modern City* (Minneapolis: University of Minnesota Press, 1999), 63–64; Mark Shiel and Tony Fitzmaurice, eds., *Cinema and the City* (Oxford: Blackwell, 2001); and Mark Shiel and Tony Fitzmaurice, eds., *Screening the City* (New York: Verso, 2003).

78. Sontag, *Against Interpretation and Other Essays*, 213.

79. Ibid., 214.
80. Ibid., 219.
81. Ibid., 224.
82. See Jameson, *The Seeds of Time,* 157.
83. Ibid., 56.
84. Ryan, "Dreams of Postmodernism and Thoughts of Mortality."

# Index

The Amherst Series in Law, Jurisprudence, and Social Thought

EDITED BY

*Austin Sarat, Lawrence Douglas, and Martha Merrill Umphrey*

*Law and War* (2014)
*The Secrets of Law* (2012)
*Imagining New Legalities: Privacy and Its Possibilities in the 21st Century* (2012)
*Law as Punishment/Law as Regulation* (2011)
*Law without Nations* (2011)
*Law and the Stranger* (2010)
*Law and Catastrophe* (2007)
*Law and the Sacred* (2007)
*How Law Knows* (2007)
*The Limits of Law* (2005)
*Law on the Screen* (2005)